IRON AMBITION

MY JOURNEY FROM SEAT 2A TO IRONMAN

First Edition: 2009

Cover designs and Layout by Abra Johnson

Iron Ambition / John D. Callos

Further information on Iron Ambition
and the companies of
John D. Callos
available at:

www.IronAmbition.com

www.Ideabridge.com

www.JohnCallos.com

ISBN 978-0-615-27891-9

Author's Dedication

I am very thankful and am deeply indebted to the many people who have encouraged me in this Ironman journey and in my career as a CEO Advisor and management consultant. Many of those people are listed in the back of this book, along with my personal thanks. While I am profoundly grateful for my entire support network, this book dedication is reserved for another group.

Iron Ambition is dedicated to those executives who toil selflessly, managing multiple priorities, dealing with urgent issues and struggling to keep morale high while under constant pressure to meet their plans, get home in time for dinner and try to maintain some level of family balance.

Too many of these mid-career executives are trapped in an endless cycle of stress with no relief in site. They keep breaking promises with themselves and they feel tremendous guilt for not spending more time with their families and friends. Many experience regret and shame for the way in which they've neglected their personal health in favor of urgent business matters. The illusion that *"one day, things will slow down and I'll have time to get in shape, fix my relationships and coach Little League"* never fails to disappoint.

I know these executives well, because I was once their flag bearer.

Today, I work with these men and women from all over the country and I know their guilt, fears, regrets and hopes. I also know that these executives will continue on this one-way path of broken promises and delayed dreams until their world is shattered and they are forced to take action.

Sometimes it's a forced job change. Often it's a divorce or a very serious health issue. But until something drastic shakes them from their rut, they are destined to continue down this path of self sacrifice and deep regret.

It's to those senior and mid-level executives who I know so well, those whom I've worked with and those with whom I will one day work, that I dedicate this book and all the suffering that led to my completion of the Ironman Triathlon.

There is a way out of the rut and I hope that you might find sufficient inspiration in my story to begin the process of breaking from the status quo. Give yourself permission to take time for your family, to be far more effective at work, to have more fun in life and to start living your dreams while you return to health and vitality.

That journey can being today, but the decision to make that first step is yours alone. The story of *Iron Ambition* is how I took back control of my life, stopped making excuses and changed everything. Follow along with me and perhaps you'll make some changes too.

John D. Callos
Long Beach/Carpinteria, CA
March 2009

TABLE OF CONTENTS

1. BACKGROUND

2. DECISION

3. MOTIVATION

4. COMMITMENT

5. SACRIFICE

6. EQUIPMENT

7. TRAINING

8. NUTRITION

9. SETBACKS

10. EVENTS

11. IRONMAN

12. LESSONS

13. GRATITUDE

14. ENDORSEMENTS

APPENDIX

INDEX

CHAPTER ONE

BACKGROUND

THE EARLY YEARS

I grew up in Orange County, California, during a period in the 1960s when orange groves outnumbered housing tracts and going to Disneyland meant a short trip down country roads.

Video games had not yet been invented and our childhood entertainment was limited to building forts in citrus groves, making skateboards from steel skates and converting Schwinn Sting Ray bikes into the first crude BMX racers. But more than anything else, we were always riding bikes. I rode my bike literally everywhere—often my father had to pick me up with the station wagon when I wandered too far from home and got lost. In those days, a dime was all that was needed to call home.

During my teenage years, I was active in Boy Scouts and earned the rank of Eagle Scout. I was also active in soccer and my summers were filled with tennis camps and swim teams. In high school I took up cross country and track (880, mile and 2 mile events), and in 1980 I made it to the state semi-finals in the 2 mile event.

Little did I know that 35 years later, I would return to my teenage past times, putting my swimming, biking and running skills to work as

I embarked on the journey of a lifetime: completing the full Ironman Triathlon with its consecutive 2.4 mile swim, 112 mile bike leg and a 26.2 mile marathon run.

But I'm getting ahead of myself. What about those thirty-five years in the middle? What happened between those years of youthful exuberance and athletics to the point where I became a middle-aged, overweight, stressed-out corporate executive?

In the early 1980s, my hopes of competing in the 3,000 meter steeplechase for the USC track team were crushed when I sustained an injury that kept me in a Lennox-Hill knee brace for six months. Athletics was out and I became a full time college student and part-time bank trainee. I graduated from USC's Entrepreneur Program and spent nearly twenty years in the banking industry holding officer positions with Bank of America, Wells Fargo, Bank of Boston, Pacific Century Bank (now U.S. Bank) and others.

In my years of banking I developed a reputation for managing projects, people and business units. My ideas on how to develop new business were about fifteen years ahead of their time; many are now standard industry practice. In my latter years, I was involved in integrating the businesses of acquired banks into our bank. I spent a lot of time in strategic planning, business development and special projects. I also developed unique systems and tools that helped me manage multiple projects and executives concurrently; at one point I had thirteen direct reports leading various business units or projects. I found that what I really loved to do most was to help these executives grow, to improve their skills as business managers and to increase their effectiveness as leaders.

BREAKING FREE TO
FOLLOW MY PASSIONS

In 1999 I left the confines of banking, cut the corporate cord and resigned my position as Executive Vice President of a NYSE Bank. In the height of the dot-com boom, I set out to build my own business, to follow my passions and build a company that focused on helping executives be their best and reach their corporate goals. I wasn't exactly certain how to do this, or what I'd do specifically, and I certainly didn't have any clients—but somehow I knew that my work would be focused on CEOs and their direct reports.

I spent a couple of weeks making lots of lists. My new business was created around a chart I developed, which looked something like this:

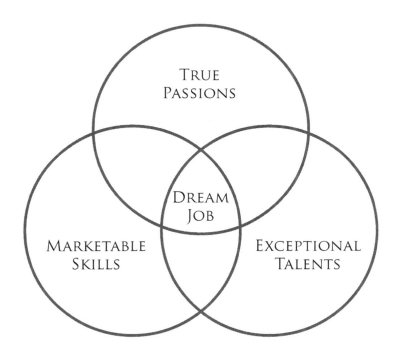

The idea of this chart was to list all of my true passions: things that I really loved to do, and when I was engaged doing them, it wasn't work at all. Next, I listed those areas where I knew I had some natural gifts, some exceptional talents, where I was likely in the top 5% or better in terms of my skills. Finally, I made a list of the skills that I knew were marketable, where executives would compensate me well for my ability to serve them and add value to their enterprise.

For example: I've always loved the beach and surfing (passion), but I have no skill whatsoever at surfing, and I certainly wouldn't get anyone to pay me to surf for them, so that didn't fit my model. What I was looking for were activities and skills where there would be a natural intersection. When I found that, I would create my dream job. And ultimately that's exactly what I accomplished, admittedly with a little nudge from my good friend Joseph Otting.

Over lunch at the Jonathan Club in Los Angeles, Joseph encouraged me to start my own consulting firm, advising banks on the methods, ideas and tactics I had developed over nearly two decades as a bank executive. While I was excited about the opportunities in the fun and fast paced dot-com industry, Joseph convinced me that I would add the greatest value to senior bankers. Bank executives would quickly see the value I could add because I had a strong reputation and knew the industry from the inside. Having been involved in some of the era's most highly-visible bank mergers would add credibility as well.

STARTING IDEABRIDGE

I started IdeaBridge in 1999 with the objective of advising bank CEOs and their executive teams on issues relating to corporate strategy, sales growth and improving their effectiveness as leaders.

IdeaBridge met with some early successes, landing a huge project with the Bank of Singapore to help them manage the transition that involved closing their branch network and re-launching the bank in an online format. This was a highly complex assignment that required my move to Singapore for about nine months.

In 2000, I received national recognition as "Business Guru of the Year," finishing first in my category in a nationwide competition. Later, The Orange County Register ran a feature article on my leadership development methods, and many of the white papers I authored were reproduced by business schools and Fortune 100 companies, including GE, Bank of America and ChevronTexaco. Soon thereafter, Microsoft featured my project management methods in several books and some of my articles appeared in a business management magazine that was distributed to 33 foreign countries.

This quick success meant that I was often very busy; I could never have kept going without the addition of the world's best business partner, Kevin Kelsey. Kevin and I have the perfect division of labor, and he has a brilliant mind that amazes both me and our clients. I still don't make any major business decisions without Kevin's thorough review.

SUCCESS TAKES ITS TOLL

But all this early success took its toll. I was either sitting at a desk, in a boardroom or on a plane, usually in my favorite Seat 2A. That was my new life, and I loved it. I took it all in, every bit of it. Every opportunity, every meal, every celebratory cocktail party. But at around the age of forty, I noticed that things were changing. My metabolism changed almost overnight, and I was quickly gaining weight.

The first sign was in Singapore, where one of the members of my project team commented that I was looking very prosperous. Of course, "prosperous" in Southeast Asia is the face-saving way of saying, "John, you are really getting fat."

Within about six years the weight just piled on until I had gained close to fifty pounds, maybe even more. It crept up on me the first year with an increase of over fifteen pounds, and then about five pounds per year thereafter. Five pounds a year doesn't sound so bad, but one day I happened upon a photograph from several years prior and couldn't believe it. I was now a fat man. I went online and found a BMI calculator that confirmed what I saw in the mirror: I was officially obese with a BMI of 31.3.

At 210 – 212 pounds I stopped weighing myself. But I could still hide an awful lot in my size 48 Brooks Brothers suits with the 42" waist. Just 10 years earlier, I had a 33 – 34" waist, weighed about 165 and wore a size 40 jacket.

HITTING BOTTOM

I had reached a low point in my self-esteem. I was disgusted and ashamed of how I had let myself go. I was embarrassed to take my shirt off on vacations and didn't even go swimming with my son Connor because I was so self-conscious. That was the absolute lowest point. I had put client work and building our business above my own personal health, and now, I couldn't even go swimming with my son while on vacation. I will never get that time back to swim with Connor as a child—the guilt and shame of that moment is still heartbreaking to this day. That was just too high of a price to pay and so I decided to make some drastic changes in my life.

My story is not unlike so many other middle-aged corporate executives that I have worked with from around the globe. Like me, they focus valiantly and selflessly on their careers, their families, their clients. When the weekend comes, they want to break loose, have a few beers, watch the game. They decide to hire others to mow the lawn, wash the cars, paint the house. Why not? They can afford it; they've certainly earned it. But little by little, just like me, their lifestyle becomes more and more sedentary and the weight just continues to accumulate, usually right around the mid-section. Look around any public venue, such as an airport or mall, and you'll see that most middle-aged men have a big belly hanging over their belt. Yep, that was me to be sure—but I finally took control, took my life back, and now have my health, pride and renewed self-esteem.

Success Follows Discipline and Focus

I have never been happier. It was an enormous amount of work and took plenty of focus and discipline; there were many setbacks and lots of pain and suffering. There were sacrifices and missed events. There were costs. Heavy costs. But in the end, I'm glad I made the sacrifices and paid my dues.

This is the story of how I accomplished this life-changing transition and those who helped me along the way. But more than my story of struggle and ultimate triumph, this is also a how-to guide filled with many lessons on business, life, relationships, health and ultimately, how to finish an Ironman Triathlon.

I did it, and you can too.

It all starts with the decision to move from the status-quo. In my story you'll find helpful tips and encouragement to complete whatever you start, and I'm not just talking about business...that's the easy stuff. I'm talking about making a commitment to do something for yourself for a change.

I'll explain how I overcame sloth, procrastination, crash diets, and every conceivable excuse. You'll see me in my unbelievable lows and my unstoppable highs. You'll see weakness and you'll see true grit. And in the end, you'll see success.

Follow me on this journey...and just maybe you'll be inspired to make some changes too.

CHAPTER TWO

DECISION

BUILD MOMENTUM WITH SMALL STEPS

It seems that getting started with anything is always the toughest part of the process.

I needed to remodel my home from the moment we bought it nearly fifteen years ago. But the task was overwhelming, expensive and time consuming. I was too focused on my career and didn't have the time for major distractions. Therefore, I only made those repairs that were absolutely essential; in fourteen years I basically did nothing substantial to improve our home.

Then one day I decided just to paint our master bath. That's all. I hired a few guys from the local paint store to help strip off the old paint and residue from the weight loss charts and graphs I had taped right above my bathroom scale.

The next thing I knew, we'd painted every room in the entire house, plus the exterior; installed a new slate roof, new exterior windows and doors; upgraded all electrical; installed new fixtures in all bathrooms and new flooring in the entire house; installed an Endless Pool, deck, and landscaping; installed new granite counter tops in the bathrooms; installed two new kitchens with all new appliances...and the list goes on. Basically, I had completely remodeled nearly every single part of our home. Few could believe the speed in which so much was accomplished on this remodel.

THE FIRST STEP:
DECIDE TO TAKE ACTION

Once a decision is made and a project gets your full attention, priorities are shifted and the speed in which things get accomplished is absolutely amazing. This law of attention holds equally true in business, on a home remodel or in the decision to finally make changes in your diet, fitness and overall health.

> From: John D. Callos
> To: Scott Gower
> Subject: The lucky hat.
>
> Hi Scott,
> It's John Callos from Carpinteria. My son Connor and I always try to help you set up your merchandise booth for Go For It Sports each year at the Carp Triathlon.
> About 3 or 4 years ago, you gave me a baseball cap for running that said "Tri" on it and you encouraged me to give Triathlon a shot. You were incredibly fit and I was incredibly fat, so it sure seemed like you were doing something right, and whatever I was doing, well, that obviously wasn't working. You inspired me to try to complete a mini-triathlon. At the time, I was merely a spectator with a 42" waist and carrying at least 205 – 210 pounds.
> Well, I wanted you to be the first to know that I just completed the Hawaii Ironman 70.3 Triathlon in Kona this last weekend.
> In the process, I have dropped my weight to 165 pounds and my waist to a size 33 – 34. I am set to do the Vineman Ironman 70.3 in July and the Full Ironman in Tempe Arizona

in November of this year.

From an obese, out of shape, over the hill, beer-swilling spectator to Ironman-bound—and I have you to thank for the initial inspiration. I look forward to seeing you at some of my races so that I can walk up to you and thank you personally and properly.

And I still wear that hat you gave me. It has become my superstitious lucky hat because it was a gift from you. Whenever times are tough or workouts not going well, I often think of you as my inspiration to soldier on. Thank you Scott.

- John

My experience has been that you don't need to have the whole thing figured out with a detailed plan before you get started. What you need to do, right now, is commit to taking some small action...today. As Nike says: *"Just Do It."*

And as I say: *"Get Started Right Now!"*

FROM SEAT 2A TO IRONMAN

Building and running a consulting and training company has taken me around the globe, usually in first class; my preferred seat is 2A.

I'd get quite irritable when crammed into the very small seats in the commuter jets that are the only way to get to certain clients. And why wouldn't I? I was a very big guy. I didn't need a seat belt extender... but I was getting pretty close on some of those planes.

So whenever possible, I always tried to secure the extra space available in First Class, Seat 2A, which was a window seat where no one would be stepping over me. It was roomy and of course, there was all the free beer and salty snacks I desired. "May I offer you an imported cheese platter, Mr. Callos?"

"Absolutely! May I have two?"

Even though I learned that beer or red wine while flying always gave me a headache, by the time I got back onto the plane for the return trip, it seemed that I always forgot how bad the headache was on the flight over. *"Coors Light, please, I'm watching my carbs."*

For me, Seat 2A is shorthand for the fast-paced but soft corporate lifestyle I was enjoying; the same lifestyle that was slowly killing me and destroying my self-esteem.

Although I was naturally gifted in running and soccer, following high school I did little consistent exercise for a period of at least 25 years. I really didn't start gaining weight until my late 30s—but as my metabolism changed and my business prospered, the weight piled on quickly.

Iron Ambition is the story of my journey from corporate excess and sloth to a disciplined and consistent program that ultimately led to my goal of completing the Ironman Triathlon.

HISTORY OF THE IRONMAN TRIATHLON

The idea for the original Ironman Triathlon was developed in 1977 by a group of athletes in Hawaii. Essentially, there was a long-standing debate about who was the best overall athlete: a long distance swimmer, a cyclist or a marathon runner.

U.S. Navy Commander John Collins, who was familiar with basic triathlon events held by the San Diego Track Club around 1974, suggested that the argument could be settled with a new event that would combine the three existing long-distance races already on the island of Oahu, Hawaii: the 2.4 mile Waikiki rough water swim event, the 112 mile Around-Oahu Bike Race (a two-day event at that time) and the 26.2 mile Honolulu Marathon. Collins is reported to have said, "Whoever finishes first, we'll call him the Iron Man."

Since that time, the sport has grown dramatically and the name "Ironman" is a registered trademark and vigorously protected by the World Triathlon Corporation. While WTC is a private company, it is rumored in the trade that they paid as much as 30 - 50 million dollars for the rights to Ironman and certain Ironman race properties.

Today the Ironman format remains unchanged. While over 10,000 athletes compete in the full Ironman each year, only the most talented will actually race the entire way. Like me, many are just aiming to finish before the seventeen-hour cutoff time, and if they do so, it will be the highlight of their triathlon career. These people are called age groupers or mid-packers. We will never be contenders for the podium, and that's totally OK with us. We just pursue this challenge for the camaraderie of the sport, to get in the best shape of our lives, and for the chance to perhaps one day earn the title of Ironman.

THE WORLD'S TOUGHEST SINGLE-DAY ENDURANCE EVENT

The full Ironman consists of a 2.4 mile open water swim, followed by a 112 mile bike leg, and concludes with a 26.2 mile marathon run. These events are run consecutively and always occur in the same swim-bike-run order. The athletes must complete the entire event within a prescribed time frame, or they will be eliminated.

Each leg of the Ironman event is timed and if a participant fails to meet the periodic cutoff times, they will not be permitted to continue in the race. The full Ironman has a 17 hour cutoff time for the 140.6 mile event.

Many people claim that the Ironman is the most challenging one-day endurance event on the planet. However, ultra marathoners, those who run footraces that cover distances in excess of 26.2 miles, may debate that opinion. And the ultra marathon purists suggest that the real ultras only begin at 50 miles, that's why I aim to complete both endurance benchmarks: the full Ironman Triathlon and an ultra marathon in excess of 50 miles.

Training for an Ironman takes an incredible amount of time, and it has been documented that there is a 90% injury rate for those who attempt this distance. To make the Ironman more accessible, the organizers recently developed the 70.3 event, which is exactly half the distance of the full Ironman.

WHAT'S A "REAL" IRONMAN?

There is great ongoing debate as to whether one is a "real" Ironman if they complete the 70.3 and not the full Ironman. Many hard core triathletes agree that until you've completed a full Ironman, the full 140.6 miles, you are not a real Ironman.

The spirit of the challenge to earn the Ironman distinction is to complete the entire 140.6 mile course. By means of an absurd example, if a participant entered a full Ironman event, but only swam half the way, only rode the bike for half the distance and ran only a half marathon instead of the full marathon, they would never say that this person was an Ironman. Therefore, the argument goes, how can we really say that a finisher of a 70.3 is a bona fide Ironman?

Technically, I suppose a reasonable argument exists that one is an Ironman if they complete an Ironman-sanctioned, Ironman-trademarked event. Curiously, after I completed two sanctioned Ironman-trademarked events: the Hawaii Ironman 70.3 and the Ironman Vineman 70.3 in Sonoma, CA, I must admit that it was tempting to say I was now an Ironman. Furthermore, many people who are not familiar with the intricacies of the event believed I was an Ironman just for finishing these events. Even my family members and some business associates encouraged me to claim the title of Ironman, since most people really didn't know the difference. They thought I'd done enough and should stop at the 70.3.

But to me, I would never consider myself worthy of the Ironman title until I had finished the full 140.6 event in an Ironman-sanctioned and trademarked event. Period. I believe it would be disrespectful for me claim the Ironman title when so many other dedicated athletes had sacrificed so much more than I had and endured far more hardships, in terms of time away from family, the physical toll and all the training necessary to complete this remarkable event.

It's just how I'm wired. Most people wouldn't know, but I would. I needed to complete the full thing. I needed to finish something big: the full Ironman Triathlon. That was my dream. This was my goal.

WHEN A MILE FALLS SHORT
OF THE FULL DISTANCE

In 1973, I attended a Boy Scout summer camp in southern California where they offered a patch for completing the mile swim. I had quietly lusted for that award for nearly a year as I had seen it featured in the monthly Boy's Life Magazine. I was a swimmer of sorts and figured I could muscle my way through the event and earn that coveted badge. But the lake was very low that year and they had to move the event to a small pool. Seventy laps in a 25-yard pool and I had my award; but it was a hollow victory. I had kicked off every lap (no rules against that) and cut the actual swim from 1,760 yards to maybe only 500; the rest of the time I was gliding under water from the push-off from each lap. That never sat well with me as a Scout and I never wore that patch. Over the years it made me feel like a cheat and I never got over that feeling of being awarded something I didn't really earn.

Do you follow my logic here relating to the Ironman and why I had to complete the full 140.6 mile event before I could accept that title?

Well, in the summer of 2005, a full thirty-two years after accepting the mile swim award from the Boy Scouts, I had the opportunity to set the record straight. I was chaperoning my son's Boy Scout troop at Cherry Valley on Catalina Island, CA. During the announcements one morning, Jordan Holloman mentioned that they'd be conducting the mile swim challenge in the open ocean.

I grabbed Jordan by the arm and pulled him aside: *"Jordan, you've just got to let me swim this thing. I need to redeem myself. I have been carrying around this guilt for thirty-two years."* Jordan was totally supportive and let me swim the event. They had two courses: one was from a dock at the harbor's shallow edge and the other course required an escort to proceed into the open ocean on the outside of the cove; naturally, I took the open ocean route because I really wanted to set the record straight. At that time, I was not in any kind of swim-shape and I barely completed the swim, but at least I finished.

The pride and relief I felt at finally completing the event without the aid of kicking off the walls was more significant that I could ever have imagined. Knowing that I really didn't earn that original award in the true spirit for which it was intended really bothered me more than I had realized. I took my new Mile Swim Award and sewed it right onto the front pocket of my size XL Adult Leader Boy Scout shirt and wore that patch with pride—because I earned it.

LIVING LIFE WITHOUT REGRETS

Life is too short to live with these kinds of regrets and I certainly wasn't going to stop at only half an Ironman; I was going all the way or they'd have to drag me off the course.

So from the beginning, I was determined that if or when I completed the full Ironman 140.6, I would proudly wear that accomplishment and distinction for the rest of my life. And it would mean all the more and be all the sweeter knowing that I earned every bit of it.

Many ask me why on earth I would pursue this crazy event. Foremost among these questioners has been my father. When he was my age, he had his own grand pursuits: he was attempting to set the world altitude record in a glider airplane, with no motor or propulsion system of any kind. I remember seeing parachutes and survival kits in the living room and there were many times he'd leave my brother, sister and me down near the airfield while he soared in the skies above Tehachapi or Lake Elsinore, preparing for his world record attempt. He even received advanced military training in high-altitude chambers to prepare for his attempt. Maybe something is triggered in the Callos men in their late forties. So while I couldn't really give my dad a good answer as to the reason why I wanted to pursue the full Ironman, in the back of his mind I think he quietly understood the need and the drive for an exciting challenge at this stage in my life.

WHY PURSUE THE IRONMAN?

Is there an answer as to why I wanted to pursue this challenge? And was it worth the time, expense, physical toll, pain, sacrifice and struggle? I really don't know anyone who has a good answer for this question; I sure don't.

I suppose the appeal is that many claim this is the most challenging one-day endurance event on the planet. Very few people have attempted this event, even fewer have completed it. Bragging rights might be part of the reason we all do it. But if I didn't at least attempt this full distance, I know I'd regret it. I just had to try.

From the moment I first saw the Ironman World Championships in Kona, I was enthralled. I thought it was absolutely incredible. How could that possibly be? Could people really do this? Is it even possible? I was stunned and amazed. I bought the DVD of the event and I have watched it dozens of times. I'm not a huge sports fan, but to me, the Ironman World Championship is my annual Super Bowl.

Watching the Ironman World Championships fueled my drive to someday complete the full Ironman Triathlon. I would never set any speed records, but I wanted to complete this endeavor—to finish what I started. To see it through. Perhaps just one time. But certainly at least once. To see how far I could push myself. To live my life without regret.

WEIGHT LOSS AND FITNESS

Losing weight is the bane of many people's existence, and let me assure you that it continues to haunt me daily. Being self-conscious of my fat belly rolling over the top of my belt was a constant mental drain and a source of deep, visceral shame and embarrassment. I wanted relief; it was constantly on my mind and I was always sucking in my stomach to reduce the visible sign of the massive girth I was hiding beneath my suits.

As an obese man, I knew all the ways in which to hide or camouflage the shameful girth. First, my suits were tailored a bit bigger than needed, so that the extra fabric in the front of the coat could hide the belly. Next, and this was very important: never take off my suit coat, no matter how hot or uncomfortable. If I was wearing casual clothes, never tuck in my shirts and always buy them larger than needed. Finally, I'd always suck in my stomach at all times. I could go from a 42" waist to the appearance of a 36" waist merely by pulling-in my stomach. But these tricks of the trade for fat men like me get old. Deep down, we all want to lose that gut. I probably wanted to lose it more than most.

LOOKING FOR SHORT CUTS IN ALL THE WRONG PLACES

I tried everything. Every pill. Every diet. Every scheme. Every Internet program. Every weight loss book and protein shake. I have done it all.

I was impatient and wanted quick results. At one point I got quick results and thought I was doing great. But it turns out that I was only losing water and muscle. I skipped meals and, unbeknownst to me at the time, I was losing a lot of muscle, only exacerbating my problem as my metabolism slowed to a crawl. I stupidly believed that skipping meals meant fewer calories, which in turn would lead to losing weight. This is dangerous, unhealthy and in the long term, unsustainable. Like so many others, I was looking for shortcuts to losing weight, but I had it all wrong.

It's an interesting dynamic that a reasonably intelligent man would be so gullible and so wrong-headed about weight loss. But think about it: the only time we ever start paying attention to weight loss or nutrition is once we get fat. It's not as if we've spent a lot of time studying health, diet, exercise and weight loss tactics when we were youthful and had a perfectly flat belly. Why would we? It's only when we see ourselves as fat and fully acknowledge that we have a weight problem that we begin to jump into action trying to find answers to this problem. We haven't had much experience in this area so we make a lot of mistakes and are easy marks. Suckers for every weight loss gimmick imaginable.

Once I made all the mistakes, bought every program, took every pill, read every book, I finally recognized that I needed to lose fat, not just weight. Fat was the killer. The more muscle I gained, the higher my metabolism would rise and I could literally be burning more calories even as I slept. However, if I starved myself by skipping breakfast and only eating salad for lunch, I would waste away as my body got its needed protein by slowly digesting my own muscle. Yes—starvation diets lead to weight loss by shutting down your metabolism and you end up getting the needed protein by breaking down your own muscle. Less muscle leads to even slower metabolism and now you are in a huge downward spiral of wasting away.

The tough lesson for me was that I had to eat in order to lose weight. I had it all wrong. In fact, I was doing the exact opposite, just like millions of others who skip breakfast and other meals. Nothing worked permanently until I stopped looking for the easy way out and buckled down for the hard, long road back to health and fitness.

THERE IS NO QUICK FIX

There is no easy, quick, safe weight loss program. I really don't know why we all look for the quick fix, but when it comes to safe weight loss, there is nothing simple or quick about it. To be totally candid, losing weight for me has been hard work. Damn hard work and it takes a lot of discipline and constant focus. The moment you take your eye off the prize, allow yourself to settle back into old habits, allow yourself a couple of days off, the weight starts creeping back faster than you can possibly imagine. Trust me on this one. Immediately following one event, I took a few weeks off and quickly gained 10 pounds. I was relishing the victory of completing the event, and started celebrating: steaks, cocktails, even three dozen glazed donut holes one Sunday morning with my son Connor. I took my eye off the prize, I relaxed my standards and had to spend another 6 – 7 weeks of very hard work to get back to my race weight. It wasn't worth it. No way.

WEIGHT LOSS SCAMS

Some people will tell you that the answer to weight loss can be found in a pill, others market a detox program, still others tell us that we can eat anything we want and lose weight while we sleep or lose 12 pounds over the weekend by sipping a special juice. I even went to the point of buying this cream that was "documented and fully guaranteed to melt fat" simply by rubbing it on my stomach. I thought it was a crazy claim, but the before and after photos were remarkable and the accompanying medical doctor's sworn statement and written affidavit were very compelling. Duped again.

It's really sad to have to admit that I was so gullible. Thousands or perhaps even millions of us overweight people are eager to find a solution. We are easy marks and huge targets, willing to try anything to help us regain a bit of our self-respect. Anything that will help us take off that weight. Anything that will free us from the shame and constant mental anguish of being fat. I know, because I lived this way for so long and eagerly tried anything and everything that promised a solution; it's still a daily struggle.

Finally I've realized that these were all scams. I had to learn for myself, the hard way. But when you've tried everything and it always failed, or you got very quick results only to balloon up again, one day you wake up and realize that there is no easy way to losing this weight. I've finally learned the answer for permanent weight loss and it was the very last thing I tried. Why? Because it was the hardest thing of all.

THE SECRET TO FAT LOSS

What's the secret to losing fat and keeping it off? First, it takes a combination of a lot of exercise where you are breathing relatively hard and sweating. I see so many heavy people in the gym just barely moving on the exercise bikes. They are so deeply engrossed in the overhead TV, a novel or *People* Magazine that the pedals are barely moving at all. It's no wonder that the weight is not coming off. Unless they work hard and work up a good sweat for at least 40 - 60 minutes, there will be no change. Nothing. I've done that: reading reports, writing white papers, proofreading proposals or evaluating research while sitting on an exercise bike. My advice: when at the gym, work out. Hard. Get sweaty and get your heart rate really pumping for at least 45 minutes, non-stop. Don't bring novels, newspapers or any other distractions. Stay focused and work hard.

If you've ever watched the popular TV show, *The Biggest Loser*, then you've seen the dramatic changes that these people have made in reshaping their bodies and losing fat while increasing their lean muscle mass. The transformations are truly remarkable. But what you won't see are the contestants casually reading a magazine or engrossed in a novel while on exercise equipment. No way. These people are working extremely hard, they are sweating profusely and some are working to the point of vomiting. No one said losing weight is pretty. There are no tricky camera angles or secret formulas; theses people are just working their guts out, pushing extremely hard, they are totally focused and they are watching their diet very carefully. That is exactly what it takes to lose weight; there's nothing easy about this process.

A major component of successfully reducing fat is the need to carefully monitor what you eat and how often you eat. Portion control, timing of meals, the right mix of food types, the number of meals per day, etc. These are all critical factors to losing weight and keeping it off.

I've learned (the hard way) that no pill, magic cream, Hollywood "weekend cleanse" or miracle food-combination will ever melt your fat away. What will generate results is: a lot of exercise, a lot of sweating, a lot of discipline and tremendous focus. I think that most people don't stick with their programs because it's simply a lot of work. It's tough and many days you will be walking around limping, sore and very much in pain. The only way I could keep at it was that I had to set some goals and assemble a group to hold me accountable; I learned that I could not do this on my own.

Setting and Achieving Big Goals

I realized that I needed to set big goals with deadlines. I decided that my first big goal would be the Hawaii Ironman 70.3, followed by the Ironman in Sonoma, called the Vineman 70.3, and finally, in November 2008, the full Ironman 140.6 in Tempe, Arizona. At the time, these were totally unrealistic, incomprehensible goals. I had no idea how I would ever complete these events, but the goals were crazy enough to get me really motivated and that was exactly what I needed.

Next, I told a lot of people about the events I was training for. If I didn't see it through to the end, if I stopped training, I'd have to tell everyone that I quit, and I certainly didn't want to face that discussion.

I also needed the additional accountability of a coach to make sure I stayed on track, did all the workouts and prepared intelligently.

So I decided that what I needed to start looking for was a specific training program and coach that could help me get started with some smaller events, then lead up to the longer distances in a safe and sane progression.

I'd already read dozens of books on health, exercise, diets, fat loss, weight loss, super foods, miracle cures, Navy SEAL workouts, cardio ball workouts and every triathlon and cycling book I could get my hands on. I learned a lot, but I was not applying what I learned. Instead, I needed to have someone who was a coach, who I would be was accountable to and who could work around my current level of sloth and help me improve, injury free, to the point that I would successfully finish some of these shorter distances. This would be my first step, and this was my plan.

I lacked the discipline of working out consistently, but when I finally did get my size 42" waist out the door, I would push so hard and try to run so fast that inevitably I'd get injured. My internal pace-clock from my high school running days would tell me that I really needed to pick it up and run faster. And every time I did...whap. I got an injury and was out. I would quit.

I needed a coach that understood my hyper-competitive background and could balance that with the reality of my hyper-extended mid-section. I needed to work into this very slowly and methodically in order to avoid the injuries that constantly resulted in setbacks and quitting.

FROM PODIUM TO PARK BENCH

In high school I was a constant podium finisher; state-ranked miler, 2-miler and cross country champion (3 miles in 15:48), but due to a knee problem that was exacerbated due to my 40 – 50 pounds of extra weight, I was now in constant pain. Even on weekend Boy Scout outings with my son's troop, I had to hike with two trekking poles in order to support my knee; I was always bringing up the rear because my painful knee problems prevented me from keeping up with the rest of the troop.

For many years, standing in lines at amusement parks and at the movies, or just walking around shopping malls, was unbearably painful. I always needed to find the closest park bench and take a seat in order to get the weight off of my knees and heels. Nearly everyone I knew was aware of my knee problem and it was extremely frustrating. I can totally relate and sympathize with those who are so overweight that they need to rely on motorized carts for improved mobility. I understand the unbearable joint pain. Unless you've really been obese, it's difficult to understand how painful that extra weight is on your heels, ankles and knees.

In my case, the knees were a constant problem since college and so I finally went to a nationally-recognized orthopedic surgeon who had literally written the textbook on certain knee operations. I was convinced that I needed to have my knee replaced and I was 100% committed to immediately scheduling the surgery. I had the knee checked with an MRI and multiple x-rays as well as a very thorough physical examination and strength test. The conclusion: I was faking it. Well, actually not faking it, but they could find nothing structurally wrong with my knee. It was just the pressure of all that extra weight.

I concluded that losing weight had to take priority over speed and needed a coach that understood that weight loss was the primary objective. I was also looking for a coach that understood that I had some long standing injuries that we had to work around, especially my knee pain. In addition to all this, my goal was to slowly get in shape so that I could begin consistently training for the Ironman.

During this period, I swam occasionally at the YMCA and went to the gym once a week to work with a personal trainer that my dad had hired to help me out, but my weight was not going down. Something had to change—so I set out on a quest to find a coach who could help me achieve my goals of weight loss and avoiding injuries while working toward completing a half Ironman, on the way to my ultimate goal of finishing the full 140.6 mile Ironman Triathlon.

CHAPTER THREE

MOTIVATION

THE CURVY PERSONAL TRAINER

My ever-expanding girth and pudgy face caught the attention of my father, who, in his characteristically-blunt style, confirmed what I already knew: "John, you're getting pretty heavy." So for my birthday he went to a gym near my home and purchased a block of sessions with a personal trainer.

Like so many others before him, my dad got talked into a long-term package of sessions with the youngest, fittest, most attractive co-ed trainer in the gym. The moment I set eyes on my curvy new trainer I knew this wasn't going to work.

I needed someone rough and tough; a real jerk that wouldn't accept my excuses or my complaining. This young girl just wasn't right for me and I told the manager that we needed to change this arrangement immediately. I only had one session before I was transferred to someone they thought would be a much better fit. But the problem with the new trainer was that he had a huge chip on his shoulder since I wasn't comfortable working with his good friend, the hot young co-ed. Whoops...that trainer wasn't going to work either. Finally I was matched with Jim Clark and it was a perfect fit.

PUMPING IRON

Jim was the perfect combination: someone who understood my limitations, but at the same time, pushed me hard. He was about my age, had a son about my son's age and he was supportive of my goals. Jim was in fantastic physical condition both in terms of muscular development and aerobic capacity. We met two to three times a week and I made quick strength gains. The growing number of iron plates I was lifting was evidence of my improvement under Jim's training. After a few months, I was doing bench flys with 50-pound dumb bells, but I still wasn't losing any weight.

I felt I needed some cardio exercises in addition to the weight training, so I found and ultimately hired a fantastic U.S. expatriate running coach who works online from his retirement home in Mexico. He had a very logical and straightforward approach to slowly and safely increasing my running mileage each week. He also had terrific ideas about icing, stretching and massage that were very helpful. However, despite the running and the constant weight training workouts, I was still not losing weight and was getting progressively more frustrated every time I stepped on the scale for my weekly weigh-in with Jim. It became something of a mini-obsession that only another heavy-set person could really understand.

I bought every book on the subject, every tape, and I tried every weight loss cure and system I could find online. Sometimes I felt so disgusted that I just wanted to stop eating altogether, just skip meals, but I learned that slowed down my metabolism and only made matters worse. My trainer's answer was always to be patient and keep lifting. But I was impatient and wanted faster results. During this period I had also been watching the television reality show called "The Biggest Loser." The show may be melodramatic and overdone, but the contestants made some remarkable transformations and I began to research the methods of the show's trainers.

"BE IN SHAPE WHEN WE MEET..." PREPARE TO SUFFER

My search for the trainers' methods and tactics ultimately led me to a young doctor in Santa Barbara, CA, by the name of Dr. Robert Wilcher. When I approached him, I had one clear goal and nothing else: I had to lose this weight. Not only would I feel better, I would also be able to cycle faster up those hills and jog easier, and most of all, I knew that my knee pain would subside and my confidence would skyrocket.

Dr. Wilcher is a chiropractor, personal trainer, coach and accomplished athlete. He runs a fitness facility in Santa Barbara, CA called Killer B Fitness and he trains many athletes and executives. He is a very competitive athlete himself, having competed in two half-Ironmans and other races, and he understood my drive and desire to finish a triathlon.

Dr. Wilcher was a real student of running efficiency and other techniques that enabled him to assist his clients in significantly improving their times and overall fitness levels, as well as reducing their risk of injury. Furthermore, he focused on improving health, nutrition, fundamental core strength and balance. This seemed like the perfect fit, except for the fact that his studio was located over one hundred miles from my home. We agreed to meet the next time I was up at our family's weekend beach shack in Carpinteria, which was only twelve miles from Dr. Wilcher's office.

When I met Dr. Wilcher, I repeated my overarching goal of weight loss and made it clear to him that everything we did together had to be working toward getting from 191 pounds and a 41/42" waist down to about 160 pounds with a 32/33" waist. The other stuff (half Ironman Tris, bike races, etc) had to take a back seat to my primary objective of weight loss.

In addition to the weight loss goal, I was looking for an overall, integrated approach to training for all three disciplines. Since Dr. Wilcher is a chiropractor, I hoped he could also help me with a constant muscle knot deep in my upper left trapezoid. This trigger point always seemed to flare up on the bike or after long hours working on the computer.

I really liked Dr. Wilcher's style, approach, constant follow-up and advanced knowledge of the skeletal-musculature system as it related to core strength, injury prevention and overall health. He was also no pushover. He was tough and a straight-shooter, which was exactly what I needed. Here's a good example of some training and nutrition advice he gave me in an email:

From: Dr. Robert Wilcher
To: John D. Callos

If we are talking about losing weight, then we are talking about burning calories. Lots of them. Please give up the weight training program with Jim. You are better off doing the elliptical. Go for 30 - 40 minutes and then do some planks and sit-ups, then go back to the elliptical or bike or stair master for at least another half hour. Lifting all that weight without cardio is not going to burn enough calories to melt all that extra fat that you are carrying. If your time is limited for exercise then you've got to give up the heavy weights and go cardio and core.

Trust me, you need to be in shape for when you see me next. I'm not kidding. You will suffer if you're not in shape. What it takes to get in really good shape is hard, consistent and efficient exercise. Heavy lifting is not your objective unless you're training for a bodybuilding contest.

Let your trainer get mad at me, but I don't think your weight loss objectives will be met in your time frame by just lifting weights. You must do cardio as well. I'm telling you right now, it's not easy, but it gets easier and more fun when you start seeing the pounds come off. You've been with this guy for quite a while, but with no weight loss.

If you're with me, you'll see a result in 1 week, but you've got to do what I say. You've got to find a way to burn 1000 calories a day. The first 2 weeks will be difficult, but when you get more efficient you can go faster and weight will come off faster.

If you can try a shake in the morning, mix the following in a blender:

1 handful of berries (frozen is easier)

1 tablespoon coconut oil or flax seed oil

3 raw organic eggs

1 scoop of Master Multiple vitamin mix by Life Essentials

1-2 cups soymilk, water or almond milk

Don't forget to have your 2 glasses of water every morning right when you wake up.

-Dr. Wilcher

So I got started with Dr. Wilcher even though the distance between us was a big problem. I paid him upfront for six months so that I would have the motivation to keep going once we got started. Because the distance made frequent in-person sessions difficult, this relationship evolved into a daily email correspondence arrangement with constant updates. Regrettably, the distance proved to be too much to handle and we did not get as many one-on-one training sessions as I had hoped. However, his daily correspondence and encouragement really helped.

Finally, I started losing weight because he was straight with me. He told me what I knew and had experienced, but what few would ever say: "Losing weight is hard work and you are going to be in pain. This is going to hurt. And you'd better be in better shape next time I see you because this is going to be difficult."

Man, was he right. His sessions were killer; like nothing I'd ever experienced. No weights or fancy equipment. Just isometrics, balancing and using heavy medicine balls for all kinds of torturous drills. But that's what it took—his workouts inflicted more pain than any piece of gym equipment and I got much stronger. Now I understood the value of core strength and balance. The tough workouts were paying off.

The six-month arrangement with Dr. Wilcher resulted in reasonably good weight loss and so I decided to sign up for the

Carpinteria Triathlon that would be held in September 2007. I needed a triathlon-specific coach now that I had a solid base from Dr. Wilcher. My search led me to a triathlon and running coach named Amanda McCracken and we started working together in May 2007.

A New Triathlon Coach Enters the Picture

Amanda understood that I really needed to be held accountable, and I also needed to get started with something that would get me into the habit of waking up early to complete my workouts. We decided that I would report my daily progress and get started by doing a basic fitness test so that she could get a fair sense of how much I was really capable of doing at this early stage.

I asked Amanda to design a program that would consistently result in two pounds of weight loss each week, principally through increased exercise as well as discipline with meal portions and frequency. I had just about four months to get in shape for the Carp Tri, hopefully injury free.

In 2005 and 2006, without any training or preparation, I had entered the Sprint Triathlon in Carpinteria, CA. This was just a 500 yard swim, a 10 mile bike and a three mile run. I remember so clearly that in 2005 I told my wife to wait for me at the swim exit on the beach, as I had expected to be the first one out of the water. Why wouldn't I? I had been on swim teams as a youth and swam on this same beach my entire life; this was my home turf. My wife couldn't believe it when I dragged my sorry duff out of the ocean in dead last place. Yep. I could barely make a 500 yard swim at that time. I was doing the backstroke, the side stroke, the dog paddle...anything to make that swim. My overconfidence in the swim leg of the event was shocking. I did OK on my bike, which I'd borrowed from my dad, but I nearly died on the simple three mile run. The next day I couldn't walk up or down the stairs of our beach shack. I was destroyed.

2006 was not much better, although I did have a wetsuit that year which made the swim much easier. As my friend and world-class triathlete Scott Gower says, "The wetsuit is like legally cheating.

It's permitted by the rules, and you should take every advantage that's allowed."

2007, however, was going to be the year that I actually trained for the event. I told Amanda that I was focused on improving my time. So once we got the weight down, I really wanted to focus on triathlon-specific training for each of the three events.

We determined that the biggest issues were going to be the run and the swim. I could always muscle my way through the bike, but the hard stuff would definitely be the swim and the run.

Amanda immediately came up with a great plan to help me ease into the training, even when my business travel schedule took me away from my typical training grounds.

Here's an example of one of her early plans:

Wednesday, Thursday
and Friday's plans while traveling:

- 10 minute warm up, stretch 10 minutes, 20 minutes running, more stretching
- On Thursday, try to negative split that main set of 20 minutes of running, that is to say, choose an out and back course; go out for 10 minutes at an easy pace and then see if you can return before reaching the 20 minute mark; cool down with another 5 minutes of jogging

Saturday and Sunday's plan:

- 10 minute jog (warm up) near the beach (not on the beach if the sand is not firm)
- easy swim in the ocean, depending on how long you can sustain this...maybe 15 minutes?
- stretch for 10 minutes (IT band stretch is important)

Do the following set of core exercises on Wed, Fri, and Sun:

- 2x15 pushups, focus on maintaining a firm core
- 2x30 crunches, focus on pushing your belly button into the ground
- 2x15 oblique crunches
- 2x15 seconds of planks
- 4x15 seconds of Superman (lying on your stomach, arms extended out in the air like Superman)

These should be a good start. Let me know how it works out for you.

Amanda wanted me to focus on functional exercises more than weights. These exercises included pushups, Hindu squats, pull-ups, floor exercises with the ball, crunches, etc. All these exercises use one's own body weight and are functionally useful. And this new functional strength actually came in handy from time to time.

CORE STRENGTH HAS BENEFITS
FAR BEYOND TRIATHLON

Soon after I signed with Amanda, my car was being serviced and my wife offered to give me a lift to the office. But our son Connor was running late for school, we hit some bad traffic, and we needed to stop by a gas station as well. To make the extra stop to drop me off at work would have meant that Connor would certainly be late for class. So when we stopped to refuel, I just jumped out of the car and said that I'd walk to the office.

They couldn't believe it, as my office was still quite far away and I was wearing dress clothes for work. But before they could stop me, I started jogging down the street. Instead of going the three miles or so on surface streets, I thought I'd jog alongside the freeway margin, then jump a fence into the concrete-lined San Gabriel Valley riverbed, go under the 605 freeway, then jump another fence and crawl through a couple of drainage pipes and concrete culverts. I know it sounds crazy, and it probably was, but I knew the way and had done it before when I was a bit younger.

Anyway, I had to climb chain link fences, and then bend extremely low doing a sort of duck walk to get through the concrete-lined culvert. Next, I needed to get through another small concrete pipe that went under the freeway. But when I got there, the water was knee-deep and there was no way I could ever make it through. So I had to decide to either retrace my steps through the freeway system, culverts, riverbeds and bike trail (about a mile of fence jumping), then start all over again and do the entire three miles on regular surface streets—or instead, jump two secure chain-link fences and sprint across the freeway, make it to the other side, then jump that fence right away (before I got caught) and climb back down into the concrete drainage ditch and continue on my way.

I was so committed at this point that I decided to climb the freeway embankment and chain link fence, and then sprint across the freeway. The point is that all the pushups, pull ups, squats and core strength training came into critical play that morning in my dash across the oncoming freeway traffic. Sure, I could have taken the long way instead. I could also have just been more patient and arrived late at the office, or I could have called someone to get me—but none of those options were as fun or exciting.

That experience really taught me the value of functional and core strength and balance versus specialty weight machines. Frankly, in Los Angeles, one never knows when they will need to do what I did that morning. I was actually caught in the LA Civil Unrest in 1992, and I have also seen the devastating impact to freeways and other infrastructure due to earthquakes in California. I know firsthand how these kinds of skills can come in handy when one needs to improvise in order to get home or to reach safety. It later dawned on me that I would not have been able to save myself, my family or anyone else in my formerly out of shape condition. I was glad to see practical application for all this work and it was exciting to see the gains I had been making.

There Will Always Be Ups and Downs

As we worked together, Amanda walked me through several rough spots when I felt discouraged and off-form, showing me the difference between breakdown and breakthrough:

Subject: Workouts
From: John Callos
To: Amanda McCracken

Hi Amanda,

I am just not feeling it today. Strange. Some days, I'm totally excited to complete double workouts; other days, I just don't seem to have the drive.

I was reading a bike magazine and realized that my poor nutrition was the cause of the bonking in the pool. It does make sense to me that skipping lunch is not good. But it is interesting that I can go from dinner to my morning workout without any nutrition and I am totally fine, but I cannot go from a light breakfast to skipping lunch and jumping into the pool for a really hard workout.

Your ongoing challenge will be to keep me corralled because I do need adventure and challenges and fun, and crazy experiences like my urban escape through the drainage control ditches and over the freeways, or a 112 mile bike ride or a crazy swim, or running-walking-swimming from Santa Barbara to Carp by taking the train up with nothing more than a swimsuit, running shoes and a cell phone.

Breaking up the workout into those interesting sets you suggested was actually fun and much less boring than just swimming laps back and forth, so that made the workout go by faster. Please try to keep things challenging and exciting.
-John

This was her encouraging reply:

Subject: Workouts
From: Amanda McCracken
To: John Callos

Hi John,

You'll have those days when you question everything and doubt the purpose of training. Don't get down on yourself about that...you have to listen to your body. There's a time to push yourself and a time to give in. I think letting go a little today is no problem. You have been going full steam for quite a few days, on top of a lot of travel.

Running is proven to burn the most calories of the three disciplines. This is a key piece we must address and a factor that will either enhance your training or make it unbearable. I know it isn't fun for you right now, but we've got to slowly build you up.

I will do a better job this Sunday with creating a week of more adventurous workouts. Maybe two workouts per week with some crazy variety. I'm not trying to baby you, but I want to build you up slowly so when the breakthrough workouts are dished out, you are ready to conquer them rather than breakdown.

With training and weight loss, I want you to ease into it without throwing everything else in your life (marriage, fatherhood, work, etc.) out of whack. That's partially my job as a coach too. I feel somewhat responsible. Your emails are insightful and continue to show me where you are at, physically and mentally.

-Amanda

Injury-wise, things weren't all smooth sailing during this time. In August 2007, some problems were creeping in and I promised myself I would be completely candid with Amanda—I needed to do that with my coach, and I knew I had her support, even when things didn't go exactly as planned.

BROKEN ANKLE

One injury that dogged my workouts was that I had begun favoring my right leg in order to save my left ankle, which I had recently broken by an extreme rolling of the ankle to the outside. This injury occurred quite suddenly when my left foot landed on a very hard and raised rut left from a truck tire going through a muddy dirt road. When this injury occurred, there was a loud snap or "pop" and I knew instantly that there would be trouble.

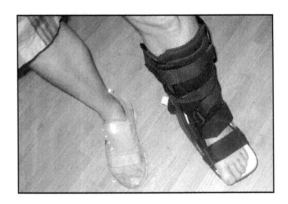

At its worst, the ankle was the size of a very large grapefruit, about three times its normal size, and my entire left foot was bruised (dark black and purple) from the tip of my toes all along the bottom edge of the outside of the foot, up past the ankle. It did make a remarkably quick recovery, although not by any means complete— the ankle was only a third bigger than normal, and all visible signs of bruising were gone. It was still extremely stiff in the mornings and painful to the touch, but it did loosen up a lot by mid-morning and the more I walked on it, the more it seemed to loosen up.

Due to this ankle problem I started to favor my right leg and foot in order to take the pressure off the broken ankle. Essentially I was walking around like the leaning Tower of Pisa.

Picture this: you know if you walk in the sand just after a wave has rolled up on the beach and quickly retreated? You walk barefoot on that soft, wet sand and it leaves an impression, but not really of the entire foot, just the outside of the foot, the heel and toes. Well it was that outside skinny portion of the bottom of my right foot, the part that would leave an impression in the wet sand, which was very sore, just like a bad bruise.

As a result, the side-bottom of the right foot was bruised and very sensitive to touch or pressure. It really hurt to walk on the right foot, plus the left ankle was still painful—not that bad to walk on, but it hurt if I touched it or if it rubbed against the side of my shoe.

I was sorry to have to report this to Amanda, because I had never been more eager to really kick the running into full gear in order to get moving on our 60-day plan leading up to the Carp Tri. But it seemed I had to cool my jets for a bit before I caused the ankle to get worse. I really should have taken the time to stay off of both feet for a few weeks in order to allow these problems to heal properly.

THE HOME STRETCH
LEADING UP TO MY THIRD CARP TRI

In the days leading up to the Carp Tri I was still icing the left ankle a lot. My great friend Kelvin Shields brought over a special ice bag with a screw top that held crushed ice, and I used that 2 – 3 times a night for a total of about 40 to 60 minutes. In addition, I was experiencing something weird—I felt, for the first time ever, an incredible stress and pressure to get all my workouts done, so much so that they were always on my mind. Constantly. And if I couldn't get one done, I felt very guilty. I wondered if others felt this way—it was really stressing me out, way more than even work.

Amanda was not the source of the pressure, nor was she generating the stress; it was just my extreme desire to deliver as promised. But I was feeling very anxious about these workouts, and I asked Amanda whether this was normal and if her other athletes felt the same pre-race jitters and stress. She confirmed that this was all quite normal.

Amanda continued to encourage and coach me through a broken ankle and other mishaps to ultimately achieve a new personal record in my home town race, the Carpinteria Triathlon. Despite all the issues, excuses, missed workouts, travel, and injuries, Amanda's base training helped me pull off my best results ever.

I could not have been any happier, excited or proud. My time was far better than the best-case scenario that I had planned. I was stunned. I set new personal bests in each event, and I owed that all to Amanda and her training program. She was awesome and she did a terrific job.

SOME GOOD THINGS
MUST COME TO A REGRETTABLE END

In October 2007, a bombshell was dropped on me. The owner of Amanda's coaching company had cut some deals with various product companies to sponsor his athletes...all of them. He mandated that beginning in 2008, we were all now required to purchase and wear the uniform that prominently displayed his company name and its sponsors.

Ostensibly, this would make us all feel like we were part of a team, plus we'd be getting some discounts on certain products. But the requirement felt so heavy-handed and obviously one-sided that I couldn't accept it. I had nothing against the company, its owner, or Amanda. The gear looked fine and it probably would be really cool to tell my friends and associates that I was on a triathlon team. But why should I be asked to pay for and race in the company's gear just to meet the commitments that were made to the owner's sponsors?

While I totally respected the decision of the business owner to change his policy and require that athletes purchase and wear his company-branded race uniform, I disagreed so vigorously with his demanding style and approach that I could no longer be affiliated with his company. Philosophically, and on so many other levels, I just completely disagreed with his business approach, which mandated that I had to wear his uniform or I could not enter a race. I felt that was just plain ridiculous. This led to the extremely difficult decision to end my wonderful coaching relationship with Amanda.

I signed up for a coach, not to be a sponsored athlete. I wanted to make my own choices about whose gear I would use or whom I decided to represent. And my choice was to represent my great friend Tom Whittaker.

BE STRONG.
TOMSTRONG.

Tom Whittaker and I went to high school together in Carpinteria and were great friends. But following high school, I moved to Long Beach and he stayed in Carp. We lost touch for twenty-five years, but were brought back together when I learned that he had been battling brain cancer. Tom had beaten the cancer and was now an avid cyclist, having been deeply moved and inspired by Lance Armstrong's amazing recovery. Tom encouraged me to get into cycling and we remained in constant contact about all things cycling, including eBay auctions, constantly sharing bike parts such as handlebars and saddles, going on rides and even racing together in the Long Beach Marathon Bike Race.

Regrettably, Tom's brain cancer returned. He was very upbeat about his prognosis and remained very strong. So strong that in a show of support, we made some cycling gear with our own logo, a logo that was a play on words from Lance Armstrong's LiveStrong. We called it TomStrong Cycling and Triathlon Team, and we had the logo placed on all kinds of gear and shirts, which we distributed widely among friends, family, doctors and supporters.

But according to my former coaching company, I would be breaking the agreement with them if I wore anything other than their official race uniform. I could not honor and support my good friend by wearing his TomStrong gear during a race, and that was completely unacceptable to me.

I felt horrible about losing my coach, the one person who had really taken me so far, but this new policy was the final straw. It was emotional and it was tough, but it was over.

Here We Go Again...
The Search for Another Coach

Of course, at that point I had no coach at all and no real prospects. So I began the search to find someone that could help me stay focused throughout the long months of tough work ahead as I progressed toward my first big test: the Hawaii Ironman 70.3 Triathlon on May 31, 2008.

In November 2007, I scoured the Internet and all triathlon-related magazines and podcasts in order to assemble of list of potential coaches. Money was not an issue for me—whether it was $100/month or $1,100/month, I was just looking for the best overall fit for me.

I sent the following letter to each of the potential coaches on my list:

From: John D. Callos
Subject: Looking for a TRI Coach

I need an experienced Triathlon coach who has completed some Ironman triathlons and who is up to date with current training programs, techniques, etc. I want a more personalized approach to get me to my first 70.3 in May 2008, then I want to convert to a more standardized, proven plan that will help me be well prepared for my first full Ironman. I don't want to race these events, I merely want to finish with a smile on my face, cross the line on my own and not get too hung up on every minute of my final time.

Overall, the most important thing for me is to take training in stride, keep it consistent and above all, do whatever possible to minimize the risk of serious injuries that could potentially sideline my dreams of an Ironman finish.

I would like to talk to you about coaching me for the next six months to make sure I am totally prepared for Hawaii 70.3 half Ironman on May 31, 2008. I do not intend to aggressively compete; I just want to treat it as a hard workout day, not an intense race. I also have the Vineman 70.3 in July 2008. I need your assistance in planning my race calendar for

2008. I want to keep things fun and exciting but not overdo it, so I will need your advice on scheduling various events.

All of this should lead up to making certain that I am able to complete a full Ironman in late 2008.

I am a 46 year old male business executive. Recently, I have run four sprint Tris and finished roughly in the bottom third of the age-groupers. I am not fast, but I do have the ability to get my endurance built up reasonably well. About six weeks ago, I went for a very slow run and ended up going 15 miles without stopping. This was amazing and I loved it, but because I did not have the necessary base training, that one run caused a bout of plantar fasciitis, which sidelined me for a month.

I have world class road and TT bikes and I like to swim. I have completed a Total Immersion swim weekend, but don't have quick easy access to a pool for consistent workouts (I'm researching an Endless Pool at the moment). My most recent Sprint Tri was completed at about 1:20 and I was very happy with that time (I ran with a broken ankle). I am 5'9" and my weight is 172 or so, which is down about 20 pounds from last spring and over 40 pounds from my heaviest weight. My goal to get down to about 158 pounds. I have a 36-inch waist, down from 42 inches, and my goal is to get down to a 33-inch waist. Losing weight is the primary motivator for me. Having these races scheduled and confirmed really helps to keep me motivated, but I need a coach to keep me accountable and focused.

My three long-term goals are to complete a full Ironman marathon, a 50 mile run and a double century (200 mile) one-day bike ride. Perhaps the goal of completing a full Ironman in just 44 weeks from now, starting pretty much from scratch, is just not feasible; I will need your opinion on this. Running is obviously my weak spot, but if we keep it focused and work it up slowly, I hope to avoid injuries and do fine. I want to train very consistently so that I can do everything possible to avoid a DNF (Did Not Finish).

I am willing to work hard in training sessions so that I will be prepared as I can possibly be. I can spend as much as 8 hours each week in training, although I want to take Mondays off.

So what are your thoughts on all of this? Please let me know.

- John

Most of the people I contacted were either top professional Triathlon athletes who had coaching businesses on the side, or they were the world's most notable coaches with books I had read and enjoyed.

The replies began arriving immediately. Most would not take me on as I was just too much of a novice. Others were glad to take my money regardless of my current level of fitness. Most did not require that I wear their uniforms, and I was surprised that many had Ironman programs where I would have a much better idea of the workouts well in advance. I liked knowing several weeks to a month in advance what I had in store so that I could plan my travel and meetings accordingly.

They were all good, but I wanted to make sure I chose the perfect coach. I had no desire to seek a new coach a third time around. I wanted someone that I could relate to, someone who was strong enough to reel me in and not let me intimidate them; if they were too agreeable, it wouldn't work. I also needed someone who was analytical, who was also a tremendous athlete and thought like an athlete, someone with whom I had a natural and easy chemistry.

During this search I had been listening to a variety of Podcasts on triathlon and multisport. My favorites were, and remain:

- Phedippidations
- Endurance Planet
- IM Talk
- The Competitors
- EN Triathlon Podcast
- Fitness Rocks
- Simply Stu
- *Tri Talk Triathlon Podcast*

They were all fantastic, motivating and informative in their own ways, but I really connected with and related to the host of the Tri Talk Podcast, a wonderful, energetic and inspirational man with great integrity; I knew that David Warden would have to be my top pick for my dream coach.

David is one of the world's leading researchers on Tri-specific training issues, the top Podcaster and an incredible coach for triathlon. We shared a very strong interest in researching the facts, numbers and science of training. David works very closely with Joe Friel, the father of all Triathlon training and the author of many Tri-specific training books, including the bestselling Triathlete's Training Bible.

I added David to the top of my list of dream coaches and started an email campaign to try to convince him to take me on as an athlete:

> From: John D. Callos
> To: David Warden
> Subject: One more athlete for your stable.
>
> Hi David,
> I know from your Podcast that you are booked-up and do not have any space left to coach additional athletes. I greatly respect your desire to limit the athletes that you work with in order to provide them with the best coaching possible.
> I know all of that, but I would still really like to be added to your stable of athletes. I will not ask for the level of personal attention that you might normally provide. I have submitted a detailed application and hope that you will consider me. I have the Hawaii 70.3 in May, the Vineman 70.3 in July and the Arizona Ironman in November 2008.
> I need a coach and a detailed plan to take me through all of this. I do not want to get some pre-programmed download, but rather, have an expert help me figure this all out in order to be ready for Arizona IM on November 23, 2008, one year from now. I am only doing this for the pride of finishing strong, knowing that I have trained well and appropriately.
> I am looking for an annual plan, starting basically

from scratch. I have not been training for the past 60 days. My training goal is to stay as injury free as possible, and I would like to incorporate some basic strength training.

I have some of the world's best equipment, but I am not yet doing great in the aero position on the bike. I need more practice on this, and in fact, I am thinking of setting aside my road bike and just using the tri bike in order to get more time in the aero position. Biking in Los Angeles is extremely dangerous, but I still do it. It is also quite hard to get in the longer rides without a lot of stop lights.

Running was my passion throughout high school, and I was very competitive. Now at 45, I have not done much for 25 years. I have dropped from 199 pounds to 169 since the summer and this will play out very well in my running. My goal weight is 158 and that is not too far away for me. This weight reduction is going to have a huge difference in my running, and especially, in my knees. I have had knee problems in the past, but that was because I was so heavy and out of shape. Once I am back to regular, consistent training, this should hopefully improve.

I really like knowing in advance what my workouts are going to be, and how many hours per week in each discipline. That way I can plan around my significant travel requirements. I want to take off all Mondays and I want to work hard on weekends, typically with brick workouts.

If you finally agree to take me on as a consulting client, I will not constantly bug you or ask for help, and I will never ask for free advice or pressure you in any way to do anything for free. You are the best in the world and I am happy to pay you for your consulting services. Please re-consider my application and take me on.

-John

P.S. Your Podcasts are awesome. I can never get enough and I listen to them over and over. I love the fact that you really do a lot of research.

The next day, I received his reply: it turned out that his new contract would not start until December 1, so he had a small window of time where he could consult directly with me if we started to work right away. He was open to the idea of helping me and wanted to discuss how this potential arrangement might work. We had a phone conversation, during which he reviewed my goals, strengths, limitations and race priorities, and then we discussed various options in terms of the frequency and amount of contact we'd have to review my challenges, issues, workouts and overall progress.

THE COACHING RELATIONSHIP

I wanted someone who would work with me, hold me accountable, and yet understand that there would be times when I absolutely could not complete certain workouts due to my travel schedule.

David was perfect in all respects. He was not a cheerleader coach, rather, his coaching was based on science and tracking data. I recorded every run with a heart rate (HR) monitor and GPS wrist watch (Garmin Forerunner 305). I would then forward my pace, HR, distance and all other relevant data to David every day via an online tracking and training log called TrainingPeaks. Progress was monitored and tracked, and then David would develop new workouts based on my recent results.

David always paid attention to how I was feeling and any injuries I was dealing with. There was one time in particular when he gave me some advice about laying off workouts; I was not happy about it, but in the end, he was right.

Subject: Important Update and Compliment
From: John D. Callos
To: David Warden

Hi David,
I was not happy with your recommendation to cut back on hours this week. I was actually quite eager to put in

major hours—so when you suggested that we should make this a recovery week to avoid any further deterioration of my aching hip, I was not pleased.

But in retrospect, I am so glad that you made that unpopular call.

My hip was aching all night just like the old days—so if I had stubbornly stuck to this week's plan, I would have likely destroyed my chances for the Arizona Ironman. Can you believe that?

Being a coach is a lot different from being a cheerleader or a workout partner, or just robotically recording the next week's workouts based on some proven workout formula culled from a training book.

A good coach knows his or her athlete, their capabilities, their goals and desires, their limitations, their motivations. The great coach goes the next step to modify plans, races and workouts based on the athlete's feedback, progress and injuries.

I am so proud and glad to have you as my coach.

You made a tough call, but just 12 hours later I can say it was the absolutely right call. I will not do any cycling until tonight in order to give the hip a little more time to rest.

- John

I owe it to David, not just for training support, but for emotional encouragement as well, especially listening to me when I ramble and fret about constant injuries, missed workouts and unfortunate set backs. He was always patient and thoughtful, and in the course of working with him I have learned a lot about myself.

For example, just shortly after we started working together, I sent him this email:

Subject: Training Update
From: John D. Callos
To: David Warden

Hi David,
Here's what's on my mind:

- Fact 1: My workouts are off to a slow start due to travel, holidays, home remodeling, etc.
- Fact 2: I am getting really stressed out due to the commitments I made to you and to myself, and because of the races looming in the future
- Fact 3: My motivation is high to get these workouts done.
- Fact 4: I have lacked the discipline to consistently get up in the dark and run in the cold mornings. That is the truth.

Questions:

What is the best thing to do here? Should I try to make up all the missed workouts, do I triple-up on the weekends or just extend the base period by another week?

I would probably advise myself to:

- Relax
- Know that this will happen when starting back up again, especially with a lot of stuff going on right now in my life
- Not be foolish and try to triple up workouts on the weekends, which will dramatically increase risk of injury.
- Start over. Extending the base by a week is a smart move and will only help in the long run.
- Not worry. I have enough time if I get going again and stay focused.
- Know that David will not be disappointed; he knows I am for real and I don't need to prove anything to him.

- When I get stressed about missing a workout, see the first bullet point above, RELAX.

Lessons learned in this process:

- I MUST do my workouts first thing in the morning—absolutely, positively, no matter what, no matter how early the flight is. Never, ever assume that I can get the workout done later in the day. It must always be done the very first thing in the morning or I will not get it done.
- While David has asked me to split some workouts if possible, I know that my schedule will not permit this.
- Do not triple-up workouts on Sundays just because I have Monday as a workout-free recovery day.
- Endless Pools take a LOT longer to install than the salesmen tells you when you are buying the pool.
  Any thoughts David?
  -John

And this is what David replied:

Subject: Training Update
From: David Warden
To: John D. Callos

John,

I like your analytical approach. Let's break this down:

I am not disappointed in you at all. If you think all my athletes meet all of their workouts, you're wrong. That is beauty of having a coach: to help change the plan when necessary.

You will miss workouts. It is impossible to do every scheduled workout unless you are a sponsored pro athlete training full time. For someone as busy as you, you have to manage your own expectations of yourself and recognize that this will sometimes happen, and it is OK.

Always focus on "where do I go from here?" Don't focus on what you've missed or what you could have done. If you were trying to drive from LA to Vegas and you made a wrong turn and ended up in Bakersfield, you wouldn't say, "how do I get back to LA and then to Vegas?" You would say, "how do I get to Vegas from HERE, where I am right now?" We can get you to your Ironman goal from here, no problem.

There is still plenty of time to get you ready for the half and full Ironman. Don't sweat it at all.

We can change your schedule such that you won't have any workouts separated. We can get them all done in one shot each day. This will mean some long workouts, but I want you to have a majority of your runs on fresh legs, not on dead legs. Having these done in one workout will become fairly difficult in March, and extremely difficult in August, but we can definitely do it.

Everything else you wrote is right on, except the part about me being disappointed.

-David

Meeting Joe Friel, The Father of Triathlon Training

Prior to working with David or any of my coaches, I had purchased literally all the books in print and all the DVDs in circulation that were focused on triathlon training. Curiously, many of these materials were written or produced by Coach Joe Friel or they featured his perspectives on training and racing. Coach Friel is one of the world's most recognized authorities on the scientific approach to triathlon training.

Coach Friel and David Warden are close associates and I was deeply moved when I received an invitation to meet Coach Friel. However, it later occurred to me that I may have received that invitation by mistake. It took me a moment to process this, and then I replied:

Subject: Dinner opportunity with Joe Friel
From: John D. Callos
To: David Warden

Hi David,

I'm not sure if I received your email by mistake regarding the dinner invitation with Coach Friel. I think it might have been intended just for your pro athletes.

Coach might have preferred that my slot be given to one of the pros, especially if this is a special invitation-only event. If, however, it is a large gathering or conference, I would not just be interested—I would be honored and grateful to attend. I have studied his books, watched his videos, read his blog.

There will be no hard feelings if this was sent by mistake—I totally understand that these events are usually reserved for the top echelon of pro athletes, sponsors, race directors, etc.

If Coach Friel knows for sure that you have invited a total beginner and is still OK with this, then I am totally onboard for sure.

Just let me know. Thanks.

-John

I received a reply from David that, yes, the email was indeed directed to me. He told me that Coach Friel knew who I was, and he had even gone to him for advice regarding me specifically. Coach Friel's offer was sincere, and I was encouraged to attend this purely social visit.

Meeting Coach Friel for me was like meeting a rock star. This was also the very first time I would meet David Warden face to face. It was a tremendous evening and as I had suspected, there was a professional triathlete at our table. Coach Friel was very approachable, a great listener and seemed to take great interest in my transformation. When he asked me questions about my progress, he really listened intently and gave me his full and complete attention; he absorbed it all and was very sincere. He was also very complimentary of David Warden.

The sort of coaching relationship I had with David was exactly what I had always been looking for, and I was extremely fortunate to be working with him. We shared such good chemistry, and the great thing was that he was completely committed to my goals throughout the entire year. So when things went wrong or I got hurt, he still kept everything in perspective and kept his eye on the prize: the Full Arizona Ironman in November 2008.

Chapter Four

COMMITMENT

Progress at Last

At the beginning of 2008, I was satisfied with my workouts and had learned that I was better off having more accountability to get these done consistently. I was not feeling badly about things, even though I was only training three to four hours each week.

I was having fun, wasn't injured and was finally settling back into a normal life after the holidays, a major home renovation and the huge task of installing an Endless Pool. Once I had the Endless Pool up and running, I could tell that it would be an excellent cross-training tool.

I was no longer worried about the swim portion of triathlon events and strangely, my worst event, the run, had turned into my favorite. I loved to run because it was liberating and exhilarating, just like it had been as a kid in the citrus groves and as a record-setter and medal winner in high school track and cross country. I just had to constantly keep reminding myself that I needed to be patient, stay within my abilities, to be smart and remain disciplined about not pushing too fast, too soon; things were going too well now to risk getting an injury.

So I was proud of what I was doing and happy to tell my family and friends about my goals. I also met a goal that I'd had for over 20 years:

I could finally fit into a size 33 waist for my pants. At the beginning of 2007, I was about a 40" waist. But since August 2007, I had lost at least 25 pounds and I felt fantastic.

Getting Respect at The Gym

My leg muscles were visibly growing and becoming extremely defined, even after twenty-five years of complete inactivity. Part of this definition was the leaning-out process, but there was also a new level of fitness returning to my body, and I was slowly beginning to feel more like an athlete than a workaholic at the office (I was never a couch potato, but I was really living the soft life of dining out, cocktail parties, first class travel, and the like).

I was enjoying the weight lifting portion of my training, but it was different from just going to the gym to bulk up like all the other guys. I had been using the YMCA gym because they also had a pool, and one day after my swim I wandered into the weight room. Near me was a huge, muscle-bound guy covered with tattoos. He walked toward me with authority and swagger, removed the pin from the top of the stack of iron plates I had just been lifting and slammed it into the bottom of the stack. I could hear the thunderous beat of rap music blaring from his headphones in between his grunting as he violently hurled the entire stack of weights with each rep.

And there I was, standing at a lat pull down machine with just two plates totaling about thirty pounds. But after just seven reps this hardcore lifter collapsed in a heap, while I kept going to my full 30 - 35 reps in my AA training phase.

He looked over at me and took out one earphone; I thought he caught me staring at him and I was worried. Before he could say anything, I said, *"I'm training for an Ironman; for me, it's all about major reps with light weights in order to build my endurance. I wish I could bulk up like you, man, you look awesome."*

He gave me a slight nod of respect that I will always remember, and then simply said, "Cool." He got it, and he respected it. He made me feel great.

The Corporate Athlete

An athlete is always who I was growing up; you'd never see me without a ball of some kind and there was never a period when I wasn't training on a school team. I earned six varsity letters and was both President of the Letterman's Club and the ASB Director of Athletics. When my career took over, I became an athlete at work—essentially, I was a workaholic, putting in more hours than many thought humanly possible. I built my reputation on that work ethic, on the ability to outlast everyone else. What I couldn't achieve with talent or raw intellect, I'd make up with hard work and total commitment; whatever it took. Period. I know dozens and dozens of executives who do the exact same thing; most of them end up regretting it later in life, just as I did.

Working selflessly at the expense of family, friends, hobbies, interests, vacations...that's a strategy doomed to fail at some point, and if this is your course, then sooner or later you will deeply regret this decision. I know that I did, and that I still do regret putting everything in my life in a secondary position to excelling at work and serving clients, no matter how outlandish the request, how early the meeting or how many events I might miss at home. I was a fool, but I honestly didn't see it at the time.

Just like so many other executives, I just didn't see it when I was in the thick of so many moving pieces and projects; many people don't. In my consulting work with executives, I'll often visit with an executive who is running so fast and working so hard and doing so much multi-tasking that they end up speaking extremely fast and use verbal shortcuts to make a point, speaking in only half-sentences and leaving out the rich details that bring clarity to a given assignment or task. They leave their own people scratching their heads wondering exactly what was requested. This ultimately leads to confusion and inefficiency in business, let alone the health impact of running around constantly in a state of stress.

Fortunately, I took my life back, built a company around my passions and talents and was on the right path. But as I began to experience quick success in my own business, I started retuning to my old habits and needed to get control again, so training took on a renewed focus and priority.

FEELING THE COMMITMENT AND PICTURING THE FINISH

Now that I had my life back and was working out regularly, committing to a formal fitness program was the natural progression of things. I believed I could transfer my highly disciplined work ethic in business to David's training program. Just two to three years before, I was ashamed of myself and had very low self-esteem; but now, at the start of 2008, I felt terrific and my self-esteem was improving as the weight started coming off. I was encouraged by this progress and excited about my potential future in triathlon, and I was committed to sticking with my formal training program.

It might sound unbelievable, but at that point, deep inside me, I absolutely knew that I could go out there and do a marathon. I was pumped up, enthusiastic, and very grateful that David Warden had agreed to take me on (even if just on the sidelines, until an official spot opened up).

MY TRAINING PROGRAM

Generally, I tried to work out for 9 to 15 hours a week. But add to that, the time taken to prepare for workouts, get dressed, and changed, mix various concoctions of energy drinks, plan my routes for runs and bike rides, maintain my gear, record all of my results and update my training log—the weekly time commitment was probably closer to 20 – 25 hours.

I planned on working out six days each week and taking Mondays off. Including all the preparation and pre-workout planning, I had to allocate about 2 – 4 hours each weekday, depending on the workout, and the weekends were always at least twice as long.

Some weekends involved significant time commitments, such as completing a 75 mile bike session or brick (bike session immediately followed by another hour of running). Certain periods in my training cycle required workouts in multiple disciplines, and many times I did three different workouts in a single day.

My training included running, cycling, swimming, weightlifting, various drills, core exercises and stretching. Training also required that I got plenty of sleep to properly recover, so that meant about 7 – 8 hours each night, plus the occasional nap on the weekends (I should have done this more often, but didn't). I also had to be judicious about proper diet, nutritional supplements—and going for sports massage.

The risk of injury increases when muscles are not pliable and flexible, and thus there is the need for stretching and consistent sports massage. Sports massage is not a luxury. This was a very important part of the overall training regimen, even for age-groupers and mid-packers like me. This wasn't a spa treatment with candles and light touches; it was usually quite painful, with heavy pressure and deep tissue manipulation called Shiatsu. Shiatsu is a technique of Japanese origin, and I am told that the name literally translates as "finger" (shi) and "pressure" (atsu). And believe me, the finger pressure is not relaxing, especially if you get someone who really knows what they are doing.

THE SWIM WORKOUTS AND THE ENDLESS POOL

Originally, my swim workouts took place at the YMCA pool, but this became totally unpredictable due to unannounced closings for over-chlorination, or sometimes just because the college kids who guard in the morning couldn't get up in time to open the pool. It was ironic because we'd have three or four guys waiting to get into the pool at 5:00 am sharp, all of us in far better shape than the sleepy college kid, but we were not allowed onto the pool deck until they could get someone to guard for us. Finally I had it with missed workouts and ruined training schedules, and I went through the long, painful and expensive process of installing an Endless Pool.

My Endless Pool is an above-ground, 7 x 12 foot, 2,500 gallon pool with an extremely powerful hydraulic motor that creates a current of up to 3 mph. I swim in this current like a salmon swimming upstream. I typically swim at about 1.85 - 2.25 mph. I have not been able to sustain speeds in excess of 2.5 mph for an entire 30 minute workout. Since there are no walls for kick turns as in a lap pool, there is no resting, no relief.

The Endless Pool is an incredible piece of training equipment for triathletes, competitive swimmers, or just those seeking better fitness in a non-impact way. The pool also has very powerful spa jets and an extremely powerful heater, which allows us to use the pool as a huge hot tub or spa. Not only is this fun for the family, but it is also a great relief for muscles that are sore from running or biking.

While the pool was extremely expensive, I will say that it's definitely better than an in-ground lap pool because there are no walls for you to kick off. You are swimming in the current the entire time, with no rest and nothing to hold onto or kick off from—so you are getting the real experience of an actual open water swim.

PREPARING FOR CYCLING AND RUNNING WORKOUTS

Getting ready for long rides on my bike would take at least 30 minutes of prep work: I would have to oil the chain, top off the air pressure in the tires to exactly 115 pounds, prepare/mix two bottles of liquid nutrition, check seat bag for tubes, air cartridges and patch kit, pick out the bibs and bike jersey, make sure my cell phone was charged, plan the route, and gather all other stuff that I was going put in my jersey (credit card, iPod, emergency info, cash, GU packets, license, etc.)

I have learned that the prep work to get out the door can be very time-consuming, and sometimes could even get me so distracted that I'd actually run out of time to get the workout done, which would then compromise my entire day and I'd walk around angry, frustrated and disappointed that I had stupidly missed the workout. This, in fact, happened more times than I would care to admit. So, to minimize the risk of a missed workout, I would usually try to prepare everything the night before.

Tips to Complete Your Workouts

Here are some helpful hints I've learned over the years to help make sure I get my workouts completed, no matter what:

- Create some travel rules for your office, such that they do not put you on flights that are too early in the morning.
- If you do have an early morning flight, then get up two hours earlier and still get the workout in. There is no other way, because flights get delayed and your best plans of getting a workout done upon arrival may invariably get derailed.
- Go to bed much earlier than you have been accustomed to and get at least 7 – 8 hours of solid sleep.
- When the alarm goes off, never push the snooze button. Instead, LEAP out of bed and get on with your day immediately.
- No email access prior to your workouts; stay away from the computer. This must be a no-exceptions rule.
- Prepare all your gear and plans, charge your GPS watch, have all of your clothes and shoes laid out, and check everything the night before. That way, you can roll right out of bed in semi-REM consciousness, get into your gear and start your workout.
- Never negotiate with yourself in semi-REM sleep during the precious few minutes just before the alarm goes off. Never say, "Ah, I'll get up in just a few more minutes," or, "I can get this workout done tonight because I have a light schedule." Never renegotiate with yourself when you are half-asleep; your workouts will always lose.

The Laws Governing Workout Probabilities

Through my vast experience of missing many workouts, trying desperately to get them in last minute and my compulsion to attempt to control the details of my day, I have developed two laws of predicting workout completion. I think that these may be universal laws that could apply to nearly all athletes.

The Law of Creeping Demands:

"The chance that something totally unexpected and urgent may derail my evening workout increases exponentially when I am traveling or skip my morning workout."

And the Callos Corollary of Semi-REM self-negotiation:

"The odds of missing today's workout increase exponentially by every minute I hesitate to immediately leap out of bed past 4:30 am."

BENEFITS OF EARLY MORNING WORKOUTS

Despite my best intentions of working out after business hours, I learned time and again that my best chance of completing a workout would be to start first thing in the morning. Trying to set time aside in the evening was very risky because legitimate things would unexpectedly pop up, nearly every single time. Also, I could have a tough day, be completely wiped out and not be in the mood, not be in the right frame of mind or not have the right energy level to even get started. It was far better to get up earlier and just do it. There really cannot be an exception to this rule or workouts will definitely be skipped.

Having said that, I didn't always get my workouts done in the mornings. Often, my workouts required a break between them, so there was no way to get them done all at one time. On many days, I worked out in the morning, and then again in the evening.

Here is an interesting lesson, one that proved yet again that I should do the workouts first thing in the morning, no matter what:

I was in Portland on business and found a fantastic pool at The Riverplace Athletic Club. It was an indoor pool in a beautiful wood building reminiscent of an old barn. It was only for lap swimming and the pool bottom was lined with some kind of soft rubber which made it unique and fun.

So on my first night in town I went to check it out. I was going to swim a mile, and I even brought my lap-counting beads to make sure I did the full distance. But because of so many meetings that day, I'd only had oatmeal and some berries for breakfast and nothing else for the entire day. When I reached the pool it was about 6:00 pm, but despite my great desire to do so, I just had no gas in the tank and couldn't complete the workout. I got a bit over three-quarters, and that was it; I had a major bonk.

I was determined to make up for lost time the next day and was looking forward to jumping back into the pool first the very first thing in the morning. They opened at 4:30 am, my meetings for the next day had been whittled down from three to just one at 8:00 – 9:00 am. Since my flight was not until 3:00 pm, I slept in and changed my plan to do the meeting first, then go to the pool later and swim for an extra long time: two hours from 10 am – 12 noon. I was very excited to get this two hour workout done and even ordered a large breakfast to give myself the energy for my late morning swim.

But when I showed up for my 8:00 am meeting, they told me that the executive was stuck in a storm in Denver and the meeting had to be cancelled. My company had learned of the cancellation and had rescheduled my flight to get me home sooner—a car was waiting downstairs to take me to the airport. I had to rush, and I barely made my earlier flight home. I was disappointed because I was really looking forward to that long swim.

The point is that no matter what, I always had to try to get my workouts done the very first thing in the morning, regardless of how early it had to be, even 3:00 am; that's another one of the great benefits of having your own Endless Pool.

A Memorable Early Morning Workout Experience

As tough and cold as early morning workouts can be, I've had some really unforgettable adventures. One morning in April 2008, I hit the road at 5:30 am and made my way toward Orange County through Laguna Canyon and out onto Pacific Coast Highway for the return trip. It was a total ride of at least 65 miles. I had done most of the prep work the night before, which allowed me to hit the road quickly in the morning.

Leaving my house so early on my bike was an entirely different experience. New sounds, new smells, and things just looked different in the predawn hour as compared to the mid-day sun. Also, I noticed that on an early Sunday morning, there was far less traffic than I'd typically experience during my weekend rides. I felt much safer in the light traffic of early Sunday morning, so I decided to ride through the typically-busy area called Little Saigon.

Little Saigon starts in Westminster and Garden Grove and is predominantly located along Bolsa Ave. Vietnamese-Americans constitute 30% the population, but there are also large numbers of Cambodian and Laotian immigrants residing in the area as well. Many of these residents arrived during the second refugee wave in 1980, and now they own a large share of the businesses in Little Saigon, which was especially noticeable as I passed by the restaurants, bakeries and grocers.

The early morning sights, sounds and smells of these different restaurants preparing for their Sunday patrons was a remarkable and memorable experience, especially so early in the morning.

As an aside, some of the best foot massages and body manipulations can be obtained in this area along Bolsa. For only $20, one is provided with an Asian-style massage, deep tissue foot and calf massage and an array of twists and contortions to manipulate the joints and stretch ligaments. It's an incredible deal. These massages are unique in that one remains fully clothed and the massage takes place in a unique massage chair that also folds flat. These massages take place in a large room where perhaps 20 people are all getting massages at the same time. It's a unique experience and I highly recommend it.

TRAINING AT NIGHT

I have had a lot of experience of night workouts because I foolishly slept in or thought I might get the workout done after business hours. I've made a lot of mistakes working out at night and I've learned some important safety measures I'd like to pass along.

If you must do a workout at night, go way overboard with precautions. Always wear a reflective vest if you are running outside at night, use flashing LED lights both in the front and back, and don't forget to carry a very powerful handheld flashlight.

Here's why: first, a headlamp, which is what most people recommend, does not give you proper perspective and you cannot see dips or ruts in the shadows (I've learned this the hard way). Secondly, you can take that high-powered handheld flashlight and point it right at cars that may be coming at you. This alone has likely saved me at least two times while out running late at night on the busy streets of Long Beach.

Also, I recommend the strongest possible light beam you can find. The reason for the super-high power beam is that it can also be used to ward off animals and would-be knuckleheads that might try to approach you in the dark; if the beam is strong enough, it will temporarily disorient them. And before you ask: yes, this happened to me as well. I was running up the San Gabriel Valley Riverbed trail when I was approached by an aggressive individual around midnight. I pointed that halogen high beam straight into his eyes and he immediately dropped to his knees, clutching his eyes. We both learned an important lesson that night. Of course, anyone will tell you that running at night can be dangerous, and it is. The reason I had been running very late that night was because my flight had been delayed, and as often happened, I had negotiated with myself in my half-REM sleep earlier that day, that I could run when I got home early that afternoon. Wrong. Murphy's Law kicked in again. That's why I say again, "Do the workouts first thing in the morning, no matter how early you have to get out of bed."

Sometimes the Time Commitment is Overwhelming

Sometimes the time commitment required to complete all the training workouts can really be a challenge. Fifteen hours a week may not seem like that much on paper, but you really need to add as much as 15 – 30 additional minutes per workout for preparation time alone.

And of course, you also need to add in the procrastination factor, which is the little internal debate about whether it is:

- Too cold
- Too early
- Too dark
- Too rainy
- Too hot
- Too late
- Too foggy
- Too close to dinner
- Too windy, etc.

The procrastination factor is just one more thing that you have to fight-off to get yourself moving. Depending on the day, this factor can add another 5 minutes to several hours (especially if you have something more exciting to work on).

So a 15-hour workout schedule actually will take about 20 hours. And even more hours when you factor-in additional stretching, special meal and shake preparation, gear prep and so on.

A 20-hour weekly time commitment may not seem like all that much, but when you consider that you really must get a minimum of 7 - 8 hours of sleep each night for recovery and to be well rested for the next day, that only leaves only about 16 hours each day for everything else. After work, personal hygiene, meals, commute, family time, Internet browsing...there really is very little else that one can manage to do other than these workouts.

So when we did manage to get up to our weekend beach shack

on vacation, I would have a big pile of reading to get caught-up with, especially all the great triathlon and biking magazines. Plus I might have every intention of watching the Tour de France or to review a DVD of the Ford Ironman World Championships. But more often than not, none of that would get done because my workouts, and all related preparation, had to take priority. If I didn't do the workouts first thing, the day would quickly fill with other family activities, web browsing, goofing off around Carpinteria, and I would have no opportunity to fit in the workouts. This was especially true if my great friend and cousin-in-law Chris Barsh happened by and invited me to the Carpinteria Island Brewery for a couple of pints of our all time favorite Island Blonde Ale. It's a Kolsch-style ale brewed from five different types of malt, with a liberal dose of Czech Saaz hops, so good in fact, it won 1st Place at the California State Fair. One glass of Island Blonde invites another, so if I headed over to the Island Brewery prior to getting in my workout, the odds were 100% that I wouldn't get a workout completed that day. I tried to rationalize my Saturday afternoons at Island Brewery by considering this a multi-tasking and time management coup: I was spending quality time with Chris Barsh and also doing my Carbo loading. But the reality is that it would be very difficult to drink enough beer to have a significant carbo loading impact. When I was really carbo loading before important workouts or races, I would skip the beer and go straight to the Carbo-Pro by SportQuest.

THE TIME COMMITMENT
AND PERSONAL RELATIONSHIPS

When pursuing the Ironman dream, many people must pull together to support you, especially if you are married, have a family or are working full time. The importance of a support network cannot be overstated. The time to get everything done has to come at the expense of something. It's as simple as that. Where do you find an extra 15 - 20 hours a week? You surely cannot cut back on your sleep; when you are training this hard and for so many hours, you must have the proper amount of sleep for your body to repair and rebuild.

The time required for these workouts—including all the

planning, preparation, data recording, reporting and analysis—comes at the expense of relationships, work, keeping up the house, and other hobbies. In my case, the time came from work, from the elimination of essentially all TV, casual reading and keeping up the house. I hired out a lot of things I would have normally performed on my own, and for the first time in my life, I was actually paying someone to wash my cars. (As a weekend ritual and hobby I used to always take great care and pride in washing and waxing by hand our two Porsches, a BMW and April's beloved Range Rover.)

The Ironman pursuit requires one to be exceptionally well organized and to have systems in place to ensure that things don't start slipping through the cracks, because believe me, they will if you are not careful.

That's where your support network really comes in. This pursuit can stress work, family and outside friendships. If your critical relationships are not solid and in good standing prior to starting your Ironman training, I would suggest that you really shore up those relationships first and have a candid discussion with your work associates, friends and loved ones about the toll your training will likely have them; do not underestimate this impact, as it will be greater than you can imagine. You will likely miss events, have more difficulty making all of your meetings, and your friends may begin to notice that you just aren't around as much as you used to be. You may even have to relinquish your seat at the end of the brewery during training season.

COLDS, THE FLU
AND BEING SICK

In my profession as a CEO Advisor, speaker, executive coach and trainer, I have to travel. A lot. Traveling is tough on the training schedule, and it's even harder when you're sick.

People tell me I tend to get sick quite often and I'm convinced that this is due to the combination of my body being in a constant state of build, tear-down, repair, and then all the travel, the confined spaces on planes, and frankly, meeting so many people and shaking so many hands. At the conclusion of some of my speeches there could be as many as 50 – 100 people that I meet. All those people came from different locations; they shook hands with friends they hadn't seen in a while, and so on. It's a little scary.

I'm not quite a germophobe, but I am trying to be extremely careful about large groups, speeches, public areas while traveling and especially my personal space on airplanes.

My schedule often required me to have multiple meetings, do some speeches and a couple of workshops in a single trip. Sometimes the only thing I could do all week long was a 30 minute run followed by some calisthenics and resistance training in my hotel room using the rubber exercise bands that I always carry with me when traveling.

On one trip in Denver, I found an outstanding club and paid a daily fee to use their facilities. I did the weight training and swim portion of my workout, but then when it came to the run portion, I just didn't have it. I felt really bad and funny and strange. I ran for 15 minutes on the treadmill and couldn't handle it, so I went down to the pool and swam again.

I went back to the hotel and was up most of the night with a stomach ailment. I still had to conduct a two-hour workshop/speech the next morning, but I was quietly dying inside. I was so dehydrated from the stomach bout that my lips and mouth were all chapped.

Just recently I was on a plane and the guy sitting right next to me was coughing the entire flight. Worse, the guy directly behind me was coughing so violently – and without covering his mouth – that I could literally feel the expelled air hitting the top of my head. I was furious, but what could I do? And yes, I got sick; I probably psyched myself into getting sick because I kept thinking the entire time, "These guys are going to get me sick!" So sick in fact that I was in my bed nearly 100% of the time from Thursday until Sunday with the worst flu ever. Not to mention how disappointing it is to lose 4 - 5 days of fitness.

I follow this rule about working out when sick: if it's just a head cold and sinus congestion, it's generally safe and OK to work out, but if you have any chest congestion, working out is to be avoided.

A Rollercoaster Month Begins

May 2008 started out well; I successfully completed a really tough week of training. It wasn't easy, but I did it, and it was at least a great start to what would end up being a crazy month.

Subject: John Callos Weekly Update
From: John D. Callos
To: David Warden

Hi David,

I am happy to report that I completed all the hours this week. It was tough and took a lot of time. But my wife April encouraged me to get out there, even when I was dog-tired, and I just finished everything at about 9:15 tonight.

I am doing the proper hydration, I am refueling after my workouts, and I am getting plenty of sleep. But I feel overworked. It is interesting because I am putting in my best effort, and I am returning home thinking that I have set new records in power—but I find out that my times are actually worse or my power is less than I thought.

I did the following level of training volume this week:

- Bike: 140 miles
- Swim: 3.5 miles
- Run: 20 Miles
- Total workout time: 14.5 hours

The highlight of my week was a long bike ride at a pretty good cadence. During that ride, I am happy to report that I broke three new Critical Power Records in terms of watts on the bike. The ride was 72 miles long and took 4:23 with an average speed of 16.4 MPH on my road bike.

The low note of the week was the running. My long run on the weekend was very slow and I walked many times after trying to force myself into a Zone 3 HR, only to bonk every time. I'd walk a bit to recover and try hard again, only to have to walk again; finally I just settled into a slower pace and finished the workout the best that I could.

The week started off very slowly and poorly due to this horrible stabbing trapezoid problem from the aero position while on the bike. I know that I complain about this a lot David, but the pain is just so severe. It is literally like someone is stabbing me in the back with a large butcher knife. I stop and rub or put pressure on that large mass of knotted muscle, but it doesn't really do anything other than to remind me that I have a huge knot back there. I have now switched over to my road bike and am feeling much better. Not cured, but in less pain; plus there is the added benefit that I can actually turn my head to see traffic because the pain is less severe.

This trapezoid muscle problem is a serious issue and massage is not working at all. Someone told me it's an acute flare-up of something called a trigger point, and they can see physical knots of muscle in my back. We have got to figure out what is going on, and why.

In summary, I could use a break and am glad things are easier this week.

Thanks for not beating me up about being so down and out about my trapezoid problem; this was extremely discouraging after all that work. I am living in constant, daily pain.

-John

David congratulated me on completing the most challenging athletic week of my life, and then reminded me that the process of improving fitness was actually the process of breaking down fitness, and then recovering so that the body could reach a new balance, which would be higher than it was before.

That being said, he told me that no one was going to break new records in fitness during a 14 hour workout week, which was preceded by a 13 hour workout week. I was at the height of my training volume, and my body had never been more stressed, but I was doing well.

This was an immense comfort and relief, and things were going well—but that's exactly when real life hijacked the rest of my training plans.

By the middle of May 2008, I found myself being pulled in many different directions in a single week with a Boy Scout campout, business, workouts, etc. I was really feeling the stress. Plus, my business partner had just left on vacation, and the worst of all, my dad was rear-ended and landed in the hospital in intensive care for three days.

I am the eldest son of the eldest son in a Greek family—and with that distinction comes certain expectations for pulling the family together in times such as these. So on top of everything else, I had this most important issue of all: my dad needed my help, his doctors needed to be contacted and advised, and the family needed constant updates.

This is just the reality we have to deal with while still trying to get the training completed. You learn to get in the workouts whenever you can.

TRAINING WHILE TRAVELING ON BUSINESS

My anxiety about completing all my workouts was exacerbated by the necessity of my hectic business travel schedule. Because of the economic downturn, we anticipated a potential impact on our business and planned ahead by hiring a sales professional to help us meet more CEOs. As a result, many of my days were often packed solid with CEO meetings. With all that in mind, I needed to figure out how to keep all the plates spinning while not letting my hard-earned fitness level come crashing to the floor.

Since I was going to be on the road so much, it looked as if the only thing I could definitely do were some runs and a series of in-room exercises (push ups, leg lifts, sit ups, etc.). I knew for sure that there would be no excuse not to complete these. Weekends were usually free, so that could be for longer bike rides; but mid-week cycling and swims were difficult to near impossible while I was traveling.

I also had to adjust my training schedule based on the available time I had while traveling, as well as the equipment or facilities I had access to at each location. For example, I needed a real pool to do my swim workouts, not just a wading pool or a lima bean-shaped hotel pool. These things had to be coordinated in advance: not all pools were created equal and just because a hotel claimed to have a pool didn't necessarily mean I could schedule a swim workout at that location.

Similarly, the gyms in many hotels, even some of the best, are just totally inadequate and I usually had to try to find a local health club instead.

I would forward my schedule to David and he'd try to develop a training schedule around my travel schedule. Here's an email that I sent to David so that he could try and plan some workouts around my schedule:

Subject: John Callos Travel Schedule
From: John D. Callos
To: David Warden

Hi David,
This is going to be a difficult week. Please try and work with this schedule:

- MON: Home, but I will not have much time for long workouts. I will definitely do a swim for 45 – 60 min, and a run if I can.
- TUES: I will leave for Las Vegas around 12:00 noon. Best option will be a longer bike ride in morning or a brick (estimated 3 hour bike + 45 minute run)
- WED: I'll be in Las Vegas at meetings, after which I will fly to Portland. Best chance will be a long 2.5 – 3 hour run in morning. No swim, No bike.
- THURS: I will try to swim a 1,000 meter time trial at the Riverplace Pool in Portland, starting very early in the morning. I may also throw in a run along the Willamette River jogging trail or do weights after the swim.

- FRI: I will be back home but arriving late the night before, and likely will be beat. I will try some moderate workouts in the morning, but after that I need to be in downtown Los Angeles for meetings so will only be able to manage at most 90 – 120 minutes (bike or swim or both). I'll be attending a late night football game at Servite High School with the family, so an evening workout will be out of the question.
- SAT: I'll be heading to our weekend beach shack in the morning. There will be no time to work out before we leave. I can do a run or bike in the mid-afternoon in the Santa Barbara foothills. (Estimated 2.5 hour bike followed by 45 min brick run)
- SUN: I'll still be at the beach shack. I will do a long bike ride and run brick. I will need to make up for lost time during the week of travel. (Estimated 6 hours on the bike followed by a 1.5 hour brick run)
- MON: Still at beach shack. I will try to do an easy swim for 1 hour at the Community Pool (Olympic size) and/or a recovery run for 45 minutes.

    Thanks for working around this schedule David.
    -John

However, Murphy's Law and the Callos Workout Corollaries often kicked-in. Here they are again:

The Law of Creeping Demands:

"The chance that something totally unexpected and urgent may derail my evening workout increases exponentially when I am traveling or skip my morning workout."

And the Callos Corollary of Semi-REM self-negotiation:

"The odds of missing today's workout increase exponentially by every minute I hesitate to immediately leap out of bed past 4:30 am."

TRAINING JOURNAL ENTRY:
Family & travel commitments

I am disgusted that I missed this workout. Connor had his graduation from Freshman formation and April did not tell me about it until this morning. I dropped him off at 5:30 am then came home, and she told me we had to get ready for the ceremony that lasted almost all day. Then, afterward, there was a party and celebration and then they went to the movies. It was a series of plans that I was unaware of, got swept into and my day was completely shot for the workout. When am I going to learn that I MUST get the entire workout completed in the morning, even if I have to get up at 2:30 am? I cannot wait to get it completed later in the day because something inevitably pops up out of nowhere. Today was the perfect example. Yet again.

Despite David's careful planning, my best of intentions and my generally positive attitude, sometimes I would complete only 2 hours of workouts in an entire week.

I spoke to David regarding my concerns about falling behind on my training program, wondering if it might make sense for him to just tell me to:

- Get in "x" number of hours on a bike
- Get in "x" hours of swimming
- Do a long ride of "x" time
- Do a long swim of "x" time
- Run for "x" hours
- Do at least one long run of "x" hours or miles
- Do "x" number of weight sessions, etc.

and then I'd just go off and try to find a way to fit these workouts into my travel schedule whenever I could. Then I'd make up the shortfall on the weekends with epic training days of 6 – 8 hours. I was worried that a strict daily schedule was going to be really difficult to maintain and that I was going to fall behind. For example: I may not have access to a pool, a gym or a bike on the specific days a workout called for such equipment. Plus, whenever I missed a workout, I felt genuinely bad about myself for wimping-out and making excuses. This was really starting to cause me stress.

Worst of all, I feared that my stress level would increase as I'd be constantly stressed out about trying to get in a particular workout on a particular day, or worse, end up constantly missing workouts despite my best intentions. Therefore, I reasoned that if I knew I had all week to accomplish just a certain number of hours for each discipline, then I could do my best to find a way to fit them in whenever I could and make it up on the weekends.

I knew this was outside the bounds of the formal Joe Friel training program, but this was the real world for many business executives and consultants. If we could base my workout weeks on cumulative hour goals, I'd have a better shot of getting everything completed. Further, I could reduce the self-imposed stress of missing a particular workout, just so long as I made it up later that week. This was not the ideal physiological approach to stress and rest, but this was the only way that I thought I could complete all the workouts.

David rejected this idea and instead, custom-planned all of my weeks based upon my travel schedule. Often, he'd modify the schedule based on cancelled flights and other legitimate obstacles that prevented me from strictly adhering to his scheduled workouts. One time in Minneapolis, even though we selected a hotel because they had a pool listed on their website, the pool was nothing more than a heated indoor wading pool for small children. I had to contact David to find something else for me to do instead.

THE IRONMAN LIFESTYLE AT HOME

The Ironman Triathlon is not just an event or a sport, it's really more of a lifestyle. To me it has meant changes to my sleeping habits, my diet, what I do in my free time, who I spend my time with, what I read and how I prioritize and organize my life.

I've organized my activities around this lifestyle and have made major changes to our home in order accommodate my training. For example, I have converted a portion of our garage into a bike shop. The bike shop has four walls, a workbench, TV, DVD, VCR, computer CPU and monitor, Internet access, a closet for bike clothes (called "kits"), peg board for every conceivable bike tool, literally hundreds of bike parts, Kreitler Rollers for indoor workouts, Power Meters, heart rate monitors and other electronic bits, seven different road bikes, a time trial bike, extra wheel sets for different kinds of roads, even a lounge chair and side table to take notes while I watch triathlon training videos. The list goes on and on.

And then there is the Ironman Café. The Ironman Café is our former prep kitchen which has been fully converted to support my Ironman lifestyle. First and foremost is the Nespresso machine, which makes perfect espresso every time.

Next is a refrigerator filled with drinks, gels, oils, and food items specifically for the Ironman diet and nutritional needs.

All the cupboards are filled with hydration bottles for running and biking, and nearly every shelf is filled with nutritional supplements, protein powders, energy drinks, and my all time favorite Carbo-Pro. All the drawers are filled with overflow items for my races such as travel bags, my wetsuit (which fits very nicely in a large shelf under the stovetop), my hydration pack for ultra running, etc.

The dishwasher is always filled with my most recent water bottles, and it has been customized to handle all the plastic bike bottles and hydration systems so that none of the caps can slip through the grates and get melted in the drying cycle. It's the perfect solution for keeping all my bike bottles clean and out of sight.

But what about all the clothes and workout gear? Enter: the Ironman bathroom.

The Ironman bathroom has been totally retrofitted for the sport. The most incredible item is a super efficient, compact washer/dryer unit made by Haier. This unit washes and then immediately dries my workout gear, all in one step, all in the same unit, all in the Ironman bathroom. It is just fantastic. The unit is very small and has been fitted under the counter, just like a built-in dishwasher, but instead, it's a combo washer/dryer in one compact unit; I really do love this machine. The moment I return from a workout, the gear goes into the washing machine, and by the time I return in the evening, it's there for an evening workout. No workout clothes on the floor or smelling-up the family laundry basket. I take care of my own workout clothes and am happy to do so. These are high-tech fabrics that need special attention and care. The Haier compact unit is absolutely perfect and it couldn't be simpler to use.

I also have a chin-up bar, the bicycle frame from my first Triathlon mounted onto the wall, my race medals for inspiration and a Tanita scale (which measures body fat, water weight, muscle mass, total weight, etc). The bathroom has a full wall of cabinets that have been fitted with small boxes that hold all of my Tri-related workout clothes and shoes. There are individual containers for running shorts, bike jerseys, running shirts, socks and gloves, bike shorts, and an entire rack of running shoes. No Ironman bathroom would be complete without a small pharmacy of items for treating everything from blisters to muscle strains to severe pain. I've got it all organized in medical boxes; it's a veritable doctor's office of medical supplies. One box is my special crash cart with every conceivable medical item needed to deal with my constant toenail problems and blisters. The Ironman bathroom is just the perfect set-up and I am the only one who uses the room, so my gear is always safe.

We have committed all of this space to 100% Ironman lifestyle functionality. We still maintain another kitchen, other bathrooms and plenty of space for other things in our lives—but the bike garage and the separate Ironman wing of the house is testament to my family's commitment to supporting my Ironman lifestyle.

CHAPTER FIVE

SACRIFICE

TRAINING BEGINS TO TAKE ITS TOLL

The pursuit of the Ironman dream takes an incredible toll, not just on the athlete, but also on his or her family, friends, finances, job and work associates. I often think of this pursuit as a very selfish endeavor and sometimes tell people that it is a colossal waste of time, especially in the heavy weeks when most of the weekends are committed to training.

The time commitment away from one's family is enormous. Multiple five to eight-hour workouts on the weekends are not unusual, especially during the heavy build weeks. Uploading and recording all the workout details and power, HR and GPS course data can take an additional 1 - 2 hours. Once the data is input, the research and analytical side kicks in and I'll spend time studying how I did and discussing this in my blog and my online training journal on TrainingPeaks.com, as well as in emails and regular phone conversations with my coach.

All this training takes an enormous amount of time, so it's very helpful to have a support network.

THE SUPPORT NETWORK

My wife has been mostly amazed, amused, accepting, supportive and understanding. Connor has been terrific and it feels great to have a 15 year old son who is so proud that his dad is accomplishing these endurance events. There have been many, many times when I was just too tired to accomplish various workouts, only to have my wife rib me, pressure me or use some kind of reverse-psychology to get me out of the door.

I know what she's doing and how she's working me, but it always does the trick and gets me moving. Sometimes she'll say, "Yeah, don't work out. You don't need to. You know you are totally ready for the Ironman." This of course is effective sarcasm that gets me out the door pronto.

Other times she'll say, "Go on. Come on, just get out there and get going." Other times it's just the reality angle that works best: "You know, if you don't do it now, it is going to be bugging you and stressing you out all day long. Why not just get it over with right now?" Somehow, she can read me well enough to know when to push just the right buttons. This has been an amazing means of support. Without her ribbing and words of encouragement, I'm certain that I would have skipped some of the more intense workouts that were critical to my preparation.

Sometimes Connor knows how to push me along as well. The night before my first 70.3 in Hawaii, I was pacing the floor of our hotel at 3:00 am. I had just finished my pre-race meal (four hours before the race to allow time for it to digest) and Connor showed up with words of encouragement that I will never forget for as long as I live.

I was really worried about the swim and Connor knew it. He had scouted the swim course with me earlier that day and we were both shocked at the length of the course when viewed from high atop the staging area for the bikes. Connor just sensed that I was still worried and he got up and came to me and gave me a huge hug and said, "Don't worry, Dad. You've got this. You've got it!"

Having my son support me like that was priceless. It also marked the first time in our lives when the little boy who always needed support and encouragement had crossed that line into young adulthood; the point where he was now mature enough to sense the needs of others and to offer support. This was a powerful father-son moment triggered by Ironman, and it's a moment I will remember and cherish forever.

Another support mechanism was my coach, David Warden. As I mentioned before, David is one of the world's leading experts in the science behind Triathlon and the world's most effective training methods. Since he only works with a very small cadre of athletes, I am extremely lucky and grateful to have him on my team. Because of this, there is a subtle self-created pressure that I put on myself—I never want to let David down, especially since he took a chance on me. I wanted to prove to him that he made a good decision to work with me. Furthermore, I really loathe having to report that I didn't complete all of my workouts as scheduled. Knowing that David reviewed every workout and all my power and HR data was enough to get me out the door on some of the tougher days where I would have wanted to skip the workouts.

My business partner Kevin has also been incredibly supportive. I would either arrive at the office late or leave early, especially during daylight savings time. The extra work often fell onto him, but he never complained. He helped by trying to start meetings as late in the morning as possible (like around 10:00 am or 11:30 am), and when I was traveling, he would ensure that meetings were scheduled in a way that would not prevent me from doing critical morning workouts. Kevin also helped provide my advance calendar and meeting schedule to my coach, who needed to work my training plan around all the travel and multiple flights of each trip.

To claim there was no impact to our business would be to ignore reality. While it is impossible to calculate the cost, I believe there was a negative impact. I was not around as much, I was tired, I was irritable; sometimes I was in awful pain, and often I left early or arrived late in order to see different doctors. Client servicing never suffered, but our top line revenue could definitely have been enhanced if I were more actively focused on the business and less focused on triathlon.

It's just the reality of the endeavor; something has to give. And through it all, Kevin was nothing but completely supportive in all respects, despite the costs this endeavor placed upon him and our company. Kevin was also a fantastic help to conduct research to find doctors with a great reputation in the areas where I had ailments, such as the hip and knee problems.

THE TOLL THAT IRONMAN WILL HAVE ON YOU AND OTHERS

There is simply no way to maintain a completely normal life while training for the Ironman event. You might as well face the situation squarely and figure out if you (and your support network) are willing to pay the price.

- You will be going to bed a lot earlier (I go to bed at 8:00 pm – 8:30 pm; it used to be 10:00 pm – 11:00 pm).
- You will be cranky and short-tempered, especially during your long weeks. If you had a short temper before you start this endeavor, it will likely be greatly magnified by your training.
- You will be sore a lot of the time; you will be limping and aching. You will likely complain about it. At first you will get sympathy, but that won't last long. Too much complaining can grate on people, trust me on this one.
- You will be tired and not as fun to be around at times; perhaps most of the time during your hard weeks.
- You will be preoccupied and not always present or able to give your full and complete attention to your spouse, children, work associates, extended family and friends.

- You will definitely be spending a lot of money on such things as equipment, coaching, bikes, travel, race fees, nutritional supplements, bike repairs, race uniforms, books, power meters, HR monitors, a body fat scale, GPS watches, an Endless Pool, gym fees, association dues, equipment bags, wetsuits, aero and road helmets, custom bike fittings (a must), race day souvenirs...the list goes on and on.
- When you spend this much money, one can't really get on a spouse about their spending habits...even if they already have 137 pairs of shoes, 27 purses and 18 winter coats. Do you really want to go there? Do you really want your spouse digging through your bike shop receipts, examining all of your high-tech clothing purchases? (Castelli's top of the line bike bibs are around $260, add a jersey and you are close to $350 just for a single bike kit).

AIM FOR SOME LEVEL OF BALANCE

The support from family, work associates and friends is very important. Sure, I could still have finished the full Ironman without this support, simply because I was just so determined to do so. But I know for an absolute fact that I finished healthier, faster and happier with the knowledge that I have so many people who love me, who are pulling for me and have supported me throughout this incredible journey.

I must stress that it is important to have balance, and I have incorporated family time into my training schedule as well. This doesn't have to be mutually exclusive. For example, if my wife and I were going to dinner and I was supposed to meet her there after her shopping, I would leave my keys at home and jog there, which was about 2.5 miles away. (On one occasion, I got there and found out that they had relocated. So I jogged home for another 2.5 miles, got in my car and met her at the new place. Lesson learned: call in advance and confirm the location.)

Or if we were going to meet for lunch and April asked me to get there early and save a table, I would get on my fixed gear bike and race over to the restaurant. I'd meet her there, and then pedal home. It was a quick 10 miles, but every bit helped. I would also return videos by putting them in my backpack and running over to Blockbuster instead of driving, if I needed cash, I would often run to the bank instead of drive.

I also was "that dad." The dad who would ride his road or triathlon bike to Connor's football games, wherever they were held; away games were always the best because it allowed me to get in some longer rides. It was quite a scene to show up at those games with my bike kit, but I was still able to get in the bike ride and watch the game. It was also fun for Connor to show his friends and coaches how his dad was working out. Sometimes, when I had a brick workout to complete, I would ride the bike to his games (20 miles or so), run around the football field before the game and during halftime, then ride home. Other times, I would actually run to his school, which was close to twenty miles away, or I would have April drop me off on the way to Connor's school, and I would run 15 – 18 miles home. No kidding.

DISCIPLINE IS THE KEY

One of the pitfalls I've learned (the hard way) is that working hard without discipline is a recipe for disaster. Just pushing harder and harder, without the discipline of rest, diet, stretching, hydration, fueling/nutrition and staying within my ability or prescribed HR zones, can lead to huge problems. These include serious injuries, bonking on rides, a plateau in training progress, or even a trip to the hospital in the case of serious hydration deficiencies.

We must have the discipline to stay within our abilities and tell ourselves "NO" especially when we come up with some harebrained idea in the middle of the workout.

Examples? Sure, I have plenty.

- Trying to set a new personal mile record on the Cal State Long Beach track without being warmed up; as a result, pulling a calf muscle and having to skip the next three days of workouts.
- Not stopping to pick up water bottles or nutrition packs if

they drop on the road, and then either bonking or suffering from dehydration.

- Deciding on a whim that it might be interesting to ride the 112 miles from Long Beach to Santa Barbara, without any cycling base and in the middle of a freezing winter windstorm. Not turning around when it got really cold and extremely windy because that would be admitting defeat.

- While on a recovery day, getting into a heated race with a cyclist who passed me on the Pacific Coast Highway and chasing him down to Laguna Canyon, only to find myself totally spent and barely able to make the return ride home into a headwind.

- Trying to set a new record during my weightlifting session and pulling so hard and so quickly that I threw out my back on a seated rowing machine and had to be helped off the machine by others in the gym. That little stunt cost me at least two weeks of training time.

- Trying to ride to the top of a mountain just to be able to point and say I conquered that peak, even when I was unprepared and woefully under-trained for the extreme grade and very dangerous descent.

- Getting so mad at a car that ran me into the curb that I chased him down at the next stop light, placed my bike in front of his car to stop him, squirted my sports drink at him and challenged him to get out of his car...that was just plain nuts, but on the plus side, I did set two all-time high power wattage records trying to chase him down, and those records remain intact almost a year later.

- Thinking it would be really great bragging rights to say that I ran from Carpinteria to Ventura (16 miles) when my longest run prior to that was only about 6 miles. This idiotic move cost dearly—I lost 4 toenails and developed plantar fasciitis, setting me back at least a month.

I could go on and on. The point is that we need to be disciplined about our training; hard work alone is not the answer. Working out really hard when that's not part of your plan is just plain foolish.

We must turn our backs on the fun and exciting diversions or tests if they are not part of our overall training plan and strategy. Sometimes, that is really hard to do because you will have a lot of extra energy and feel totally capable to do more, to ride further, to lift heavier weights, to run faster. But any of these can lead to unanticipated injuries, which will really set your training back by days, weeks or even months.

We all work hard. But champions, I believe, have that extra bit of discipline to hold back despite the strong desire to push even harder. Champions understand that training is a process, not a single event.

It's my belief that you really need all three: patience, discipline and hard work (when it's part of your plan). Champions are patient and disciplined, and they work hard when their workout calls for extreme effort. But hard work without discipline can only lead to disappointment, and ultimately, injury.

RECORDING YOUR THOUGHTS WHILE WORKING OUT

I strongly recommend some sort of a system to capture all of your random thoughts and to-do items that will inevitably pop into your head during all your hours on the road, in the pool and in they gym. For example, I keep waterproof note pads in my shower, at my bedside, by my Endless Pool and in my car. I swear by the Rite in the Rain waterproof tablets available at www.riteintherain.com. I also have a special notepad integrated into my wallet (www.Davidco.com), a separate note-taking system for my iPhone and a to-do list integrated into Outlook that utilizes the principles of David Allen's GTD methodology.

It is important to have quick access to these note systems because you'll start thinking a lot more than usual and you'll need to capture those thoughts. In addition, since you will be pulled in many directions and not have as much time in the office or at home, things will start to slip through the cracks if you don't use a leak-proof system to capture and follow through on those items.

I am also a huge proponent of GTD (Getting Things Done) by David Allen; I have been using their products and systems for nearly ten years and swear by them. Look him up at www.Davidco.com. As a consultant, I've tried nearly every system and I can state with confidence that there is nothing better for me or my clients than the GTD system. I strongly recommend attending one of their seminars held throughout the world. These are not inexpensive, but the value is 100s of times the price you'll pay for the event. If you want to get started right away, then at least buy David Allen's books and start implementing his GTD system.

KEEPING FOCUSED

Sometimes when we try to juggle so many things in order to get all of our training completed, we can become distracted. A perfect example of this occurred in September 2008, just barely two months away from Ironman Arizona.

Due to a series of urgent conference calls, I had to move my morning bike ride to the afternoon. But to save time, I loaded my best bike onto the roof racks of my new BMW 5-series and headed off to work. The plan was to leave the office a bit early, get two to three hours on the riverbed bike trail and be home for dinner by 6:30 pm.

All was well and I was feeling good, so after the ride I stopped by my local butcher shop for some free-range chicken for a post-workout BBQ. I was still in my cycling kit and my butcher took notice of this strange apparel. As a lifelong butcher, he enjoyed his product to what appeared to be an unhealthy level, and he was very interested in some ideas to improve his health. We got to talking and I lost track of time.

On my way back home, I was apparently distracted thinking about ideas for him—because I drove right into my garage with my most prized bike still attached to the roof of my car.

The damage was absolutely incredible. The rack, which had been very firmly attached to the roof, was ripped right off the car. In the process, it gorged massive dents at three points where the rack had been attached to the roof of the car. As the rack scraped across the roof, metal on metal, the roof was scratched and deeply indented. Plus, the sectional garage door was knocked right off the tracks and was so jammed-up that it had to be taken apart to be removed for repairs.

The 100% carbon fiber bicycle, however, came out of the situation with nary a scratch: it was still totally intact. The exception was the handlebar, which took the full blow as the only contact point with the concrete wall above the garage. All I can say is that Zipp makes incredibly strong handlebars and fantastic wheel sets. The handlebar was fine, and it appeared the bike was still in perfect shape.

The car was not so lucky. The damage was substantial, although fortunately I had a very reputable dent-removal company that repaired many of the dents and put the rack right back on.

Lesson learned: If you put a bike on the roof of your car, ALWAYS take your garage door opener and put it into your glove box. If you have a door opener integrated into your car's electronic system, put a small Post-It or piece of athletic tape over the button to remind yourself.

Get Ready to See the Doctor...
Often

Another major cost (financially, physically and mentally) of Ironman training that needs to be emphasized is: You will likely be going to see doctors and specialists much more frequently.

I have been to see more doctors in the past 12-months than in the past 30 years combined. My Ironman training regime has resulted in the following ailments or injuries:

- Broken ankle
- Hip problems that required four visits to an orthopedic surgeon for x-rays, an MRI and evaluations totaling over $7,000
- Knee problems that required thousands of dollars of additional x-rays and evaluations
- Belly-button hernia
- IT band problems in both legs
- Knotted trigger points called myofascial pain syndrome that required close to a dozen separate visits to doctors, dozens of deep-tissue sports massages in the upper trapezoid area and at least five Cortisone injections

- Black toenails, toenails constantly falling off
- Many Podiatrist visits and treatments
- Physical therapy
- Huge and very deep blisters that took weeks to heal
- A year-long plantar wart problem that required podiatrist surgery
- Plantar fasciitis
- Bleeding hemorrhoids (likely from bike)
- Four visits to dermatologists for diagnosis and removal of suspected pre-cancerous growths from sun exposure ...and the list goes on.

The whole idea of completing an Ironman is to test one's resolve, and there are very few opportunities in modern life where one can literally test the ultimate limit of their physical and mental boundaries.

As such, it has been said that over 90% of all those training for an Ironman incur at least one injury that requires over a week of recovery. Look at any Ironman event and you'll see athletes who've pushed themselves to the point of collapse, exhaustion, dehydration and even passing out.

Injury reared up in May 2008, the week just before my first Hawaii Ironman 70.3. I tried to downplay and ignore it until I finally couldn't, and I had to tell David.

Subject: Week in Review
From: John D. Callos
To: David Warden

Hi David,

I am injured in some way; I will be attempting to get an x-ray soon. I have something going on with my hip flexor, the hip joint itself, as well as some sort of nerve thing that is triggered at the point of my sit bone, going right through the center of the hip socket and down to my shin. I am guessing it is a nerve problem, but I am worried that it may possibly be a fracture, so I must check it out with an x-ray.

It only hurts on the bike and when I am sleeping in bed, which of course, I find very strange. It does not bother me when running or swimming. There is no particular event or trigger that I can trace this injury to, but this has really been a slow burn since the last quarter of 2007. This shooting pain that is waking me up at night has been happening for about three weeks now.

Training is extremely difficult on the bike, as when the hip starts shooting daggers down my leg it is unbearable and at that point I can only pedal with one leg and let the other one merely coast along, locked into my pedal cleat.

No matter the diagnosis, I am still doing the 70.3. My will is strong and I want to work hard. It is just difficult to tell the leg to move when that nerve thing hits. I am not superhuman in terms of ability to work through pain (I know that I have a very low pain threshold), but I will do whatever I can to complete all workouts and to finish the 70.3 with my original race plan.

I am in no way looking for you to ease up or give me a pass to take it easy. I will not use this situation to get a break from the workouts. I will make up what I owe you in terms of hours.

I really prefer to not acknowledge this injury, but I promised you complete candor at all times, and I really do not want to go to the doctor because I am afraid of what I might find. I do not want my dreams of an Ironman finish to be crushed.

That is my greatest fear right now. I do not fear the work that lies ahead in terms of training, I fear a diagnosis that may sideline me.

I love this sport and what it has done for me. People don't recognize me; I have been physically transformed, and this is just the beginning. You have been the impetus to transform my life through triathlon training, and this has done wonders for my self-confidence and getting my health back.

Meanwhile, I will continue with your plan. The biggest problem is going to be on the bike, but if the pain is too severe, like the other day, I will simply turn around and come home. No heroics here. I am too old to try and prove something here. I need to stay smart and use my head. So please do not worry that I will do something stupid.

Whatever the diagnosis, if any, I will give it to you straight and unfiltered. Then together we will figure out what to do to keep me on track.

-John

David was very concerned about me. He felt that this injury had been underplayed and that perhaps I had been trying to tough it out. He wanted to take it very seriously.

However, he also thought there was a very good chance this would not keep me from finishing the Ironman. We could maximize our chances by going to the doctor promptly and getting the problem diagnosed and addressed immediately. I was to stay off the bike for a week or so and just do a lot of swimming and running instead.

The good news was that I had already completed the biggest volume week, which was the most important, and I had already done several 3 hour rides and long runs. David was confident that because of my excellent base and consistency, I would still be prepared for the upcoming Hawaii Ironman 70.3.

Dealing With Hip and Nerve Problems

Kevin did some research online and found a nationally-recognized hip and sciatica nerve specialist who agreed to a phone consultation with me. Ultimately, this specialist ruled out my biggest fear of sciatica. I also saw my general practitioner who performed a lot of tests on flexibility, and I scheduled a visit with a very well known orthopedic surgeon and nerve specialist/expert by the name of Dr. Alan Feldman.

He was part of the Long Beach Orthopedic and Sports Medicine Specialty Group. This group works with some of the pro sports teams in Los Angeles; it had physical therapy, in-house x-rays, the whole deal. They were sports-specific and my doctor was a four-time Kona Ironman finisher, so he was a perfect fit for me. He completely understood my drive and need (compulsion) to complete a full Ironman. He was totally supportive.

I had the Hawaii Ironman 70.3 coming up shortly and my hip pain was getting worse.

TRAINING JOURNAL ENTRY:
The Hip Flexor Dilemma

This was likely my worst day ever on a bike. It was horribly hot and my hip flexor was KILLING me. It is now to the point where it starts right at the tip of the left sit bone, then goes (into my actual hip joint) through my lower back and then down the front and outside of my leg, down though the outside of the left shin bone.

I was cursing and tearing up from the pain. Then as soon as it came, it would go away after maybe 45 seconds. Then it would come back 2-3 minutes later. Once the pain stops, it cannot be replicated, even if I try to force it or push it, it will not happen. It just comes and goes on its own.

When it hits, I lose the ability to push or really control the leg like I want to...it sort of goes numb in a very painful way. I came home and told April it was the worst, most painful day on a bike in my life. But the thing is that I want to push harder, I want to ride longer, I am willing to work to the max, but this is totally unbearable. And why is it that all this stuff keeps happening on the left side?

I still could have managed to limp through the ride, easing up and maybe even getting off the bike to walk a bit. If it happened in the 70.3, I would still finish the whole race. It does not bother me on the run. But my hip pain keeps me up or wakes me up EVERY night.

The doctor sat me down with some very bad news that felt like a death sentence.

Based on his review of my condition he believed that a ligament deep within the hip may be pulling away from the bone—essentially detaching, in layman's terms. He also believed I was developing an early case of arthritis in the hip socket area and the tissue (the bursa sac) cushioning the hip ball and socket area was worn very thin.

He believed that the hip was referencing pain from the socket area into the hip flexor and groin area, and it appeared that there was some kind of pressure or inflammation near the base of the spine that was causing a nerve to be pinched or compressed in the sit-bone area when I am on the bike. This nerve compression was referencing pain all the way down my left leg and is particularly irritated while in the aero position on the Cervelo TT bike.

What did this mean?

Well, he did not change my workouts at all, and he said I was good to go for the race. Whew. That was an immense relief. But he said I needed some nerve tests, an MRI, during which some dye would be injected deep within my hip socket so the doctors could really understand what was going on in there.

He did some nerve and reflex tests on the left side and it was clear that there was nerve damage, weakness in certain muscles, significantly decreased flexibility on the left hip flexor as compared to the right, and poor reflexes when tapped with that rubber mallet. As he was going through the tests, it was clear even to a layman like me that my left side was behaving and responding differently to each stimulus he applied. We didn't need an x-ray to understand that something was obviously different on the left side.

It was not just one thing that caused this hip issue. It seemed that this problem had been slowly developing over time, instead of being caused by a shock or sudden impact injury such as a tear, snap or break. And whatever was going on, it was clearly isolated 100% on the left side.

On a positive note, Dr. Feldman was very impressed with my overall physical condition and what he said was excellent overall muscle tone and development. He was pleased with my overall health, fitness and well-toned leg muscles. That just made me proud and happy—what a transformation. He recorded all of his notes and comments into a digital recorder, carefully reviewing all aspects of my physical condition, my health, my goals, my training schedule and all the relevant details of the injury, including the results of his tests.

He told me that after Kona, I was to return to his office for more detailed tests, but I was free to continue training. He understood that stopping now was totally out of the question for me. Since the pain was so deep within the hip socket, it could not respond to ice or heat, so he gave me some very powerful NSAIDs (non-steroidal anti-inflammatories) and said I could use them on race day as well.

Voltaren and Celebrex were the two NSAIDs that worked miracles. There was no pain at all when I took them, and I was taking no pain medications of any kind, just the NSAIDs.

Over time, however, the hip pain returned and continued to plague me constantly, especially at night while in bed or on my bike. In August 2008, ongoing hip problems forced me to slow down a bit and get an MRI done, since it was the only way to really learn what was going on deep inside my hip joint.

HYPONATREMIA:
BE CAREFUL WITH NSAIDS ON RACE DAY

It has been well documented in medical literature that using NSAIDs on a race day is risky and potentially dangerous. The reason for the concern is the way in which NSAIDs may limit the proper functioning of the filtering process of the kidneys due to decreasing the blood flow to these organs, and also interfering with a hormone that regulates salt retention in the body. Whenever the body's ability to regulate salts and electrolytes is compromised, we increase the risk of developing hyponatremia.

Hyponatremia is somewhat rare, but occurs when the salt in your blood is diluted from too much water. This typically occurs when an athlete consumes extremely large quantities of plain water without adding electrolytes or salts through gels, tablets, capsules or sports drinks. Hyponatremia can also result from physical conditions that impair the body's ability to excrete water (such as the problems exacerbated through the use of NSAIDs). When the levels of salts and electrolytes are low, your body's cells can start to malfunction and swell. Mild cases can be treated with intravenous fluids, and we see that a lot on the course. But in acute cases, there can be rapid swelling of the brain and organs, which can result in a coma and possibly even death.

I left Dr. Feldman's office with a firm warning to ensure that I stayed properly hydrated during the race and in all training sessions whenever I was taking the NSAIDs. It would be vital that I develop a written hydration and electrolyte replacement strategy for the race, as well as a back-up plan if I were to lose any electrolyte supplements during the race (dropping the bottle of capsules during the bike ride has caused many athletes serious problems later in the day).

As for the trapezoid problem from the bike, he said that was more common than I would suspect, but in my case it may be an old injury, probably from reaching for something a bit too heavy and a bit too high overhead. My best guess is that this occurred about ten years ago when I attempted to bring down a very heavy mountain bike that was hung very high from our garage rafters; the moment I reached just a bit too far, I felt this tear and an electrical-shock sensation in that left trapezoid, and it has never been the same ever since. Over the years, that muscle tear formed some scar tissue that doesn't stretch like a normal muscle and so it just knots-up and stays in a contracted state.

Therefore, whenever I stretched that area on a bike or any other activity, it pulled and tugged on that scarred muscle and it quickly became irritated. He could definitely feel a very tight knot in my upper back. He gave me some medicated Lidocaine patches that I applied directly over that knotted trigger point and this was expected to reduce the pain. But it really never worked well.

Getting an MRI of the Hip

My Orthopedic Surgeon referred me to an MRI specialty center for a procedure that would hopefully identify the problems deep within my hip socket. The first step was to inject a dye deep within the hip. The needle for this procedure was the longest, biggest needle I had ever seen. I was told that this was one of the longest needles used because it had to penetrate so deep into the hip socket; thankfully, there was very little pain. Once the injection was complete, I was wheeled over to a large platform and told to relax and stay still as they quickly whipped out a roll of medical tape and made numerous wraps around my feet. Once my feet and legs were completely immobilized, they slid me into a giant MRI machine that was very cramped. Thirty minutes later, it was done.

With the MRI photos in hand, I went directly to my orthopedic surgeon. The diagnosis was that I was likely suffering from a chronic case of bursitis in my hip which ultimately caused the bursa sac to swell up against a major nerve.

(While this sounded reasonable and plausible at that time, eight months later, I remain unconvinced that this was an accurate diagnosis. I still don't believe that we conclusively know what is really going on deep inside my hip joint and the nerve that is giving me problems.)

The silver lining in all of this was that I was still permitted to continue on my Ironman quest, and surgery was not going to be required. My worst fear had been that I had a broken hip and all hopes of Ironman glory would be crushed—so anything other than that diagnosis was actually great news to me.

My workouts changed following the formal hip diagnosis. I was prohibited by David from doing any more serious training for a while. I could no longer do my high-speed track workouts at an all-out pace, nor could I continue with high tempo runs or run down hills. I needed to throttle back and stay focused on a slower pace which would result in far less bone-jarring compression. I took Voltaren twice a day in an attempt to reduce the swelling in the hip socket area.

Despite the reduction in training intensity and the use of NSAIDs, the hip problem was never fully resolved. At times the intensity of the hip pain receded, but I was left with a daily, low-grade ache that was more or less constant. The strange thing was that it did not seem to hurt too badly on the runs, but flared up on the long bike rides and, for some inexplicable reason, when I lay in bed at night the pain was horrible and often woke or kept me up.

The hip pain ultimately became so unbearable and constant that it became a real quality of life issue, so I sought additional perspective. I was referred to Dr. Jeffery Ho, a pain management specialist who is recognized as an expert with these kinds of chronic pain issues, especially in athletes. He understood my need to complete this Ironman quest and he was committed to reducing the pain I was feeling.

Just one month prior to the Ironman, I resorted to Cortisone steroid shots that went very deep into the hip socket. Dr. Ho pulled out that same huge needle I had seen when they did the dye injection for my hip MRI. He explained that this particular needle was probably the longest needle that could be used to make an injection into the human body. Having been through this once before, I was not about to watch him perform the injection, nor did I want to even look at the needle again.

Despite my greatest hopes, I did not experience tremendous relief from the Cortisone shot and was really disappointed. I was on a daily regimen of Celebrex and a long-lasting painkiller called Ultram. The two in combination provided some relief.

The only way to altogether stop the hip pain was to stop working out, which was not a viable option at that point. I did not intend to stop so close to the full Arizona Ironman—I had just come too far for it all to end like this.

LEG LENGTH DISCREPANCY

So many issues and injures were happening on the left side of my body that I had a strong suspicion that I was bio-mechanically misaligned, had a leg length discrepancy or some other internal hip problem. I thought that perhaps the cartilage padding in my left hip socket might have been worn down enough to cause me to have a slight difference in my overall leg length. I think that this might be corrected with a wedge in my left shoe. I have had a lot of time to think about this, a lot more than the doctors, and it seems to make sense. Remarkably, 100% of my injuries have been on my left side.

My left foot was devastated with the largest blisters I had ever had, many of my toenails had fallen off or have turned purple—just on the left foot, ONLY the left hip hurts, ONLY the left trapezoid hurts, only the left everything...the right side is 100% perfect.

I now wear a small silicone gel pad in the heel of all my left shoes. I'm not yet convinced that this is the ultimate answer, but it does seem to help.

WHEN INJURIES BEGIN TO SURFACE... BE SMART, NOT STUBBORN

Injuries first start as minor inconveniences. A subtle twitch, a funny feeling, a stiff muscle, an ache that wasn't there before. These are the first signs. Rarely does one just run down the road and then all of the sudden...SNAP and something rips or tears or breaks.

It's far more likely that we will experience an odd sensation, soreness or a single muscle fiber that seems out of place, is twitching strangely or is aching while the others surrounding it are just fine.

So what to do when this occurs?

The first thing I learned is to slow down. Check it out. Try to figure out what is going on. Massage it a little, walk a little. If in doubt, slow down or walk. Yes, there is a bit of an ego blow to start walking when you're wearing all this high-tech gear, with all the latest and best gadgets strapped to your waist, wrist and chest—but I have learned the hard way that it's always better to just suck it up and be smart, to save myself for the next day.

Let me digress with a perfect example:

I was in Portland on business and had purchased the latest and best running shoes from the local Nike Town store. I was told that this particular model was made with some new, high-tech foam apparently developed exclusively for the Space Program. Further, they were part of the LiveStrong line, which I strongly supported. They also had this bright yellow moon boot type of a sole that just screamed to the world that they were latest, greatest, newest model. So naturally I just had to buy them. '

I loved those shoes. I returned home a few days later, having just worn the shoes around town, the hotels and while traveling. I decided to take them on my weekend long run that Saturday. Of course, I should not have worn those shoes on such a long run and I absolutely knew better. That's why I double-socked and even put some anti-blister lube on my feet prior to the 15-mile attempt.

Like clockwork, the hotspots started to develop around the fourth mile and they got progressively worse with each successive step. Did I call home for a ride? Of course not; that would be admitting defeat. What if this happened in the Ironman? I'd still have to find a way to finish.

I started to walk, then it got so bad that I sat on a bus bench with my head in my hands in total disgust. Why would I do something so stupid? Was I trying to sabotage my chances? I know better and yet I still did this, but why? I just couldn't believe how stupid I was. Even in my high school running days and as a youth in Boy Scouts, I always knew that you had to break in your shoes little by little. This was a huge mistake and I was caught in this conundrum: should I finish what I started, or should I turn around and go home? The answer might be completely obvious to an observer, but when you're in the middle of a workout the answers are not always so clear.

I really struggled with this and ultimately did the smart thing and turned around before the blisters got too bad. I thought that if I ran on the grass of each person's front lawn, it might be easier; but that didn't work either. So instead of just walking, I came up with another idea. Again, in the middle of these workouts, thinking is not always clear.

My great idea? I decided to take off the shoes and just run in the double-pair of socks. So there I was, running down the big city streets in my socks, carrying one bright yellow, Lance Armstrong LiveStrong, high-tech space foam shoe in each hand, wobbling from side to side due to the blisters. What a scene.

Instead of just blisters, I actually subjected myself to the huge risk of a bone bruise or even a broken metatarsal. The foot has 26 bones, 107 ligaments and 32 muscles and tendons. It's an extremely delicate piece of equipment, and definitely doesn't respond well to running on concrete without shoes.

Ironman or Just Bullheaded?

There is a big difference between what we should do and what we often end up doing, especially in the heat of a workout or a race situation. It's the difference between being patient, smart and disciplined and being just plain stubborn and foolish.

Of course I know that difference, but more often than not, I catch myself saying:

"You want to be an Ironman? Then start acting like an Ironman and pick up the pace. Tough it out. Be strong. Be a man. Be an Ironman. Are you going to quit during your Ironman debut like you are quitting right now? Suck it up. Navy SEALS don't quit. David Goggins doesn't quit. What would David Goggins do? You are a Navy SEAL on a mission and the world depends on you crossing that line. Connor needs medicine, all the roads are closed due to a natural disaster and the only way he can get well is if you get home prior to sunset. So you must pick up the pace and arrive at the front door before the sun sets. Gut it out."

This is often my self talk on workouts. Tough thoughts to be sure, and this stubbornness often gets me to ignore the warning signs. But to be patient, smart, and to ultimately go the full distance, we must pay attention to the very first signs of trouble.

Be Smart and Deal with it Now

Before we get a blister, we always get a hot spot. This is a hot sensation where the skin is rubbing against the shoe. We can take a couple of minutes and deal with it right away, or if we are bullheaded, we ignore it and then pay the price for the next 7 - 10 days as the raw, oozing blister festers and is aggravated all over again with each successive stride on the run or the chlorine from the pool.

I know I must slow down and figure out what is going on when these things hit, whether it's a hot spot that will likely turn into a blister or if it is a twitch or funny pull in a strange place due to overexertion. Like David Warden tells me, "Keep your eye on the prize."

And the prize is not finishing the workout in record time or toughing it out through an obvious early warning signal just to prove that I have what it takes. The prize is finishing the full Ironman race.

What good is it to finish the workout at record pace if you have to spend the next 3 - 5 days limping around and recovering?

Many times I needed to adjust my perspective: being an Ironman was not just about being tough and stubborn. An Ironman must also be smart. Smart about pacing, about nutrition, about rest, about balance. And smart about paying attention and taking appropriate action at the early warning signs that an injury might be looming.

Muscle soreness while training is common and by itself, is really not a big issue. Usually, sore muscles are caused by microscopic tears in muscle fibers. The soreness typically goes away within a few days. This is exactly what training involves: breaking down muscles and rebuilding. That's why proper nutrition, hydration and rest are so vital to training improvements.

But when muscles remain sore for weeks or even months, and the pain is centered in a particular spot, you could have a trigger point problem. Trigger points are typically found in muscles, tendons and ligaments. Technically, the doctors call this "myofascial pain syndrome."

TRIGGER POINTS
AND MYOFASCIAL PAIN SYNDROME

These are very sore, long-lasting aches and they sometimes produce sharp electrical-type pain. They are often caused by trauma, repetitive strain or pushing beyond any reasonable norm.

I have had a consistent problem in my upper back, in the trapezoid area. My trigger point nearly always flares up when I do long bike rides, and 100% of the time when I am in the aero position on the Time Trial bike or hunched-over my desk for an extended period of time (I have poor desk posture to be sure.).

Essentially, it is an acutely knotted mass of muscle strands in a very specific spot. The muscle is in constant and palpable contraction (shortening of the muscle) that will not release, and it results in a taut band and a hard fibrous nodule, lump, or knot. No amount or rubbing or massaging or pressure will relieve the pain. Aggressive deep-tissue massage will tend to break up the knot a bit, but typically, there is a lot of bruising that goes along with the deep-tissue, very high pressure massage. Plus, the relief is only temporary at best, and never complete.

I have tried literally every recognized cure for this problem, including:

- sports massage
- deep-tissue massage
- heat packs
- electrical stimulation
- chiropractors
- anti-inflammatories (NSAIDs)
- prescription pain killers
- physical therapy
- electromagnetic therapy
- weight training
- Lidocaine patches
- Cortisone injections
- Lidocaine injections
- wet needling
- and finally, rest.

Of all these, only one thing worked...rest.

However, since rest was not an option while training for Ironman, I went back to Dr. Ho, my pain management specialist.

The goal was to deactivate the contracted muscles. One option was to paralyze the muscle with Botox, and this would normally have been a viable option. However, since my trigger point was located in the upper back and shoulder region, there was a very slight risk that I might lose the ability to fully control my shoulder due to the temporary paralysis of the muscle. Odds of this happening were low, but due to the risk, they didn't want to attempt that. Instead, we tried the "wet needling" procedure.

Wet needling involves the injection of a mixture of steroids, Lidocaine and Cortisone directly into the muscle knot. A significant amount of care is taken to precisely identify the muscle strand, and once identified, a shot of the mixture is injected right into that specific little fiber. Then they move up the fiber ever so slightly and inject the fiber in another spot along the muscle strand, and another, and so on.

What they are looking for is for the muscle to start twitching or firing. Once they physically observe the muscle twitching then they know that it is beginning to release from its contracted state.

As the four or five injections were made, I could feel the muscle release and the doctor was pretty excited when he saw the muscle firing and twitching, which was the visual cue he needed to confirm that this process was working.

Three hours later, the spot was still sore, not from the shots but probably from the excessively hard rubbing and pressure that I had been constantly applying to this spot over the past few days trying to relieve this knot. Over the course of my Ironman training leading up to the full Arizona Ironman, I had at least five wet needling procedures.

This wet needling process is clearly a controversial procedure and many professionals will say that it's not worth the risk. But when you're in severe pain you'll often resort to measures or practices that you'd otherwise reject outright.

I'm Really Suffering Here

In the mid-90s I was responsible for making some extremely difficult decisions involving businesses we had acquired and the people who ran those companies. I was under a tremendous amount of stress and started skipping meals, getting very little sleep and often working over 100 hours a week. I considered this a challenge, and like an athlete, ignored the pain, ignored the danger signs. It got to the point where I started having daily headaches. These headaches got worse and worse to the point where I was taking 8 – 12 Excedrin tablets every day.

I had developed a severe migraine headache problem from all the stress, but I was too busy to deal with it or to see a doctor. Sound familiar?

Well this continued for six years where I ultimately had ingested over 20,000 Excedrin in my daily battle to stave-off these migraine headaches. I never went anywhere, literally nowhere, without Excedrin and Pepcid AC. Did I know that I was doing damage and potentially subjecting myself to the risk of stomach ulcers? I suppose I knew it, but I felt that this was just my lot. I had migraines and had to put them down, until one day, the result of ignoring my health almost took me down—permanently.

ACUTE VERTIGO RESULTS IN AN AMBULANCE RIDE

In the mid-90s I had a severe cold but kept working anyway. I was using a lot of Afrin but just couldn't get my sinuses to clear-up. Ultimately I contracted a severe sinus infection, but didn't see a doctor; again, I was too busy. Instead, I just ended up taking Afrin every day... all day long...for several weeks. I had to constantly excuse myself from meetings just to get a couple of more squirts of Afrin so that I could breathe through my nose.

I was on the freeway heading to a meeting when I needed a squirt of Afrin but had none left. My sinuses were so clogged that I started having a severe headache and my ears became completely clogged up as well; the pain of this sinus and ear canal pressure was like an ice pick being jammed into each eardrum. So like a skin diver does to equalize pressure in deep water, I pinched my nose and blew very hard to try and get my ears to clear up and release some of that pressure.

The moment I tried to equalize pressure I developed a severe case of vertigo. It was exactly as if the entire world was a huge spinning top: I could not make up, or down or left or right. Nothing. I was 100% totally helpless and going about 65 mph in the fast lane of the Los Angeles freeway system. This is exactly what happened. I had no control and was totally helpless. The only thing I could do was to slowly apply the brake while in the fast lane and try to keep both hands on the wheel without turning; I couldn't see anything except flashes of spinning colors, but I could sure hear all the cars honking.

I was taken to the emergency room in an ambulance and recovered without incident. But my family doctor got involved and took me off all the Excedrin and Afrin. I lost a week of work while I recovered, took the much needed rest and detoxed off of Afrin and Excedrin. With a single prescription of Inderal, I was cured of daily migraines forever. For emergencies, I have Imitrex, if needed, but that's infrequent.

A Simple List Makes all the Difference

Putting things off and hoping they'll get better is a recipe for disaster, as I learned on that day on the freeway. Now when I have issues, I deal with them immediately, no matter what the potential outcome, I'd rather deal with it upfront and right now than to wait and possibly make things worse. This certainly applies to health-related issues and injuries, but also business matters and personal relationships. It really applies to everything in my life.

I've created a separate category in all of my to-do lists that's titled: "What's Bugging Me?" Whatever is on my mind, whether it be an injury, a broken sprinkler head, my 1965 Porsche 356C that's not getting attention, a problem with a utility company I need to correct, a strained relationship in need of repair, an old friend that I am not keeping up with...it doesn't matter...if it's on my mind, if I have been procrastinating about it or it is bugging me, it goes on that list. These items are some of the first things I try to attack every day when reviewing my weekly plan. I attempt to do the hardest things first and just get them out of the way. I just find that I am happier, more present and available, healthier and certainly more calm and relaxed when I deal with issues immediately, rather than putting them off. And when things pop into my head, as they often do on my long runs, my hours in the saddle or swimming in place in my Endless Pool, I immediately write them down in my David Allen note taker wallet, my Rite in the Rain waterproof pad or record them into my iPhone using the 'Jott' voice recording and transcription service. Nothing slips through the cracks.

I know that it's tough to keep all those plates spinning, but it only gets harder when you've got to find another 15 – 20 hours a week (minimum) to get your Ironman training and related activities completed.   Therefore, I find it essential, and make my strongest recommendation to others, that they'll need a leak-proof system to record all of their to-do items and then when they get back home or to work, to focus on getting the toughest things done before lunch.

CHAPTER SIX

EQUIPMENT

THE TRIATHLON COMMUNITY

USA Triathlon (USAT) is the sanctioning authority for more than 110,000 triathletes. USAT maintains detailed records of our membership and has found that triathletes are a highly-educated group, with 86% of all registered triathletes reporting a four year college degree or higher. Further, 28% of USAT members reported income in excess of $100,000, and statistics on Ironman athletes show that their average income exceeds $160,000. Triathletes tend to be educated, curious learners, hungry for information and appear to have plenty of disposable income. As a result, many triathletes are eager to purchase the latest and best products that promise to improve their race and training performance. Triathletes have also been credited with many of the most productive recent advancements in cycling technology and aerodynamics.

If a triathlete is analytical, has some excess income and wants to improve their results in multisport events, they will be drawn into product research and the constant opportunity to upgrade in order to shave grams or improve aerodynamics. And there is no lack of technical and wind tunnel data to support their purchasing decisions.

Like many other multisport athletes, I was like a kid in a candy store with so many new products constantly being advertised, each promising to shave time, weight or both. I really enjoyed getting deep into analyzing my equipment options and studying the published reviews; I bought the world's best products in every category—but not without first making a lot of mistakes.

THE WETSUIT

Thinking I would save some time in the 2007 Santa Barbara Sprint Triathlon, I decided to just swim with a surfer's rash guard, which is a very thin, nylon-Spandex shirt. But the moment I hit the water, my body went into shock and I could hardly breathe; I was gasping for breath and it felt as if my lungs had collapsed. I immediately began hyperventilating due to my panic and the shock of the very cold water.

Immediately following the Santa Barbara triathlon, I went on a search for the world's best triathlon wetsuit. I was looking for warmth, comfort, flexibility and superior buoyancy in a wetsuit that would be very easy to remove quickly in the swim-to-bike transition area, called T1.

Some of the wetsuits I evaluated cost over $700, but my search ended with two finalists: the QR Superfull or Xterra Vector Pro X2. I contacted Matt from Xterra for advice, and he gave me helpful guidance on selecting a new tri wetsuit, explaining everything and really taking the time to carefully size my suit. I had been struggling with binding in the arms and shoulders of my prior wetsuit, which was why I tried the Santa Barbara Tri with no wetsuit at all—my prior full suits had been difficult to swim in and they caused severe chafing because they were so restrictive.

I finally decided on the Xterra Vector Pro X2. The suit was perfectly sized for me based on my extensive consultative conversation with Matt.

Prior to my next race, the Carpinteria Triathlon, I took a few minutes to warm up in the water and check out the suit for the first time. What instantly struck me was the incredible buoyancy of the rubber used in this suit. It was amazing. I felt like a cork just bobbing along on the surface of the water. The effect was like nothing I'd ever felt before in any wetsuit.

Paying top dollar for a great wetsuit was well worth it in terms of increased buoyancy and a great fit, without being overly restrictive. Two other things were immediately apparent: there was no sensation of cold or being wet in any way. The water simply did not leak in at all. There wasn't any leaking through the back of the neck like I had experienced with my cheaper wetsuits, nor the instant shock of the cold water when just using a rash guard.

The next thing I noticed was that this wetsuit did not feel restrictive at all. I had full and complete arm motion with no sense of binding. So no energy seemed to be wasted fighting the suit; instead, the suit worked in tandem with my natural motion.

I was ready to go and loved the new suit. I never looked back in terms of the price; it simply didn't matter because it was a terrific suit. Lesson learned: I should not have purchased the cheaper suits to see if I would like triathlon, I should have purchased the best suit from the very beginning.

When the cannon went off at the start of the Carpinteria Triathlon, I jumped into the water with a newfound confidence. Instead of waiting for everyone to go in and then enter at the back of the pack, I raced those guys right into the waves at a full sprint. I had never felt such confidence and it was 100% due to the wetsuit. I no longer had any fear of being held under the water by the mass of swimmers at the start of the race or at the first buoy turn.

I was so excited by my new wetsuit and I swam so effortlessly that I got off course and ended up swimming out to the wrong buoy, the one for the Olympic distance course. But I turned around and still recorded a time that was about 3 minutes and 30 seconds less than the exact course from the prior year. The T1 time was better as well, because the Xterra Vector Pro X2 nearly just removed itself as if on cue; it slipped off with only the slightest bit of encouragement.

Amanda, my triathlon coach at that time, could barely believe the improvement in time, and there was no doubt that the Xterra Vector Pro X2 had much to do with that. It was the perfect wetsuit and I had supreme confidence knowing that I was using one of the world's best products designed specifically for triathlon. I am extremely happy with this product.

Following my new record in the swim, which to that point had been my weakest event, I thought I could do even better if I only had my own lap pool at home.

From Wetsuits to Lap Pools

Chris Barsh, my great friend and cousin-in-law, had a lap pool growing up in Huntington Beach. I first saw their pool during a 4th of July party about thirty years ago, and even as a teenager, I had lusted for a lap pool, one just like the Barsh family had in their side yard. I had been talking about the Barsh family lap pool for over thirty-years, and now I was in a position to do something about it.

But the problem with a backyard lap pool for a triathlete is that it is very difficult to build one long enough (25 meters) to get a satisfactory workout. A solid flip turn at each end of the pool can significantly reduce the number of strokes per lap, and so one is essentially gliding under water nearly as much as they are swimming. In the actual race, there would be no walls, no kick turns, no resting. So a small, backyard lap pool would not adequately simulate the actual open water swim event of long course triathlon.

Then along came Endless Pools. Imagine an adjustable flow of water coming straight at you, just like river, and you are a salmon swimming upstream. The company calls their Endless Pools a "swimming machine" and another way to look at them is like a treadmill for swimming. All this in a compact 12' x 7' footprint. The pool takes up very little space, you determine the speed of the water flow, and there are no lines, pool closures or restricted lap swim pool hours to contend with; it's just the perfect solution.

I really wanted something like an Endless Pool. It would help my swim training because there would be no walls to break up the workout and take mini-rests by kicking off each wall. For example, I calculated that swimming in the 25 meter pool at the YMCA was really only about swimming 20 yards with at least 5 yards on each lap used up by the flip turns and wall push off.

The only problem was that Endless Pools are extremely expensive. There was no way that I could ever justify the incredible extravagance. Just like Warren Buffet, who calls his Gulfstream IV-SP jet "The Indefensible." Some things you just cannot justify with straight logic, but you do them nonetheless.

I began evaluating Endless Pools and their few competitors, receiving DVDs and brochures from Endless Pools and another from SwimEx. I liked what SwimEx had to say and they really seemed to be a high quality company. But I just couldn't figure out how we were going to get their 20 foot pool into the backyard and how to dig such a large and deep hole. The downside to the SwimEx pool was that it had to be placed into a concrete lined pit in the ground; their pool would arrive by truck on a giant pallet that would have to be lifted over my house and set down into the backyard.

I called the SwimEx people and learned that it would cost about $38,000 - $40,000 to build, ship and install the pool with the options that I wanted, likely even more when all was said and done. It was quite shocking because the pool was advertised at about $22,000, but the reality was that it would cost nearly double the advertised price to actually get it into the ground and operating smoothly.

Following my SwimEx research, I headed back to talk with Endless Pools about their new Fastlane product. It was a free standing pool with the motor unit, but it was only a vinyl-sided set up, not a real in-ground fiberglass or stainless steel pool, and it didn't have tiles, jets or benches. It was built only for one thing: to swim against a moderate current without having to make flip turns. At about $12,000, the Fastlane product seemed to be a reasonably-priced alternative to Endless Pool's flagship product.

The cost of an Endless Pool is listed at about $20,000 - $25,000, but the real numbers are far different from the basic package.

In addition to the basic pool package, which is assembled on site either above or below ground, indoors or out, you'll certainly want to add some extras. The electric pool cover alone can be as much as $4,500. But it doesn't stop there. How about a swim mirror to check on your stroke? Got it. How about lights? Yep, need those for swimming late nights and pre-dawn. What about a swim meter to indicate your speed, pace and workout distance? That's an absolute must, but that'll cost extra. Want a swim step so someone can get out of the pool? You'll need to order that as well. How about four hydro-massage jets for a Jacuzzi-like experience? You bet, especially after a long bike ride. I could go on and on regarding the extras.

THE REAL COST OF AN ENDLESS POOL

In my case, I thought I was getting the deal of a lifetime because I was able to locate a pre-owned Endless Pool from a private party with a beach front estate in Malibu. I called Endless Pools to verify the data provided by the owner and discovered that their pool came with a custom-made $6,000 electric security cover and many additional extras and upgrades. All this for about $12,000. My best estimate was that to configure a new pool exactly the same as the one I was buying would probably cost about $33,000. I would save well over half the cost, and I was elated.

But let's just look at the REAL numbers:

- $12,000: The initial cost of the Pool
- $9,000: Installation cost
- $2,000: Prep and pour a new concrete slab
- $1,500: Upgrade electrical service to power the massive hydraulic pump
- $5,000: New gas pool heater to replace the small, inefficient electric heater that had raised my electric bill by $2,000 in the first month alone.
- $2,500: Build a wood deck around the pool for a platform and easier access
- $2,000: Flagstone to face the outside of the pool structure
- $1,500: Labor to install the stones and the coping
- $2,250: Extra parts, new parts, service call on the cover and the electrical
- $300: Landscaping around the deck

The total cost turned out to be about $38,000, and I am certain that I have left out a lot of things. Endless Pools will never quote you how much it is going to cost for everything, but these are the real numbers.

Enough about the costs; what about the performance and value?

I love the pool. It has been a great tool and I am a much better swimmer because of this pool. It has operated flawlessly for over one year. I have not had a single issue or problem and I am very happy and proud of this pool.

It does take a little adjustment to get used to the pool's current. The current comes from the front of the unit in a smooth, waveless motion, and it is also drawn back and down into a grate at the back of the pool. The water is returned to the front where there is a huge propeller safely housed in a solid stainless steel compartment. Totally 100% safe.

One interesting discovery with the Endless Pool is that your feet are drawn-down a bit by the power of the returning current. The faster the current, the stronger the downward pulling motion on your lower legs. You'll get used to it though, and one nice benefit is that when you get back into the lake, ocean or community pool, you won't believe how much faster you are going without that pull on your legs; it's an amazing difference. You feel like you are just gliding right along the surface.

I am the first to recognize that the installation of an Endless Pool was a crazy and unjustifiable extravagance. Had I known that it would cost about $40,000, I never would have considered it. Never. For that price I could get a lifetime membership to the finest health clubs in the world. But it's done, and I don't regret it at this point. Plus the Endless Pool is portable and can be disassembled into sections and easily transported when I move full time to my avocado ranch in Carpinteria.

I also like the hydro-jets, which I can focus on parts of my back that get trashed from riding in the aero position on my time trial bike. And the really great thing about the pool is both the convenience as well as the ability to practice at exact pacing. If I wanted to complete my 2.4 mile Ironman swim leg in 1 hour and 20 minutes, then I knew that I had to just set my pace meter to 1.80 mph, and that would be the exact pace I would have to swim in the event. I can adjust the speed to whatever I like, although it can easily get to the point where it is just too fast. The pool is infinitely adjustable to the perfect speed based on whatever my workouts require.

The Endless Pool has also been used as a family hot tub from time to time. We upgraded the heater to an actual swimming pool heater (thus the $5,000 cost). That allows us to superheat the water in about 2 hours from about 88 degrees for my typical swim to 101 degrees for a hot tub experience.

The pool holds about 2,500 gallons of water and it is very easy to maintain. Endless Pools sells a kit of mineral pellets that are placed into the filter that significantly reduce the required maintenance or addition of harsh chemicals to the water. This product alone takes care of everything you'll need to do, except for chlorine. The company recommends just about a cup of plain household bleach once per day. When I am going out of town for a while, I use bromine tablets in a floater and this has worked to maintain an excellent balance. The water tests perfectly, yet it's extremely simple to maintain.

Because the huge propeller and jets mix up the water so thoroughly, any particulates in the water will naturally get carried through the heavy filter unit and there has never been a need to vacuum the pool in over one year. The water remains absolutely crystal clear and tests perfectly. Caring for the pool is nearly effortless, but whatever effort is required is actually quite fun. The stainless steel benches and housing can be easily kept pristine with a Scotch Brite Pad while I am in the pool.

The pool can be installed indoors, outdoors, above ground or below ground. Below ground installations are quite expensive. At the same time, if you just install this 4.5 foot tall box on top of an elevated slab, it can be unsightly.

What we did was to pour a solid concrete pad, and then build a deck around the front and side of the pool that allowed for easier access with two stair steps. Then in front of the elevated deck, we planted flowering bushes to soften the whole look. So you'll see the lawn, then the flowering bushes, then the deck, then just two feet of the stone facing of the pool. This approach enabled us to break-up the massive box shape and soften the overall look. I just love the way it all turned out. I actually like it much better than if it were an in-ground unit.

The pool is definitely an excellent training device. I wouldn't go so far as to say that it is a must, but it sure is a very convenient, fun and practical piece of exercise equipment that could possibly last a lifetime. And if you move, you simply have an installer come over to unbolt the solid steel panels and reassemble it later; the pool itself is nearly indestructible. All you'll need to do is to buy a replacement liner, which are very attractive and even look like real ceramic tiles.

THE BIKES...OH THE BIKES

Triathletes can spend a fortune on their bikes, and often do. I am no exception. I have a LeMond Revmaster indoor trainer, which is excellent for cadence workouts. I also have a fixed gear bike to help me learn to pedal more efficiently in what they call "perfect circles." But the real story begins with my road bikes and my time trial bike.

I started using a steel bike that my dad gave me. In its day, the LeMond Zurich was an excellent bike, but it was too small for me and despite significant retrofitting and new components to try and make the size 53cm frame fit me, it was clear that I needed a larger frame.

Probably the most fun part of the bike shopping process was to evaluate all the data on every possible bike. Every bike and triathlon magazine is just full of reviews on bike options, and I took it all in and made this a real research project. Ultimately, I decided on the Orbea Orca which is a full carbon road bike made in Spain. It was Bike of The Year and the exact same bike used by Team Jelly Belly in their races and on the Tour, so I figured that I couldn't go wrong.

The bike was purchased online and was fitted with the full Dura Ace component group. It was solid, fit well, and was an incredibly smooth ride. I loved that bike and still do.

But as I got more into triathlon and attended more events, I came to believe (wrongly) that I needed an even better bike that would provide more comfort in a lighter weight package. I settled on the Specialized S-Works Roubaix SL. I added significant improvements to the bike in terms of upgraded components, and I decided to use this bike as a hill climbing bike that I would leave at our beach shack in Carpinteria. The real pleasure was not just the fun of having the latest and best, but also the chance to ride on the exact same hills and climbs that Lance Armstrong and Team Discovery were training on in the Santa Barbara area. Ultimately I got this S-Works Roubaix SL down to a bit over 13 pounds, but this came at great financial costs, and I was slow to learn what the real cyclists all knew.

Think about it: whenever anyone who doesn't know much about road bikes walks up to you, they want to lift the bike up to gauge its weight. I too fell victim to all the hype around the lowest possible weight, thinking that the lighter the bike, the better. But that simply is not true.

The key to going fast over long periods has very little to do with the bike and a lot more to do with the rider. It's all the engine. Your legs and your cardiovascular efficiency; those are the keys. Next is your position on the bike and your comfort/ability to sustain that position for a long ride. It does no good to be fitted in an extreme aerodynamic position if you cannot hold that position for the vast majority of the event. And as for the weight of the bike, it is far better to lose extra fat off of your body than to spend money trying to shave 10 grams of weight off of your bike. But there are literally tens of thousands of amateurs who still have the mistaken belief that a lightweight bike makes all the difference.

Over time I came to understand that I needed to lose weight and that I also needed to ride in a more aerodynamic position. I decided to get a Time Trial bike. These bikes offer a much different hip angle, which gets one lower on the bike and also reduces the use of certain leg muscles for the next event, the run. Based on all the magazine hype and the podcast reviews, I was certain that I would have to get a full aero set-up to improve my bike times during the 70.3 and full Ironman events.

At the time, there was one top choice, the clear leader for world's best Triathlon Time Trial Bike: the Cervelo P3 Carbon racing bike. No question about it. So I bought one on eBay, directly from a bike shop. As an aside, great deals can be had in the winter months if you can locate a bike shop on the east coast that wants to move some product. I've found that during the slow winter months, you can find some terrific opportunities in those states where demand is down due to the cold weather.

My bike arrived via FedEx and it looked fast just parked in my garage. But that bike never did fit right, no matter who did the professional fitting. I had it refitted six times in 15 months, but the position always remained uncomfortable. My world's greatest TT bike was straining my neck and high upper back/shoulders, and I felt so scrunched-up in the cockpit that I was having difficulty breathing freely.

In about April 2008 it appeared that my Cervelo P3C time trial bike was the likely cause or at least a significant contributor to my trigger point problems, which were a source of constant pain. So I took the bike for yet another fitting, this time with Mike Faello at Surf City Cyclery in Huntington Beach. I really wanted to see if all these problems might be linked to the position of the aero bars and the way I seemed to be scrunched up in the front cockpit.

Mike was shocked that I was riding in such an extreme aero position for such a newbie. He discovered that my fork had been cut (buyer beware!) and was now too short to make the necessary fitting adjustments. We ordered a new fork which would provide the extra length needed to raise me higher in the front and reduce that extreme aero position. The position had been so extreme that I was unwittingly grasping the aero bars in a death grip to keep from sliding off the front of the bike. I really didn't realize this problem until Mike pointed out that the position was even too extreme for him.

Mike and I decided that the primary goal had to be comfort, and then over time, getting lower and lower down in the aero position. Prior to working with Mike, I was so low in the aero position that my neck had to bend up and back in an exaggerated position just so I could keep my eyes on the road, and this caused an enormous amount of strain in the neck and shoulders.

For a test, Mike set extra padding material on top of the bars just to raise up my position until I finally felt comfortable. It was a world of difference and improved my comfort dramatically. Even though it appeared that I would be raised up higher and might be less aerodynamic, it would still be way better than an upright position on a road bike. Now that the bike was dialed-in, we needed to look at other aerodynamic accessories such as race wheels.

My race wheels are the dimpled Zipp 606, a deep dish carbon rim that offers exceptional aerodynamics, especially at speeds over 20 mph. The theory behind aerodynamics is that we want the air to stick to the leading edge and sides of the object for as long as possible; this is actually less turbulent and more aerodynamic. Thus the dimples on my rims, just like the dimples in a golf ball, offer exceptional aerodynamic benefits. Regrettably, I very rarely exceeded 20 mph, so the wheels are yet one more example of an item with superior technological advantages that I have yet to take full advantage of.

Despite all the custom fitting and Mike's careful adjustments to make me as comfortable as possible in the aero position, I was still experiencing extreme pain from the trigger point in my left trapezoid and now, in my left hip. I could not continue riding in the aero position as the pain was just too severe, so I ended up doing much of my rides in an upright position on the time trial bike. This upright position completely negated any aero benefit of the bike, and in fact, may have been slightly less aero than my standard road bike.

I made the decision to sideline the Cervelo P3C TT bike for the Hawaii 70.3 and just use the Specialized S-Works Roubaix SL road bike. I made an appointment to get it race ready and did whatever I could to get it in aero ship-shape as soon as possible.

I knew that I would be at an extreme aero disadvantage riding a road bike, but at that point, it appeared to be my only viable option if I wanted to continue with my dream of finishing in Hawaii; the trigger point pain was just too severe to allow me to stay in the aero position for the full 56 mile bike stage in the lava fields. I might pay dearly in time, in watts, or in leg fatigue for the run, but at least I would be able to finish the ride and probably complete the run. I was almost certain that I would have an extremely difficult time finishing if I used the TT bike. At that point, I really didn't know what else I could do, except possibly changing to a different model, such as the Cervelo SLC SL frame in a road configuration. But there was really not enough time to build up a bike and get comfortable with it.

David told me that switching to the road bike was not going to break my race. Yes, there would be differences between a road bike and a tri bike: about 10-15 minutes extra due to pure frame and position drag over the half-Ironman course, more if it were windy that day. It would also mean that I would be working for an extra 10-15 minutes and would be slightly more fatigued going into the run. It was like having to ride 3-5 more miles than everybody else who would be riding a TT bike, but it would be worth it to me.

The road bike geometry puts the seat angle more shallow than a tri bike, meaning that I would use the hamstrings more on the bike, also leaving me that much more fatigued on the run. This could be mitigated by moving the saddle on my road bike as far forward as possible and the cleat position as far back as possible. However, David also thought that being so close to the race, he wasn't sure if it was worth it, plus it would take a lot of time to find someone who could make certain that the new position would not compromise me.

His verdict was: If I was dying on the tri bike, it was not worth the 15 – 20 minutes I would lose in Hawaii from the road bike. That was a drop in the bucket given the 7 hours or so that I was going to be out there in the lava fields.

There's no question that in a wind tunnel, aero bike frames consistently prove that they can save time on the road; the greater the race distance and speed, the greater the potential time savings. However, the truth is that your own body contributes to at least 70% of the aerodynamic drag, and the bike frame contributes to 30% at the most. You'd be far better off focusing on your position than purchasing the world's most aero bike frame. But we triathletes tend to go overboard over-analyzing things trying to squeeze every gram and every second out of everything, so nothing is immune to review and analysis—not even our helmets.

Triathletes have long been the leaders in utilizing aerodynamic helmets that are long, sleek, and sort of missile-shaped. These helmets may look like something out of a Jetson's cartoon, but they are proven to shave precious seconds, perhaps even close to a minute in the vacuum of a wind tunnel testing environment. However, the greatest time savings appear to be if one is consistently traveling faster than 20 mph, a speed I have never been able to maintain over a race distance. But that didn't stop me from acquiring the best aero helmet. One day, I hope to be able to sustain speeds in excess of 20 mph. Of course by that time, there will be an even better model available.

So the bottom line is: While I have some of the world's finest bikes and equipment, all of them combined really won't make me much faster at all. At my current level, speed is really up to me, not my equipment.

EQUIPMENT DAMAGE

In October 2008, I was involved in a serious bike-car accident—more about that in another chapter, but while I escaped relatively unscathed, my bike was totaled. The Dura Ace brake/shifter combo was trashed and my Zipp 606 high profile carbon rims were bent out of alignment. My Look Carbon-Titanium pedals were ground down from the bike sliding and bouncing on the asphalt and my rear derailleur was severely bent. Most disappointing, however, was the Specialized S-Works Roubaix SL Carbon frame, which took a direct hit and was smashed by the car.

I was relieved that the driver's father quickly paid to have the bike frame and miscellaneous parts replaced. While the damages were substantial, much of the bike could still be salvaged. I was relieved that the Zipp 606 wheel set and the Wireless PowerTap 2.4 Power Meter both survived (that could have been another $3,500 on top of everything else).

After the accident, I got a new bike frame. It was the 2008/09 Specialized S-Works Roubaix SL2. Emphasis on SL2. I was told by the great team at Surf City Cyclery in Huntington Beach, CA that the SL2 was the perfect bike for an older, inflexible guy like me, and yet it was still a very high performance bike. Once they built it up for me, they were all drooling over the SRAM Red grouppo with the Zipp 606 clinchers, the wireless PowerTap 2.4, the Zero Gravity brakes and the Look Carbon-Titanium pedals. This is absolutely a world-class, dream machine that could literally be taken as-is to the Tour de France or in legendary road bike races such as the Paris-Roubaix challenge. I am lucky to have this bike and really love it.

INDOOR TRAINERS

Even with what many would agree is the world's best road bike, I still remained a bit skittish in traffic after my accident. So I wanted to buy an indoor trainer—partly for fun, partly because I had a reasonably good excuse to do so and I figured April would have no problem with a purchase like that after I got hit by a car. Kevin had been very encouraging about an indoor trainer as well, as he was well aware of my many near-misses and was also the first to hear of my accident with the car.

There were a few options: CycleOps, Kinetic, Minourna, Blackburn. But I had my eyes set on that RacerMate Computrainer because it linked to real courses with live video, including some Tour De France climbs and Ironman courses.

But before I went for this huge expense, including the big screen TV and dedicated CPU, I asked David if he or any of his coaching experts thought this was a real training tool or just another fun toy that I could add to my collection of triathlon training equipment.

David responded that the Computrainer was both a training tool and a fun toy. If my intent was to do future 70.3s or longer events, the Computrainer would be a nice thing to have in my arsenal. It would make it more fun to train indoors on long rides of up to eight hours, and after my direct hit by a car, I was more willing than ever to do more cycling indoors.

The Computrainer

I purchased a Computrainer by RacerMate and am very happy with this training device. It takes quite a bit of set up and is a highly-technical product, but once you've got it dialed in and understand its functions, this unit will definitely improve your cycling fitness. In fact, the company is so certain that you will improve that they offer a written guarantee that you will improve by at least 10%.

The unit tracks HR, cadence, speed, watts and pedal efficiency. But the great thing that they have done is to link real-life courses to a video screen. So for example, if I wanted to see what it's like for a cyclist in a certain stage of the Tour de France, I can literally plug in that stage and experience the exact same loads and forces of the actual course; this is all done through your computer and an electric flywheel device attached to your rear wheel. Plus, you can monitor everything on screen in real time.

I've set mine up in the Ironman bike shop in my garage. I have a CPU linked to the Internet as well as a large screen monitor and 42" flat screen TV. I can watch videos on the big screen and my performance data on the monitor, or I can put the actual course video on the flat panel. It's really interesting because the scenery goes by as fast as it would in real time. If you speed up, the scenery speeds up, if you stop, so does the video. RacerMate provides course videos of many of the Ironman race venues, so you can really get a feel of riding the actual course by purchasing the video specific to your next event.

All my workout data is recorded and then sent to David via TrainingPeaks software. It's a slick system with a lot of technology behind it. Now this is not cheap, in fact, it's extremely expensive. But after my bike accident, I feel better about reducing my time riding on the streets of Los Angeles. I will still get out on the open road, but every mile I ride on the Computrainer is one less mile I risk getting into another accident, and from that standpoint, the unit is priceless.

KREITLER ROLLERS

I also have a wonderful set of Kreitler Rollers. These are three steel cylinders that roll freely within a fixed steel frame. You place your bike on top of the rollers and pedal in place. There is absolutely nothing to hold the bike from tipping over, nothing but your own balance and the centrifugal force of the rotating wheels and cylinders. It's counter-intuitive, but the best way to maintain one's balance is to pedal faster, not slower.

The Krietler Rollers force you to maintain excellent balance and respond with caution when things go badly. For example, if you begin to get off balance, the worst thing that you can do is to quickly jerk your bike. Instead, you must keep your wits about you and focus on getting back upright. So, in literally dozens of hours on the Krietler Rollers, I have learned to maintain an excellent line and have dramatically improved my balance. I've crashed many times on these rollers, but I am convinced that they have ultimately saved my neck on two separate occasions.

Recently I was riding in some extremely windy conditions near Huntington Beach and literally out of nowhere, a road hazard monument with a flashing yellow light blew directly into my path and there was nothing I could do. I hit the wood and metal hazard straight-on. I thought that I would certainly crash in the middle of traffic on Pacific Coast Highway, and I distinctly recall worrying that my chin was going to land on the edge of that metal bracket and I would likely break my jaw.

Strangely enough, I was able to recover my balance and keep the bike upright. I couldn't believe it, I was absolutely shocked. The balance I had developed on those Krietler Rollers was the reason I survived what would otherwise have been a very serious accident-perhaps even life threatening.

OTHER TRAINING GADGETS

Besides the obvious equipment used during multisports training, triathletes are inundated with literally hundreds of cool gadgets and gizmos that promise to improve training or race results. I have purchased, used and tested many of these gadgets. In addition to tools that monitor my progress, there are others that allow me to gather workout and race data and send these to my coach for detailed analysis. While I personally analyze all the data, I am not really certain this actually changes what I do or how I work out. Instead, I rely on David to adjust my workouts and plan my race strategies based on my recent workout data.

Here are a few of the gadgets I use on a regular basis in my pursuit of the Ironman dream:

- Garmin 305 HR Monitor and GPS watch for running and the bike
- Tanita/Ironman electrical impedance body composition scale
- iPod nano, iPod touch, iPhone
- Finis SwiMP3 (Waterproof MP3 player for the swim)
- Nike + iPod foot pod and pace calculator
- PowerTap 2.4 wireless PowerMeter
- Cat Eye bike computer
- The Back Knobbler for my chronic trigger point pain
- Gram scale for weighing food and bike parts
- Electronic hanging-scale for weighing bikes
- A complete set of Park Bike tools to outfit my Ironman bike shop
- My Endless Pool and associated pace meters
- An assortment of online training programs to analyze results
- The Haier washer/dryer combo
- Krietler Rollers
- LeMond indoor trainer
- Computrainer by RacerMate

Watches and HR monitors are really important training tools as well as fun gadgets. I have about six to eight various HR monitors and watches. One of my favorite tools was a HighGear watch that April gave me for my birthday. This had an altimeter and an onboard weather station in addition to a stop watch, countdown watch, etc. Regrettably, I ruined that watch in a high school pool doing some time trial repeats. I was clicking the lap split button every 50 meters to record my times. However, pressing those buttons permitted water to enter the case and ruin the LCD screen. It was a water resistant watch and I had used it countless times in the pool, however, this was the first time that I had ever use it to record my lap times.

I have read that the Garmin 305 and 405 units can actually be worn in the swim if you do not press any buttons. The Garmin HR transmitter is water resistant to 10 meters but the watch is not. Go figure. Take it from me, do not take the risk of pressing buttons on any watch while swimming laps, doing so is just taking a big risk.

Power Meter: The most valuable tool in my bike training and race arsenal is my wireless Power Meter. The CycleOps Wireless PowerTap 2.4 records the watts I produce as well as speed, average speed, cadence, HR and a huge variety of other data that I can use to evaluate my workouts both in real time and later on when I download the data upon my return.

The great thing about the PowerMeter is that it is a great equalizer. When it is windy or hilly or over 90-degrees, my speed can vary dramatically. But with the PowerMeter, I just look down and try to maintain constant power (watts) regardless of the conditions or impediments. I just shift gears and sometimes adjust my cadence in order to try and maintain constant power output. I no longer worry about speed, I just focus on my wattage output. This is a revolutionary training tool, and combined with my HR monitor I really have fantastic data that I can send to my coach for detailed analysis.

In addition to my PowerTap, I always try to wear my Garmin 305 GPS watch to record my location, the elevation changes, HR, speed and other data. This is always my backup in case anything goes wrong with the PowerTap, which from time to time might have some interference problems with the high power electrical lines that cross my path. I have a PowerTap 2.4 on my training wheels as well as my race wheels.

Another tool I use constantly is my Tanita/Ironman body composition scale. I track my daily weight, body mass, water percentage, muscle mass and total body fat percentage. I have learned long ago that just stepping on a scale and recording the gross weight is a recipe for disaster because I won't know if I have lost muscle or fat or if I'm just a bit dehydrated. Now I have all the details at my fingertips and I track them on large handwritten charts that I hang in the Ironman bathroom.

The other training items I keep around the house consist of exercise balls, medicine balls, dumb bells, a hard foam roller for IT exercises, a fixed chin up bar, and parallel gymnastic rings that hang and swing from a large beam in my Ironman Bike Shop.

THE FUTURE OF GADGETS

One gadget that is just starting to be found in the marketplace today is a GPS tracking device that can let family, friends and authorities know of an athlete's whereabouts at all times. Currently these devices are clunky and heavy, but manufacturers are making fast strides at reducing the size of these units. Today, one can rent these devices at some Ironman races. Your family and friends can then track your progress through the bike and run course (it cannot work in the water…yet.) They can see where you are at all times and know when to get ready to cheer you on as you pass by. This is a gadget or device that I would like to see widely available, but in a much smaller version and at a much reduced price, hopefully without the monthly maintenance fee, which has been quoted to me at about $50/month.

I think that we are going to see a lot more scientific training tools available in the next few years, especially in the area of power meters. I also think that we are going to find a way to measure watts or power from the run in a simplified manner. We could measure foot strike and some sort of power from the runner, in addition to HR, speed, pace, distance, etc.

One series of tests, tools and protocols that I would desperately like to see become widely available for a reasonable cost are:

- Developing optimal HR training zones
- Very accurate body composition and body fat measurements
- Determining VO2 Max

- Determining blood lactate threshold levels

All of these currently exist, but not all of them are readily available in a one-stop setting and the costs can be prohibitive. But one day I believe that we will find a way to administer these tests in a convenient, accurate and inexpensive way.

Beyond my ideas for needed training tools, I know that David Warden has his own ideas. As one of the world's leading researches and triathlon coaches, David would like to see real-time GPS and biometric streaming. As a coach, he would like to be able to have his athlete wear a device which would stream the athlete's pace, power/watts, altitude and heart rate back to him in real-time as the athlete trains. That way he could literally be with the athlete for any workout, and talk via cell phone to keep him on pace or on goal for that given workout. This is basically a PowerTap/Garmin device that has the GPS ability that we now see in many cell phones.

CHAPTER SEVEN

TRAINING

EPIC WORKOUTS
AND MEMORABLE TRAINING DAYS

I learned long ago that working out simply for the sake of trying to lose weight just didn't work for me. I needed something challenging and exciting. I wanted to explore new areas, point to a mountain peak and ride to the top, find a location on a map and ride there...or most recently, while on Catalina Island, instead of taking a boat to the Boy Scout Summer Camp, I would swim over from our hotel at Twin Harbors. These exciting, slightly crazy workouts make it fun and keep things fresh.

While I always try to include a few crazy workouts every month, some stand out as truly epic and I think of them often when I am tired or feel like quitting. Knowing that I was able to push through and complete these workouts, often gives me the confidence to persevere.

Ran into some rough characters and that forced me to radically speed up or they would literally run me right off the road! I got away from them, but just barely. Later on the return trip home, another inner-city group of toughs came down in a pack of 30. They passed me very aggressively and totally out of control. There was a 3-person pile-up and another guy got shot right into the concrete riverbed. I nearly crashed into a metal post, but unclipped just in the nick of time to barely avoid a major incident. It was crazy. Any radical HR changes are due to this situation.

112 Mile Battle in a Freezing Winter Storm

After a huge amount of online research and bargaining, I decided to buy a new bike for myself for Christmas in 2006. It was an Orbea Orca carbon fiber road racing bike that was universally recognized as Bike of the Year. I bit the bullet and had the bike shipped to me and then I hatched a crazy plan to map a course up to our weekend beach shack in Carpinteria, CA. My goal was to ride the entire distance on my brand new bike. It was considered one of the world's best bikes, so it had to be capable of that distance. As it turned out, the problem wasn't the bike at all...it was me.

The day I set out on this epic bike ride, the wind was howling and it was extremely cold. I left very early in the morning (in the dark) and headed up the coast toward Santa Monica. Once I passed through the heavily-congested South Bay, the LAX airport area and finally through Santa Monica, I presumed it would be a simple matter to just follow the beach all the way up the coast.

It took over 12 hours to go headfirst into that freezing wind in order to make the 112 miles, and it was the most miserable experience of my life. There was nothing gratifying about this experience and there was no sense of accomplishment at the end; only relief. The wind was blowing so hard that the beach sand along the entire coast appeared to be perfectly flat, just like poured concrete. The wind-whipped sand would constantly blast my face and legs while the freezing air made it sting. My well-oiled chain was attracting the sand and I could feel the grit with each pedal stroke.

When I finally reached the agricultural plains of Oxnard and Camarillo, the wind was blowing so ferociously that I literally had to get off of my bike, lean headfirst into the freezing wind and walk with my bike for about three miles until I reached the Port Hueneme area (half-way between Malibu and Ventura). Only then, with the aid of tall, wind blocking-structures, did I get the reprieve needed to remount my bike for the final thirty-five miles of my journey.

Despite the cold and fierce winds, I never called anyone for help, which I figured would be the same as admitting defeat. I did not want to hear, "I told you not to head off into that wind storm. I told you it was too cold. We all told you that it was too far. I could have told you that you weren't ready for such a long ride." I didn't want to hear that, and so I never made the call for help.

When I finally arrived in Carpinteria, it was pitch black. My bike light battery had gone dead in Ventura and I had literally ridden fifteen miles in complete darkness using only the headlights of passing cars to guide my way down Highway 101. When I pulled up to our beach shack, I was utterly and completely exhausted, totally spent. I got off my beautiful bike, which I now hated, and didn't get back on it again for nearly a year.

15 MILE RUN TO VENTURA

With my iPod, phone and running cap in place, I strapped on my favorite Nathan hydration belt and headed south from our weekend beach shack in Carpinteria. I thought I'd run down to Rincon Point and do an 8-mile loop, which up until that point, would have likely been my longest run ever.

But I felt great and the weather was just fantastic, so I set my target on the Oil Island, which was a few more miles down the coast in La Conchita; I was still feeling remarkably strong. So I called April and told her to get ready to pick me up, but that I'd try going just a bit further. I was running right alongside the crashing waves and could smell the pungent mix of salty sea air and drying seaweed that had washed ashore. The surfers were out, the sun was high and my iPod was set on a relaxing mix of Jack Johnson. I was moving slowly, but never felt the need to stop and walk.

As I rounded one bend in the coastal mountains, I would set my sights on the next bend, then the next. Before I knew it I was actually closing in on Ventura, which is 15 or 16 miles from my place in Carpinteria.

The one major problem was that there was no water to drink anywhere and I had run out long ago. I ultimately ran by some homes on the beach and filled my bottles from a garden hose.

This run stands out above all others because it was nearly double my longest run up until that point. It also marked the first time I ran without any pain and was truly enjoying the experience for what it was. I was enjoying the environment and it was just a fantastic day.

The bad news, however, is that I later learned that this epic run caused a bout of plantar fasciitis and remarkably, I had been running on a broken ankle. I had severe blisters and several of my toenails fell off. I was in a leg/ankle boot for about a week afterwards.

The lesson learned was that I was not prepared to increase my mileage by that amount. The long standing rule for running is to never increase your mileage by more than 10% of the previous week's mileage. I knew the 10% rule. I broke the rule. I paid the price.

CLIMBING
LA CUMBRE PEAK

I had read in a men's magazine, *Outside*, about some of the toughest things a person could do in terms of physical fitness challenges. The article suggested that one of the toughest things to do on a bike was to ride up Gibraltar Road, which snakes its way from the Santa Barbara Riviera area up to the absolute top of the 3,995 foot La Cumbre Peak.

This is the exact same road that Lance Armstrong trained on with his Discovery team, so I just had to try it.

Here is the actual write-up from *Outside* magazine that listed the climb:

GIBRALTAR ROAD:
Santa Barbara, California
Highest Point: *3,588 feet (3,995 to La Cumbre Peak)*
Vertical Gain: *3,264 feet*
Length: *9 miles*
Grade: *6.9% average*

A narrow road with fractured pavement that heads up into the coastal mountains above Santa Barbara, Gibraltar was a frequent training climb for Lance Armstrong. "The effort it takes to get up that definitely compares to some of the climbs in the Tour," says California resident and multiple Tour rider Levi Leipheimer.

I left my beach shack in Carpinteria on my Specialized S-Works Roubaix SL that was custom-built to ride these coastal mountains. The base of the mountain is about 15 miles from my house, then about another 8 – 10 miles to the peak. The road is quite steep in some parts and there is never a flat area to ease up. My legs were burning very quickly, but the views of the downtown area, the Santa Barbara Riviera, all of the Channel Islands, the coastal cities, Montecito and the harbor were amazing. Most people who live in this area have never seen the coast from this peak. It is just amazing and well worth the drive, even if by car. Months later, I took April up there for a picnic. We rode our Vespa scooters and it was a fabulous time.

It took two hours to climb that beast and only thirty-minutes to descend.

On the way up, after about an hour and a half, I stopped along the way for less than three minutes to have a banana, and because a guy was coming up strong behind me and making me very uncomfortable. I didn't want to feel the pressure of him on my tail, so I decided to pull over and let him pass, thus removing the stress and temptation to compete.

Then I got back on the saddle and ground uphill for another 30 minutes. I was really proud of myself for actually making it.

The great thing about this incredible ride is to sit on the deck of our humble beach shack and look back toward the very top, the absolute ridgeline of those coastal mountains and to know with great pride that I pedaled my bike all the way up to the top, along that ridgeline and over to the La Cumbre peak and transmission towers. I rode up literally from the beach sand all the way up the mountain and through the clouds up to the pine trees. No matter what ever happens to me for the rest of my life, I will always look to those mountain peaks with knowing pride that I have conquered them. That is truly epic.

OJAI VIA 2 KOM CLIMBS

One day I decided to ride my bike the 17 miles from our weekend beach shack, over and through the mountains to the tiny hamlet of Ojai. This is the exact same route taken in the Amgen Tour of California bike race for two years. The really cool thing is that this same route includes two KOM (King of the Mountain) peaks.

KOM peaks are where the racers can earn extra points, time bonuses or even cash bonuses if they are the first to hit these peaks. The interesting thing is that if a competitor tries to go ahead of the group and compete for the KOM designation, they may (or may not) win the bonus, but whether they do or not, they are going to be really spent after exerting all that extra energy to fight uphill. KOMs are reserved for the steepest or longest and toughest grades. So to have two of these in each 17 mile loop meant that I'd be doing 4 KOMs, which is really remarkable and very rare to have this kind of an opportunity right in my own backyard.

It was a long, tough grade, as any KOM should be. But I started feeling the hurt far sooner that I thought I should. My stomach was really hurting and I had run out of food, gels or any other nutrition. I became famished. I was extremely weak, very lightheaded and had no energy; it was literally painful, and this was one of the very few times I had this kind of experience. I was just dying out there and I still had a very long, very steep way to go. What happened to me is that I officially had bonked.

I finally made it up and over the two KOMs and coasted as much as I could down to the Lake Casitas campground snack bar. As fast as they could make them, I ate: a burrito, a taco, a hot dog, a bag of salted nuts, 2 ice cream sandwiches, 3 - 4 bottles of Gatorade, a bottle of water, and a Snickers bar. I was ravenous and out of my mind with hunger.

When I felt better, I turned my bike around and headed back over the two KOMs; I never made it to Ojai that day, but I learned an important lesson about always bringing extra nutrition on my rides. I never want to feel the bonk again and will always be prepared for future rides.

SANTA BARBARA BY TRAIN, SAND AND SEA

One day I took the Amtrak train from our beach shack up to Santa Barbara. Wearing just my tri shorts and a running shirt, I was going to walk, run and swim back along the shoreline. No matter what obstacle might possibly lie in front of me, I would overcome it by sand or by sea.

I packed a waterproof kayak dry-bag with my cell phone, some cash, my ID, water, food and my reef shoes, and I was off on the train. This was an adventure that few people in the world have ever completed. To walk, run and swim along some of these $10 - $30 million mansions on Butterfly Beach, Hammonds, Montecito, Padaro Lane and Sandyland was very exciting. Many of these places are so private and secluded that they cannot be reached by public streets or by foot unless you walk in from a long way; there's simply no access. But if you are walking or swimming down the beach at extreme low tide, no one can stop you from your journey. In California, the beach remains public property with right of way access up to the mean high tide line.

There were many places that were absolutely impassable, so I just loaded my stuff into my waterproof kayak bag and swam through and past the wave line until I could see sand again, then came to shore to continue my journey by foot. The major problem with this adventure was that there was no drinking water and definitely no stores to buy food or beverages. So yet again, I was really running low and arrived home extremely dehydrated from the beating sun and the roughly 13 - 15 mile journey by sand and by sea.

SOLVANG KRINGLE VIA LA CUMBRE PASS

My mission for the day was to secure the prized Solvang Kringle pastry the moment the bakery opened. The problem was that the bakery opened about 7:00 am, and I was about 45 miles away on the beach side of the coastal mountain pass.

Well before sunrise, I mounted the Specialized S-Works Roubaix SL and headed north to the tiny hamlet of Solvang, CA. This would be a challenging ride of just over 90 miles, the first three hours of which would be in total darkness.

I started slow and easy in order to warm up and to adjust my night vision. Even though I was wearing three layers of cycling shirts and two pairs of gloves, I was still cold and shivering as I climbed up over the coastal mountains via La Cumbre Pass and rode through the clouds; it was very damp and extremely cold.

Have you ever driven your car at night through very dense coastal fog? Do you recall what it's like when your high beams hit that fog and you are blinded? Well that was the challenge I faced riding up and over the mountain pass. It was unsettling as I made my ascent, as there was no shoulder for cyclists in many of these steep stretches, and with the thick fog reflecting the headlights of oncoming motorists, I was a bit concerned.

I made it up through and above the clouds and it was a bright starry night at the top of the pass. But then I had to descend back through the clouds on the other side of the Pass as I moved from Santa Barbara toward Lake Cachuma and the Santa Ynez wine country.

Descending through those clouds, at night, in very damp weather, was extremely cold. The cold, wet air and the low temperature conspired with my accelerating downhill speed to give me ice-cream headaches all the way down (about 4 - 5 miles).

The sun began to rise as I hit the lake and rode the 20 additional miles to Solvang. I had timed my ride to hopefully arrive for the prized Solvang Kringle the moment the bakery opened, that way it would still be fresh and warm.

Kringle is hand-rolled from Danish pastry dough that has been rested overnight before preparing and baking. Many layers of the flaky dough are shaped roughly like a giant-sized pretzel. Solvang is world famous for this particular pastry and I was going to bring one home as proof that I had actually made it to Solvang despite urgings from some not to attempt the trip due to the lack of a cycling shoulder on the mountain pass.

Well, they packaged up that Kringle in 4 large plastic shopping bags, sealed them all very tightly with tape, and I stuffed this large pizza-sized pastry into the front of my jersey. To avoid crushing the delicate puff pastry, I suspended the packaged item with athletic tape from the shoulder straps of my bib shorts and it worked great.

The trip back was much faster because I had plenty of light, so I was not as tentative. I was also pushed a bit by a few guys from one of the cycling teams who were leaving Solvang around the same time that I did. Solvang was the home city for the Discovery Cycling team for many years and the area is full of cycling lore about Lance Armstrong and his amazing exploits. Many coffee shops in town actually have signed photos of Team Discovery and other cycling teams because the area is a very popular winter training grounds.

I would do this trip again, but next time will continue through the Central Coast wine country and return via Buellton and the 101 freeway heading south back to Carpinteria. I will state however, that the La Cumbre Pass is a very dangerous road for cyclists as there just is not enough shoulder to safely share the road. Sure cyclists do make the trek up the mountain, but I feel that it is quite dangerous to do so and I'm not likely to do this again. Gibralter Road is much safer.

THE SAN GABRIEL MOUNTAINS

As the full Ironman event approached, many weekends required very long bike rides followed by an hour run or longer. There were only so many places that one could ride in the LA basin where there weren't too many cars or stoplights. My preference was the paved San Gabriel Valley riverbed bike trail.

One day I decided to see how far I could go up the riverbed bike trail. The river came from somewhere, and I was determined to find its source way up in the mountains. I rode up the entire length of the bike trail from the ocean waves in Seal Beach, all the way up into the San Gabriel Mountains, where I discovered that there were multiple dams and huge reservoirs I'd never known about. I rode up and into the mountains on very narrow roads. I discovered a tiny little campground area and an old mining town that few have probably ever seen, and all this is just 45 minutes from downtown LA.

I stopped to refuel and get more water, and I had a very difficult ride back up the mountain and down the other side into the Glendora area. Many cyclists know this area as Glendora Mountain Road, and it's quite a challenge. I ran into a lot of cyclists up there and the cool thing was that they had driven from all over southern California to bring their bikes to this location, but I had actually ridden my bike up there. I felt great about that. I told one group that I had ridden all the way up to the mountain from the beach and they couldn't believe it. That was cool and I felt like I must be getting much more fit. At that point I realized, perhaps for the first time, that I was becoming an athlete.

Getting off the mountain was fun and very fast, but then I had the long way back on the river trail in very strong headwinds. This was extremely difficult, but resulted in some of my highest sustained power ratings/watts ever. I believe that I set three new power records that day for maintaining high watts over long periods. This ride proved to me, and to my coach David, that I was definitely ready to accomplish the Ironman, so from that standpoint, and the three new power records, it was epic.

Ultimately, however, I paid a very heavy price for this ride. I had ridden my Cervelo P3C TT bike and much of the day was spent in the aero position. This caused a massive trigger point reaction that resulted in extreme pain and chronic knots. Further, the next day, my hip was absolutely killing me, and regrettably, it has never been the same since.

The funny thing about the hip socket problem was that it didn't always hurt during the activity, but rather, much later in the evening or the next day. Why? Well the best we could figure out was that all the activity caused the area to slowly swell up and become inflamed over several hours following the workout. During the ride I might not feel it, but later at night, after the long bike and run, the body started trying to recover and became inflamed in the hip area. As the hip area would swell-up, perhaps it also started putting pressure on some nerves in the interior hip joint area, referencing that pain to my hip flexor, groin area and down my leg to my shin area.

This hip situation has never been fully resolved and the pain I experience goes from a daily low-grade ache, all the way to sharp, electrical shockwaves that make it nearly impossible to control the leg to pedal. Nights are the worst. For some reason, it hurts the most just lying in bed. My own idea about this is that perhaps the joint has been swelling up from the activity and at night it reaches the apex of inflammation.

DESPERATE
AND DYING OF THIRST

One time I was so hot and thirsty that I was frantically scouring the roadside looking for any plastic bottles that might still have a few drops of liquid remaining in the bottom of the container. I was severely dehydrated from a hot, windy day that just sucked all the moisture out of my body, and I had run out of water with no stores around, no drinking fountains, no garden hoses, no gas stations, nothing.

I was so parched when I finally returned home that I nearly lost my voice—there was just no moisture left in my body to work my vocal chords. I believe that situation was so severe that I was literally dying of thirst; I was losing my vision, I was very dizzy, I had lost my depth perception and had a horrible headache. The headache caused by this dehydration episode was so severe that it took two emergency Imitrex 100 mg tablets to get it under control. Despite consuming massive amounts of water and sports drinks immediately upon my return home, I did not have to use the bathroom for another 12 - 15 hours.

On a similar note, I recently had a run where I had plenty of water in a new type of hydration belt. Because it was a new belt, I had forgotten to transfer my phone, ID and cash into the belt's pockets. I loaded up with water in my four 10 oz. bottles and was off for a 13 mile run. I had my iPod blasting an aggressive track of songs and didn't seem to hear when two of my water bottles fell off somewhere along the way. This new hydration belt had bottles that snapped into a rigid plastic holder instead of my Nathan hydration system that held the bottles in a rigid pocket or nest.

Well, I'd already finished my two front water bottles before I realized that the two rear bottles had fallen off. I was extremely thirsty and had no money to purchase additional beverages along the way. It was very hot and I was getting loopy and all I could think about was my desperate need for water. No 7-11 would let me have a bottle of water on the promise to return later with cash. This was another serious hydration problem and called for desperate measures.

I passed a restaurant in Seal Beach called the Blackboard Bistro where I used to dine weekly while Connor was at his karate class. I finally worked up the nerve to walk in there and literally beg for ice water. They were more than accommodating, and that was the sweetest water I'd ever tasted. I didn't realize how bad the situation was until I finally had some water to drink.

Later, when I needed more water, I went to a supermarket that had a self-serve beverage counter where you could fill up your cup with soda. Well I learned that these almost always had a cold water tab as well, and they always had ice. So I filled my two 10-oz. bottles with ice water and that saved the day.

I've since completely abandoned those snap-on water bottle hydration belts. Don't get me wrong, I really do think that they are a great idea, but no matter what I do, I just cannot seem to keep my bottles from popping out. I have repeatedly ordered replacement bottles, and I'd really love to continue using this system, but for me, it just doesn't work. I'll continue to stick with the Nathan hydration system that has those great nests that firmly hold my bottles in place while still allowing quick, easy ingress and egress of the bottles.

TRAINING JOURNAL ENTRY:
Poor hydration and nutrition

I got caught in a horrible wind storm. It was also 95 degrees. This was likely the hardest ride of my life due to the insane Santa Ana winds. I wanted to quit many, many times. I stopped briefly to rest several times.

I finally bonked two-thirds through the ride due to not having lunch prior to the ride; I only had 2 GU packs, with no Carbo-Pro or any other nutrition. Also, I ran out of water by being a good Samaritan and giving my last one-third of a bottle to someone who was likely suffering from heat exhaustion on the trail. I got pretty thirsty over the last 10 miles.

Also, I got a bad headache the next day. All this tells me that I have suffered from mild heat exhaustion and pretty bad dehydration. I have been drinking a lot of electrolyte replacement fluid, and my overall hydration level is now fine based on my Tanita body mass scale. It was just an overall very tough ride due to heat, wind, poor hydration and very poor planning in terms of not eating before and during the ride. I should know better, so why did I let this happen?

Important lessons learned: do not ride up the riverbed trail on hot days because that triggers massive windstorms twenty miles from home and I will have a horrible time trying to get back in the headwinds. It is deceiving on these hot days because at first I feel good and strong and am averaging great speeds; that's because there is a slight wind at my back. When will I ever learn!! However, on the return trip, the wind picks up double or triple the speed and I am riding 100% directly straight into these huge windstorms.

Open Ocean Swimming: Catalina Island

This workout sticks out more for the extensive planning and preparation than for the distance, but it remains epic in every respect. It involved swimming roughly 1.50 miles in the open water, but through three separate boat harbors, the open ocean and then a massive kelp forest.

I planned this swim several weeks in advance since I would be doing it solo, unsupervised and through very dangerous obstacles (the ingress-egress of boats and the huge kelp beds). I rigged a system that included a seven foot surf leash and ankle cuff that was attached to a skin diver's inflatable fish buoy and diver's flag. I towed this large inflatable buoy behind me as I swam. Attached to the buoy was a dry bag which held my clothes, a cell phone, emergency contact information, shoes, shirt and water. No matter what happened, I was prepared.

If I got too tired, got a cramp or had some issues, I could just hang onto the inflatable orange diver's buoy. I had a full wetsuit to protect me from the rock and kelp and I had a diver's flag that made me highly visible to passing speed boats and ferries. Plus, in the worst case, if I had to go to shore, I had some water shoes to help me traverse the rocky coastline. Planning the swim and designing the equipment may have been more fun than the actual event, but I enjoyed every moment of it.

Highlights of this journey included the massive sea kelp forests that I had to traverse and the spiny edges and small crustaceans that had attached themselves to the sea kelp; I was glad to be wearing my full wetsuit. I also had several conversations with the yachters who had never seen anything quite like this device that I had rigged. These large yachts certainly appear much more intimidating when you are bobbing around in the water at sea level as compared to admiring them from the cliffs above. It was very appropriate to have that large orange buoy towing behind me, otherwise, it would have been very difficult for the boats to have seen me in my black wetsuit, as they would never expect to see a solo swimmer so far out into the ocean.

High Performance Clothing

There's quite a lot to learn about proper clothing for training and racing. Most newbies to the sport will learn the hard way, as I did, that cotton shirts will turn to sandpaper when perspiration and salts dry on the cloth and rub you raw in all the wrong places. Bleeding nipples are an experience that I will never allow to be repeated. I ended up throwing out all my cotton workout shirts and using them as rags in my Ironman bike shop.

Based on my experience in this Ironman endeavor, I have developed some perspective on suitable and preferred clothing for workouts and races.

The Swim

The swim is rather simple. Certainly you'll want to wear a tight-fitting nylon/spandex suit and not board shorts. Some choose to swim in a bikini-style Speedo, but I find that most guys swim in longer shorts with about an 8 – 10" inseam; the women all swim in practical one piece suits. Sometimes I swim in my running shorts, which I will describe below. In my experience, only the fittest guys at the pool are ever wearing the bikini-style Speedos.

I cannot possibly describe the horror of walking out onto the pool deck for the first time, with my massive belly hanging over the front of the spandex/nylon swim shorts, my bleach-white skin and farmer tan.

I was so embarrassed because all the other guys were so tan, fit and ripped. I always chose the lane far away from the fast guys. And the hardest part of the swim workout seemed to be sucking-in my massive belly to try and reduce the appearance of my overhanging mound of stomach fat. I would break every rule and ignore good judgment by nearly running across the pool deck to jump into the water as quickly as possible, hoping that no one would notice the huge spare tire I was hauling into the pool.

In most triathlon events, we wear a wetsuit and often the athletes will wear their bike shorts beneath their wetsuit. I prefer to wear a garment called a Tri-Short. These are thicker, spandex-nylon shorts with a thin foam pad in the seat area. They can be used for the swim, for the bike and for the run. Many people would refer to these simply as bike shorts.

More recently, triathletes have been using the new speed suits as we saw in the Olympic swimming events in Beijing and the Ironman World Championship in Kona. These garments are allowed so long as they do not provide buoyancy. Some athletes race in these for their entire event up to the Olympic and even 70.3 distances. Most however, quickly change out of their speed suits in T1. I like the sleek, cool look of the speed suits, but for a mid-packer like me, it makes no sense, as the time savings would be negligible.

CYCLING APPAREL

When we get into the apparel for cycling, that's when we can really get carried away. Thousands of dollars can easily be spent on cycling clothes alone. First, let's start with some terminology: the bike jersey and shorts and socks often all match, typically with a theme, a team's name or a sponsor's name, and this matching set is called a "kit." It is NOT a "cute outfit" as April likes to say. In fact, at one time I thought it would be great if April took up cycling as well; I reasoned that maybe we could ride together on the weekends. So I took her to the bike shop and she fell in love with some of the women's cycling clothes. To encourage her, I bought her a jersey. But she has never returned to get fitted for a bike. It seems that she likes the "cute outfits" a lot more than the riding.

Cyclists refer to their garments as "a kit." It's a "kit" and never an "outfit." Most cyclists will have many kits. It's fun, but also very practical.

We must avoid chafing and therefore need high-tech, wicking fabrics that are specifically designed to deal with massive amounts of perspiration. The way we look at shorts is first to check out the fabric, then the number of panels that are sewn together to make the shorts (the more panels, the better the potential fit and the better the shorts may work with your movements), and the pad or chamois. Originally, the pads were actually leather chamois, but now nearly all pads are made of very high-tech molded foam that bends and moves without binding while also wicking away as much perspiration as possible. Cheap bike shorts are just asking for trouble—so spend as much as you can afford, as you really do tend to get what you pay for with bike shorts.

Most cyclists wear bike shorts that have long straps that go over the shoulders in a Farmer-John style like suspenders; these are referred to by cyclists as "bib shorts." These particular shorts will not slip or ride up; they really just tend to stay in place very well. When I go for my long rides, I am always wearing bib shorts. You've really got to be careful with these, however. Try them on and make certain that the straps that go over your shoulder are not too short; if they are, they'll be pulling and yanking at your crotch and you'll have a truly miserable day. I have several such bib shorts where the straps are too short; what appears to be a great bargain in the sale bin is just wasted money if you don't wear these items due to improper fit or discomfort.

I wore my tri shorts on some of my longer rides and found them quite adequate; however, unlike bike shorts, tri shorts do not have a heavily padded foam chamois. A great pair of tri shorts can cost upwards of $150, and a pair of cycling-specific shorts can cost over $200. The bib shorts can range from $70 - $400 or more. Again, I prefer to buy high quality items and would never buy anything again without trying it on. A precautionary note: the sizing of most top of the line cycling apparel is based on European sizes and they take their sizing cues from professional cyclists. What this means is that the sizes tend to run small. If bib shorts do not fit perfectly in the store, do not buy them no matter how great the deal. My preference is the Castelli brand for all cycling apparel, and I've learned that this Italian brand runs small as well.

As for the bike jerseys, these are a unique item as well. You'll find 2 – 3 large pockets in the back of the jersey and typically a half or full length zipper in the front. The pockets in the back are for food, bike supplies, phone and emergency items. Some people use the pockets for additional water bottles. I prefer the full zipper models with three large pockets in the back. I always try to find jerseys that also have a small zippered pocket to hold emergency cash, a credit card, a key and ID. No matter what, I don't want to risk losing those items, and if you don't have a separate zippered or Velcro latch to hold them in place, they can easily fall out while you are pulling other items out of the same pocket during your ride.

Many jerseys are replicas of famous cycling team kits and include matching cycling shorts and socks. I prefer a plain kit without a lot of excess advertising. Just give me a plain Castelli jersey and shorts and plain white cycling socks. I like the great fit and style of the Castelli kits, which do not include excessive product endorsements or corporate logos.

Cyclists also need different clothing for the winter months, such as warm gloves, long johns, heavier weight jerseys, arm warmers and rain jackets.

All of this cycling apparel can easily cost thousands of dollars. And of the vast amount of cycling apparel I own, there are only 3 - 4 key items that I continuously use. These are all the top-end, most expensive items; they work, they are very comfortable and I don't regret spending the money on them.

My greatest regrets are always buying the "deals" or close-outs from the bargain bins. I never seem to learn my lesson in this area; it's just so hard to pass up a great deal, but please remember the two most important things in cycling apparel are: a great, comfortable fit and a good wicking fabric. You just cannot buy a garment with great fabric at a bargain basement price; there's just too much technology that goes into these wicking fabrics and you'll need to pay for this technology in order to be comfortable.

RUNNING GEAR

Running apparel is pretty basic, but again, the fabric is the key. I prefer the Nike FitDry for basic running shorts and 2XU and Zoot as my tri shorts. The tri shorts are very similar to what you'd typically call bike shorts, but they are also terrific for running and eliminate virtually all risk of chafing between the legs.

When I first started running, I could not wear regular running shorts because my heavy thighs would rub together and chafe with each stride; it was just terrible. But over time, as I lost weight and became leaner, I was no longer required to use Body Glide or other anti-

chafing materials between my legs. Once I had lost about 35 pounds I also felt less self conscious wearing my tri shorts, and now they are my preferred running shorts.

I always wear a high performance wicking fabric shirt, often long sleeved, and I nearly always wear thin Nike running gloves regardless of the weather. Gloves serve two purposes for me: they help me quickly wipe sweat from my brow and face, and they help a bit with a runny nose. Yes, I know that sounds gross, but a lot of gross things happen when you work out in cold weather or when you push yourself to extremes in the heat. It's all part of the program if you want to train year-round for ultra endurance events.

As for shoes and socks I have some strong preferences as well. The socks must be a high performance wicking material, typically anti-bacterial. While due to my heavy size, I prefer a heavily padded sock for additional cushion, many runners prefer very thin socks or no socks at all. I also use some of the new toe socks by Injinji that have a little pocket for each toe. This design helps prevent blisters between your toes, and believe me, this can be a really big issue on very long runs. Some people also swear by using a nylon stocking as a first layer, then putting their normal running sock on top of that. It's all just personal preference. But one thing we all can agree upon is that getting pebbles in our shoes is a real pain. That's why I prefer to wear gaiters when I'm running on dirt trails or paths. I buy most of my ultra running gear from Gillian Robinson and Don Charles Lundell of Zombie Runner. Between them, Gillian and Don have completed over 250 marathons and ultras, including the Western States 100, Badwater 135, 24-hour races and multi-day runs; when I need advice they are my go-to resource. Zombie Runner has a physical store in Palo Alto and they also offer a great online store (www.ZombieRunner.com) with everything for the ultra runner.

My shoe preference is constantly changing and I have purchased literally dozens of pairs in the quest for comfort and cushy support. Here's what I have learned from my shoe experiences: Do not buy a shoe based solely on a glossy magazine ad or the most current *Runner's World* shoe rating. Do not buy any shoe because it looks fast or cool. Instead, go to the store and try them on. Run in them. If a store will not let you run in the shoes…leave.

Some of my favorite shoe stores are:

- *Fit Right Northwest* in Portland, OR and Vancouver WA
- *A Snail's Pace*, Orange County, CA
- *Inside Track*, Ventura, CA
- *Runner's High*, Long Beach, CA
- *Santa Barbara Running Co.*
- *Zombie Runner*, Palo Alto, CA

Each of these stores are staffed by avid runners who know their trade. They encourage you to run outside in the shoe and they take their time to interview you to really understand your needs, problems and style. Many have a video camera trained on a treadmill where you can try the shoes while running and they can analyze your stride and foot strike to determine if you are a pronator, supinator, heel-striker, mid-foot striker, etc. Then they will recommend the appropriate shoe.

Online may have great deals, but if you need personal attention for the fit, then please go to a specialty running store.

Once you have found a great shoe that you really love, return to the store and buy extra pairs of that exact same shoe. Avoid the temptation to search for the newest and latest shoes, always trying to best your current pair. Once you have a winner, stick with it. As for racing, I wear the same shoes that I train in. There are plenty of featherweight, sexy alternatives for race day, but I just don't take the risk. I want to stick with the same shoe that has seen me through my toughest workouts.

In the toughest part of the race I often think of how far I have come in that exact pair of shoes laced to my feet, and somehow I gain a bit more confidence that I can continue to push hard to the finish.

SPORTS MASSAGE

My experience with sports massage has been mixed. By no means do I find it relaxing and soothing. More typically, it will be quite a painful body and joint manipulation session, especially if I have sore leg muscles or knots that really need some work. Apparently, sports massage is necessary to keep our muscles supple as well as to move toxins from large muscle groups back into our system where they can then be filtered and flushed out.

We know that sports massage works and that's why Lance Armstrong has maintained his personal soigné throughout his Tour victories and was said to employ one for his comeback in running and now cycling. The soigné, or sports massage practitioner, is an expert at deeply massaging the major muscle groups in order to physically push lactic acid, ammonia and other waste by-products from the muscle groups and back into the system where these wastes can be filtered and extracted from the body, principally through the liver.

Regrettably, I have not had many quality experiences with sports massage. Too often, it was either some inexperienced person who wanted to light candles and play soft mood music, or it was an overzealous chiropractor who was hell-bent on cracking my neck (which by the way, I never allow anymore). I've had extremely aggressive therapists who were so rough that I was left in more pain than when I had arrived, and they claim that was a sign that they did a good job; I wasn't so sure about that.

I am now seeing a physical therapist and I think this may be the best form of muscle manipulation that I have yet experienced. I think he has a better grasp of the skeletal-musculature system than most massage therapists.

I don't tend to get really sore in my large leg muscles such as the gluteus, the hamstrings or the quads. Instead, I get extremely sore in the upper trapezoid area where I tend to carry stress and these crippling trigger points, which are tight bands of knotted muscles in a constant state of contraction that will not release. I am also very tight in the iliotibial bands (IT bands) on the outside of both legs and those could really use a lot of work. Daily, I use a moderately-hard foam roller on the IT bands along the outside of the legs from the hip bone all the way down to the knee. The purpose of the foam roller is to keep that IT band from getting too tight.

Overall, I am told by many doctors, sports massage therapists, physical trainers and bike fitters that my muscles and ligaments are very tight and prevent a full range of motion, so I really need to do more stretching and perhaps a bit more massage. Clearly, I have been less disciplined in this area and have paid the price with IT band injuries that have set me back as much as 60 days.

SHAVING LEGS

It has been argued that shaving one's legs can theoretically save time in the controlled environment of a wind tunnel, but the difference is only fractions of a second to maybe 3 seconds at the absolute most. Yet a large percentage of athletes are shaving and waxing. It is argued that the more practical reason for shaving legs has to do with other issues, for instance, it is easier to clean road rash wounds without having to pick through mangled leg hair, and it is easier and possibly more productive for sports massage without hairy legs. Of course, there is the argument of time saved in non-wetsuit events and on the bike, but those time savings are very, very slight, if even measurable at all.

More than anything, I think there is just a "coolness factor" in shaving legs. It does prompt questions from non-athletes and it gives you the chance to talk about triathlon. I think that's a major reason why I shave during the season.

I have also tried leg waxing. I really don't find it too painful, and if you find an experienced practitioner, it is actually quite relaxing. In between waxings, you can use a razor in the shower once a week or so to keep things in check. In the off-season from about Thanksgiving to the middle of January, I may not shave the legs at all. Then the first time back, I will have them waxed with all subsequent sessions just a quick once-weekly tune-up in the shower.

But beware: there are some small bones where the top of the shin intersects with the bottom of the knee; this particular area is highly susceptible to cuts. Look around the registration booth at any triathlon event and you'll see a lot of men who have scabs, scars or recent cuts in that exact same area. I even know of a world famous coach and triathlete who contracted a very bad infection from shaving his legs, so be careful and always use a clean razor.

As for hair removal in other areas, I find it helpful to crop the hair around the crotch area, and for good reason. Maintaining a 85 – 90 cadence while cycling is over 5,000 pedal revolutions every hour. At that rate, things tend to shift and pull and tug and generally become very uncomfortable. Long hair in the nether regions can be very irritating and you may find yourself constantly adjusting to find a comfortable position on the seat. I found it best to crop it short and be done with it. Same holds true for underarm hair; crop it a bit and you'll be much more comfortable.

If you refuse to prune the nether regions, then at least use plenty of Chamois Butter or another good quality lubricant. I thought this was really weird at first and was pretty shy about asking what it was for, but basically, you take a generous glob of this lubricant and rub it all over everything down there…yes…everything, including the sit bones, between the legs and everything else. This will reduce the risk of chafing, pulling, tugging, saddle sores and all the like. If you are really going to get into this, you'll need to buy and consistently use Chamois Butter or its equivalent.

CHAPTER EIGHT

NUTRITION

DIET, NUTRITION AND SUPPLEMENTS

Every day, I took a wide variety of supplements that producers claimed aided in the recovery of broken-down muscle fibers and helped to replenish key nutrients that were lost through aggressive, sustained physical exertion. The list of all these supplements is quite long but it's important to state that my extensive research reveals that a good, balanced diet of fresh fruits, vegetables and lean protein can go a long way toward meeting the needs to rebuild your muscles and replenish your glycogen stores.

The problem I found was that it was extremely difficult to eat well when traveling. I preferred salmon over most other proteins, I actually enjoyed eating chicken and I also loved a heaping plate of eggs with a yolk or two. I was not eating as much red meat and really didn't crave steaks as I once had. I did have a few steaks, but this was typically as a celebration of some sort, and usually with my great buddy, Chris Barsh, who is truly a connoisseur of grilled meats. I learned that during training, I didn't like how I felt after consuming large quantities of red meat, and so I ate fewer steaks, smaller steaks, and changed my preference from rib eyes to filets, which are a much leaner cut. Ultimately, I significantly reduced my consumption of red meat and ate mostly chicken and fish.

But despite my taste for salmon and chicken, it was really very hard to consume the recommended quantities of protein, so I supplemented my protein with a high protein shake about five days a week.

A lot of debate is swirling around whether or not we really need all this protein and carbs, especially in the form of processed breads, pastries and pasta. I took note of the carb debate and tried the Paleo diet as outlined by Joe Friel and his co-author.

The Paleo diet essentially states that our bodies are designed to consume foods like our Paleo-period ancestors: raw vegetables, meats when they could find them, along with anything else they could find, pick or kill. It's a pretty easy diet to follow as well. I simply had to ask myself, "Did Paleo-man have access to Cheetos, glazed donuts, sourdough French bread, baked apple pie, ice cream cones and Coors Light beer?" So it's really easy to make food choices. But here's the rub: I was lethargic and lifeless on that plan. I know it worked really well for some athletes and maybe I didn't give it a fair shot, but after two weeks, I killed Paleo-Man and went back to foods that helped maintain my energy level so that I could complete my workouts.

THE PREVENTABLE BONK

I've learned (the hard way) that nutrition must be taken just as seriously as my physical training and recovery.

One day I tried to complete a workout and all I had to eat prior to the workout was a single strawberry, half a bagel with sugarless jelly, and one bowl of Wheaties. I got on the run and had no energy of any kind. It was terrible. I bonked and was actually in pain from having eaten so little.

Luckily I was near my mom's house, and I ran in and immediately shoveled down some avocado, tomatoes, two slices of sourdough bread and some cold chicken along with a bottle of water. This was only 40 minutes into the run. My mom said I was like a crazed maniac starving for food. After I shoveled down all that food and water, I ran the rest of the way home at a much faster pace and felt fine. It didn't bother me at all to have so much food in my stomach, and in fact, I was still eating and swallowing food as I ran the first 500 yards from my Mother's home. I had bonked, which is 100% preventable by being smart and eating right.

My bonking was proof that I was not eating right. Deep down I was fighting this battle to lose weight and was stupidly sabotaging my workouts by thinking that by reducing my food intake, I would lose weight faster. I thought that if I worked out really hard on a totally empty stomach, I could burn more calories and lose weight even faster. I was wrong and I was a fool.

I've since learned that I need to burn calories from working out, not by starving myself. I have learned that I cannot go without real food and expect to have a good session of training. I can do this in my shorter morning workouts, but not go all day with little food, or I will just have no energy available for a good workout in the afternoon or evening.

David and I spoke frequently about this topic. I told him I often tended to work out on an empty or near-empty stomach. I typically had a GU packet (100 cal) if I was out for over an hour. On a 3 hour ride, I would have 2 -3 GU packets and if I could find one at a gas station or a 7-11, I'd pick up a banana en route. Typically, on a 3 hour run, I would have 3 GU packets, a banana, a bag of salted peanuts, a 21 ounce Gatorade and 40 ounces of water over 14 miles of running/jogging.

David had some advice regarding my weight loss schemes and my periodic lapse of nutritional judgment:

Subject: Nutrition Program
From: David Warden
To: John D. Callos

John,

We need to get you used to taking in about 350 calories per hour on the bike, not 100 per hour, which is what you appear to be taking in.

The nutrition should include more than just GU, because GU does not contain electrolytes. I recommend either eGels or Hammer Nutrition Perpetum; Carbo-Pro works well also if you are used to that, but you'll still need to supplement that with some additional electrolytes.

Begin to take in at least 200 per hour on your next 2 hour ride, and we will go to 200-300 on the next ride, getting you up to 350 calories per hour.

On the run, 100-150 per hour is acceptable, let's lean toward 150. Start to take at least 150 calories in your runs that last more than an hour. eGels come in 150 calories packets, so they are a convenient way to fuel on the run; one per hour is easy to remember.

Like anything else, more is not better. Taking in too much can be disastrous to your GI tract on the run. 400 on the bike and 200 on the run is upper level for you. 350 for the bike and 150 per hour on the run are good goals for you.

The reason is this: a person has about 1,500 to 2,000 calories of glycogen in their system. For your weight and intensity, you'll burn about 6,000 calories in that 6.5 hour Ironman 70.3 event. 35% of that will come from fat, but the other 65% has to come from glycogen, meaning you are about 2,000 calories short. Taking in 100 per hour on the bike and run only gives you 550 of that 2,000 deficit, but 350 per hour on the bike and 150 on the run makes up the difference.

I know that sometimes you feel fine on 100 per hour in your workouts, but that is because you have not yet exhausted your 2,000 calorie glycogen storage in any of your workouts. Let's practice now with your nutrition so that we know what to do in the race.

While we are at it, please also start to take in 20-30 oz per hour of water on the bike. Again, I know you don't need it now, but in Hawaii in May, you will, and we need to have your body getting used to that much fluid and calories.

-David

One thing is for certain, I do not respond well to super sugary-sweet drinks like Gatorade, as these tend to line my throat with a thick coating and make me cough for about twenty minutes, unable to clear my throat. I have since learned to not take certain beverages and as a precaution, I will take a Mucinex tablet prior to my races or long workouts. This addition of Mucinex is really a life saver and works wonders by helping me to avoid the constant hacking and coughing caused by sugary sweet energy drinks and some gels.

MEDIUM-CHAIN TRIGLYCERIDES

David recommended using MCTs for additional energy. Medium Chain Triglycerides (MCTs) are fatty acids that are more easily digested by the body than other fats and are also a direct energy source for the body. In this sense, MCTs mimic the function of a carbohydrate.

MCT oil is composed of caprylic and capric fatty acids. Since MCTs are used by the body as a direct source of energy, endurance athletes may find them to be a preferable and long-lasting energy source when training because MCTs fool your body into using more fat for fuel and saving precious muscle glycogen.

MCTs can be purchased at most health food stores and typically come in liquid form, like thick syrup. I've tried the MCT liquid and cannot say that I notice a huge difference, but I still use it.

Usage: 4 Tablespoons per 16 oz of fluid, taken only on the bike. This can be added to any sports drink, but in my case, I just take it straight from a flask since mine is slightly flavored and I can just barely tolerate the slightly metallic and chalky taste.

David was particularly keen that I use MCTs because he was worried that I was not getting enough calories and could bonk as I had done before on both the bike and some runs. MCTs have about 100 calories per tablespoon, so this would also add calories to my nutrition plan on the bike, and would help me use more fat and less carbs.

Another supplement David recommended is a long time favorite and one of the few completely legal and proven methods to enhance athletic performance: caffeine. Suggested use was 2mg per pound of body weight an hour before exercise, 1mg per pound every 2 hours during the bike. Generic caffeine (Vivrin, No Doz) can be purchased at any pharmacy, 7-11 or corner drug store.

The risk of both the MCT and caffeine supplements was excess urination (both products are known diuretics). If I had to pull over to the side of the road twice an hour instead of once every three hours, it would not be worth the performance gain from taking the supplement. That was why I needed to practice taking them in my long bricks in order to see how I responded.

RACE DAY NUTRITION PROTOCOL

During some races I took a protocol of several different supplements from the SportQuest people, and Ironman Arizona would be no different. This was the standard supplement protocol we developed for my races:

• *Thermolyte.*

This is a sodium supplement designed to minimize the risk of heat fatigue, muscle cramps and the onset of hyponatremia, which in layman's terms is an acute sodium imbalance that can lead to very serious problems. This supplement contains sodium, potassium, calcium and magnesium. This mixture is designed to minimize muscle cramps or heat prostration due to excessive perspiration. Since sweat contains between 2.25 to 3.5 grams of salt per liter, and the rate of perspiration in a long, hot race such as the Arizona Ironman can easily average 1 liter per hour, I would need at least 30 – 40 grams of salt during the race. That equates to at least 65 capsules of Thermolyte for Ironman Arizona.

• *Recover Amino Power (RAP).*

This is a 100% pure pharmaceutical grade amino acid compound that helps enhance the recovery process, reduces the breakdown of muscles and ammonia build-up, delays the onset of physical and mental fatigue and accelerates protein synthesis. I would take these both in training and during races. For Ironman Arizona, I would need at least 40 capsules over the course of the day.

• *Motivator.*

This is very similar to a caffeine tablet and provides a synergistic effect with the other supplements. The ingredients are somewhat similar to a Red Bull drink, with a blend of thermogenic and energizing herbs plus neurotransmitter precursors. It contains such ingredients as Vitamins C and B-6 in addition to guarana seed extract, taurine, L-tyrosine and gingko biloba leaves extract. These mental stimulants are perfectly legal and are essential when I hit the wall late in the bike and the run. I usually end up taking about one tablet every hour and perhaps a couple at a time in the latter part of the bike or run if I feel really down. This is a terrific product, but I do not recommend taking it just before bedtime.

- *Vantage VO2 Max.*

This product is designed to buffer lactic acid build-up and reduce ammonia burden. What this means is that your muscles will perform better at a higher level of intensity and for longer periods. It aids in the prevention of muscle soreness and cramping. During Ironman Arizona, I will take at least 40 capsules of VO2 Max.

- *My Personal Race Day Emergency Kit.*

I also carry a special emergency kit on both the bike and run segments of my races. This kit contains additional Thermolyte capsules which I believe to be absolutely essential. It also contains three Pepcid AC heartburn tablets, an emergency migraine headache pill called Imitrex, four Excedrin tablets and two Mucinex tablets which help suppress coughing due to excessively-sweet drinks or gels.

NUTRITION AND HYDRATION PLANNING

For Hawaii 70.3 in May 2008, I built a nutrition plan for the race where I would have the Carbo-Pro already in the bike bottles and I was going to wear my hydration belt on the run so that I could continue to use the Carbo-Pro as I had in all my training runs.

I knew that this was less than ideal for a 70.3, but that was my plan for the run: keep everything as in training, no new drinks or foods on the run or bike. I would refuse everything except for water. My only need at aid stations was going to be cold water.

I would also carry a few emergency GUs just in case I had used those in addition to Carbo-Pro from time to time so this would be consistent during the race. Espresso flavored GUs with extra caffeine would be in both my bike jersey and tri shorts.

I did not have hydration or fueling problems as I was pretty disciplined about that once I really started to understand the physiology of nutrition and hydration. The Hawaii Ironman 70.3, the Vineman Ironman 70.3 and the Bulldog 50K ultra marathon all went great without nutrition problems of any kind.

But the full Ironman in the Arizona Desert would not be this easy. I needed a different nutrition strategy because I did not have enough Carbo-Pro powder to constantly fill up my water bottles over the entire 138 miles (about 14 hours) of the combined bike and run segments.

I got in contact with the lead food scientist at Carbo-Pro/ SportQuest. He understood my dilemma and designed a custom nutrition protocol for me based on my unique physiology and weight. I purchased the entire line of SportQuest products and have been absolutely delighted with them.

For the race I used a product called CarboPro 1200. It's a liquid that comes in a 16 ounce bottle and packs 1200 calories, good for about 4 hours in a single bottle. I planned to carry that on the bike in the seat tube bottle cage. I would preload my first water bottle with Carbo-Pro powder, then get water from the aid stations every 10 miles and sip the CarboPro 1200 along with the water. I would take another bottle of the CarboPro 1200 and divide it between two 10-ounce water bottle flasks, which I would attach to my Nathan hip belt for my marathon run. I would also take some emergency gels, but the CarboPro 1200 product was enough to get me through the entire Ironman; I strongly recommend this approach.

CHAPTER NINE

SETBACKS

RECOGNIZING MY LIMITS

As with any journey of significance, there will be exhilarating highs, devastating lows and numerous surprises.

I swung from euphoria to depression, from sloth to fitness and from health to constant pain and frequent injury. There were times that I felt on top of the world, and there were other times when I felt that my Ironman dreams were shattering before my very eyes. This much is clear: Had I not told so many friends, family and clients about my Ironman dreams, there would have been many times that I would have abandoned this journey. I just couldn't face telling people that I had quit, so I soldiered on despite the setbacks.

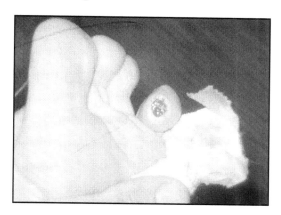

TRAINING JOURNAL ENTRY:
Injuries and Blisters

The blisters are really hampering my training, causing me to limp and contributing to poor sessions. The blisters are stinging during my swims in the chlorinated water. I had a headache almost all day. I took one of my emergency migraine headache pills and also I am back on Ultram, so my headache is gone and I am feeling better. One recurring thing is that I am getting a lot of cramps in the arches of my feet while swimming. This never really happened very often before, but it is happening more frequently. I am also getting leg cramps at night and cramps in my arches while in bed. Very strange—this kind of thing has never happened before. I am not sleeping, I am constipated from the medicine and now I am nauseous throwing up almost without warning because of the strong narcotic medicine, but the constant hip pain is so severe I have no choice, I have to just deal with it. This is absolutely not worth it. No way. I am literally falling apart!

The hardest part to reconcile was that I never lacked the heart or the desire to train and prepare, but far too often things beyond my control prevented me from doing my best. Sure, I put off some workouts, and in hindsight perhaps I made some poor food and beverage choices and allowed workouts to be missed due to laziness and poor planning.

But there was nothing I could do to fix my hip problem, my chronic and painful trigger point of knotted muscles in my upper trapezoid, or the debilitating pain of the double IT band inflammation. I wanted to work hard. I wanted to push the limits and see what I was really capable of doing. But the hardest thing to accept was that my body could no longer do what my heart and soul and raw drive wanted it to do.

Despite my desire, determination and grit to just work through the pain or the issues, I came to realize and accept that I could not go full tilt running down the track trying to beat my high school times of

1:57 in the half mile, 4:52 in the mile, 10:28 in the 2-mile or 15:48 for the 3-mile Tri Valley Cross Country Finals. Further, I couldn't just go out and try to run 50 miles on a whim just to test myself. I had to muster the discipline to hold back because I understood that my body simply could not take the strain like it used to. And that was the hardest part of all of this: the recognition of my physical limits.

Often, even when I remained completely disciplined, stayed on the program and completed the workouts exactly as prescribed, I still got injured. That was the most frustrating of all and the source of my doubts, depression and questioning about whether or not this was all worth it. I'd often ask myself in these low points: *"What's the point, what am I trying to prove, why am I doing this, how could anything be worth all this work, all this pain, all this struggle, all this time, all this hassle, all these constant injuries?"*

Nobody else seemed to be able to relate to the highs and lows better than my coach David. He remained my confidant and sounding board throughout the training, injuries and my roller coaster of emotions. He asked me to keep him in the loop and never hold back; he needed to know where I was in the training and how I was feeling both physically and mentally. Whether I was elated by setting new speed or power records, or if I was despondent over the setbacks, the constant hip and back pain, the IT band injuries, doctor visits or missed workouts, David needed the straight story, not my false cheer or my pseudo tough guy act.

I've included some examples of moments in this endeavor that were the unstoppable highs and the lowest of lows, all leading up to the Arizona Ironman. I've come to learn and understand that these are the normal range of feelings and emotions one can expect to experience during training for this ultra endurance event.

MY FIRST REAL CONFIDENCE BOOSTER

My first real confidence booster happened when I ran a 10K race held on the tarmac of Los Alamitos Marine Base in southern California. I had a terrific day considering I was just getting back into things following my broken ankle. I had followed my race plan precisely and

173

held back my speed in order to have an even pace throughout the run.

The highlight was not my actual finish time, but rather, learning that I had actually beat my former trainer who, unbeknownst to me, was also in the race. This was the first clear and tangible evidence that I was getting stronger and fitter. I was so proud of this improvement that I felt unstoppable.

Subject: First week Update
From: John D. Callos
To: David Warden

Hi David,

I think that I had a great week. I am very happy with my 10K race results because they are a textbook case of HR and pace, starting gradually and then working up more and more until the last mile where I really kicked it into high gear. I never walked, and never felt like I needed to. The pace was perfectly set based on my analysis of my most recent couple of weeks on my Garmin 305 watch. My final time was 52:30 and I know that is slow compared to what I did as a youth and what everyone else you work with does. But for me, it feels like I am really making a lot of progress and I am very happy with it.

I showed restraint when young girls, old men or anyone else passed me in the race. I kept telling myself that this was not about them, it was about trying to have the discipline to stick to my race plan. I had all my mile splits written on waterproof paper and held them in my hand the entire way, and I hit all the splits almost exactly.

One final cool thing, David: I used to have a trainer at the gym in 2007. I was in total awe of him. He would run the 5-mile loop around the university and invite me to join him, but there was no way I could even begin to keep up with him, not even for a small segment of the run. He was the most incredible specimen of an athlete and seemed to enjoy pushing me to my limits in the gym at the rate of $70/hr. I worked with him for about nine months with just weightlifting, but I ultimately left him to take up triathlon-specific training.

Well anyway, I ran across him at the race this weekend. You won't believe it, David, but I beat him in the 10K. He was really surprised that I had lost so much weight on my own and that I had placed in front of him in the finish chute. That convinced me that I am definitely making progress.

I am happy with how my training is progressing. I am confident that together, we are going to see some dramatic improvement in my triathlon development and fat loss.

Thank you for taking me on as your project. Knowing that you care enough to take the time to check on me and my progress makes me want to complete everything you ask of me.

- John

Negative Thoughts Begin to Surface

Self-doubt is a creeping, insidious thing, and worst of all, it just kills your confidence. In Ironman, you must believe that you can and will finish the event. If you don't really believe that you can finish, if your confidence is lacking, you will have a very tough time and a very high risk of DNF (Did Not Finish).

Of course I knew all of this, but when you are tired, suffering, frustrated with injuries, and you really want to push harder but your body fails you, well, that is extremely disappointing. Often, I told myself that it wasn't even worth it, that there was no way I could ever realize this crazy Ironman dream.

Just like my youthful dreams of accumulating $50 million in cash prior to my 50th birthday (my 50/50 Plan), I realized that positive thinking alone can only take you so far. At some point, you actually have to get out there and do the work and make things happen. Despite my positive mental images of finishing the Ironman and having the announcer call out, "John Callos...YOU ARE AN IRONMAN." the reality was that my body was falling apart. No amount of positive self-talk or mental imaging was going to fix my hip, my trigger point pain or my double IT band inflammation.

Ultimately, when injuries held me back, negative thoughts and self-doubt inevitably crept into my mind and started to take hold. These negative thoughts seemed to surface most when I was hot, tired, in pain, fighting stomach problems, sunburn, completely spent and exhausted and in debilitating pain. This happened a lot during long workouts, typically on the bike or on a run, although never during a swim or in the weight room.

THE PINNACLE OF SELF DOUBT

The morning of April 13, 2008, I planned a route through Laguna Canyon on a 55 mile ride. I had been up most of the night before with a stomach ailment and was really dehydrated. I did the ride anyway. No excuses. But that ride really took a huge toll. When I got home I tried to do a brick (bike-run combination workout), doing the run after the bike to simulate what I would have to do in the Ironman.

But it just wasn't going to happen. I couldn't will this into reality and I couldn't tough it out or grit it out. Had this happened during my Ironman event, my race would have been over. Period.

My plan had been to do my brick run on the soft grass of the Long Beach Recreational Park Golf Course, which is exactly two miles in circumference; I would do four full laps for an eight mile run immediately following my ride. But I barely got across the street over to the golf course and then I literally collapsed under the shade of a tree and just laid down for 5 minutes...right there in plain view of hundreds of passing cars on Pacific Coast Highway.

I couldn't help it. I was totally spent. I was absolutely exhausted and had nothing left in the tank.

At that point, lying on the grass, in plain view of everyone, I had failed, I had found how far the human body could go and I was done. There was nothing else I could do, I was immobilized; 100% totally spent.

I slowly got up and walked home with my head held low in defeat and disgust. How was I ever going to do a full Ironman? I couldn't even do half the bike distance and jog three blocks. In just seven months, I would have to ride 112 miles and immediately follow that with a 26.2 mile marathon. Impossible I thought. There was absolutely no way I could do that. I was a loser, and I was thinking like a loser. In that negative state of mind, there was just no possible way I could envision myself ever finishing a full Ironman.

FROM POST-RACE EXHILARATION TO LET DOWN

After the exhilaration of finishing my first 70.3 Tri (the Half-Ironman distance) in Hawaii on May 31, 2008, I experienced an unexpected mental crash. I would not say that I was clinically depressed coming down from the high of actually completing the 70.3, but it was very demoralizing to realize just how much fitness I had lost in the two weeks of June (three full weeks off of the bike) waiting for my hip to mend.

I couldn't run the same distance, I had limited energy in the pool and the power was gone on the bike.

Subject: Callos Week in Review
From: John D. Callos
To: David Warden

Hi David,

I am disappointed to report to you that last week went quite poorly. I fell an hour and a half short of the week's goal time, but more importantly, my motivation to get back on the bike again is gone; I cannot explain it.

I have been avoiding the bike. I only did a single bike ride all week, on Saturday, for about 1:15. I had no power, no legs, no energy. It seems that these little 30 and 45 minute rides are just totally unproductive for me because I am still stuck in the city, in traffic. It's not enough time to even get out of the city, away from the stop lights to get some consistent spinning done, so why bother? (This is just an excuse or justification of some sort, I suppose.)

I thought about fudging my numbers so I wouldn't have to deliver this bad news, but I pledged never to do that to you. We are dealing with the reality as you look at my dismal training results.

Do not give up on me, David, I have not yet given up on myself. This is just the natural sort of ebb and flow. I really hope that things will get back into a normal groove. I will make it all up this week; we will be out on Catalina Island, which I expect will be a way to recharge my batteries and supercharge my motivation.

One thing I never want to do again is take any kind of a forced layoff, so I will continue to train smart and not risk injury by overdoing it beyond your plans. This is an important lesson that, following Ironman Arizona in November, I cannot have too much of a layoff. This is just not a good thing for the way I'm wired. It's either all-in, my full commitment, or nothing at all. I blew it by taking too much time off waiting for the hip to recover and now I am paying the price in terms of fitness, endurance, motivation and the daily rhythm of training.

When I think of this as a lifestyle or a massive goal where dozens of friends, clients and family are expecting me to complete the Ironman and are holding me to my plans, then this works. However, when I just think of this endeavor as working out and staying in shape, it's not worth it.

I need to resume the discipline and the rhythm of daily workouts.

Either I am in 100% or not. Nothing half-way for me. I'm just not wired for partial activity or layoffs...I need to stay committed full bore.

-John

Malaise and Struggling to Maintain My Fitness

In September 2008, I was really worried because I was feeling totally out of shape. I felt that ever since Kona 70.3 I had gone way downhill in terms of fitness. I had completed the Vineman Ironman 70.3 in July in very good time, and I did the Bulldog 50K ultra marathon in August. However, despite this progress and these victories, I just wasn't feeling well; I was experiencing malaise and probably a bit of burnout.

This general malaise was likely because I was still battling injuries, daily (and especially nightly) pain deep in my hip, and a chronic, nearly debilitating shoulder pain from the trapezoid trigger points/muscle knots that were so painful that I could barely turn my head to check for oncoming traffic when making lane changes in my car or on my bike; this was really dangerous, and of course, very painful. I was eagerly anticipating my Cortisone/steroid shots (trigger points and my hip), which were already scheduled. I needed the relief. I was not taking any pain medication or anti-inflammatories at that time.

I also had recurring blisters that simply did not have enough time to heal properly between my long runs. I was seeing my podiatrist more frequently than I was seeing my clients, and he continued to scold me for my bathroom surgeries. I was constantly popping blisters, removing entire toenails, treating the open sores and clipping at the massive plantar wart at the bottom of a toe.

The plantar wart had been festering for over a year now and no treatment ever worked to kill the virus; the pain was constant with every step. I had developed a clear limp and by favoring the outside of my far right foot in order to take pressure off of the left side, I strained the metatarsals of my right foot and now could barely bend the toes on my right foot.

A plantar wart is unique in that it only grows on the bottom of the foot and it grows inward, that is, into the foot, not outward like a wart on the hand. This wart was just taking over and with every step, it would be irritated even more. In an attempt to deal with this, I tried freezing it off, melting it with acid...even surgery. Nothing worked. So I just started to clip away at this thing constantly, just trying to carve it out and shave it down in order to relieve the pain. Then there were the toenails. These once perfect nails were now bloody stumps. Many were black, some had fallen out and many had been helped and coaxed from the nail bed as I pulled them out with a combination of pliers and nippers. It actually provided a measure of relief to remove troubled nails rather than allowing them to remain and fester. I actually had fun teasing Connor by pulling out my toenails with pliers…it really didn't hurt and it happened so frequently that the process became something of a parlor trick. My feet were only a problem when walking in my business oxfords or when running; they were never much of an issue on the bike.

The bike had its own set of issues that revolved around the hip, sciatica nerve, trigger point and IT bands. I felt like I was losing a lot fitness on the bike because I had to force myself to stay in the saddle and resist the urge to hammer, since I surmised that the hyperextension of my hip on the bike was the likely reason for the recurring hip pain.

I only had about 75 days or so until Ironman Arizona. I wanted to do more—a lot more. But I remained smart, disciplined and didn't do any crazy new adventures or test myself. I followed our plans and power levels very carefully, but my body seemed to be breaking down in lots of areas.

Constant Hip and Trigger Point Pain

My hip pain was so bad that David and I made the joint decision to drop out of the 100-mile Tour de Poway bike race in October 2008. I lost my race fee, but it was just too close to the full Arizona Ironman and it wasn't worth the risk; we had to keep our eye on the prize.

The month of October 2008, just before Arizona, was a complete emotional rollercoaster ride. I was literally all over the place: supremely confident and unflappable at times, anxious and discouraged at others.

At the beginning of October I was not suffering any incapacitating injuries other than the constant, round the clock hip pain.

Try and picture this: You are sitting on the floor and you bring your feet up and together so that the soles of both feet are now touching flatly against each other…then, someone comes up from behind you, leans over your back and presses down hard on the outsides of both of your bent knees, pushing down toward the floor until finally, something snaps! That's a pulled groin muscle and that is the exact pain I felt constantly, but only on the left side.

The crazy thing was that I never pulled that muscle, it just felt that way. This is known as referred pain. The injury was deep inside my hip socket, but for some reason the pain was transmitted (referenced) to the groin/hip flexor area.

When I tried to ignore the pain and just be tough, pretending to be a Navy SEAL who had to endure any hardship to complete a mission, the pain would evolve into a sciatica-type nerve issue that would send electrical daggers down my left leg to the middle-outside of the shin. This caused my left leg to become partially paralyzed and I could only pedal with the right leg. Since I was locked into my pedals, the left leg had no option but to go along for the painful ride. This caused an imbalance (pedaling only with the right leg), which in itself caused further problems.

Other than the hip pain that stayed with me literally around the clock, the knotted mass of muscles in my upper trapezoid was a constant downer and contributed largely to my low points.

One of the treatment options was to use Botox injections right into the muscle. Botox is a mild form of botulism which has a paralytic effect on the muscle, causing it to relax and release the tension. The problem or risk associated with that is that there was a slight chance it could affect my shoulder movement needed on the swim. I thought the risk was worth it, but the cost per injection was so high and not covered by insurance that I elected to try another option called wet needling.

Wet needling involves multiple injections of Cortisone and steroids right into the specific muscle fiber, then following with additional injections up and down that specific muscle fiber until it released the knot. This was considered an extreme measure, but I was in such constant pain that I was willing to try anything, especially if it was covered by insurance. Following the initial treatments, the pain had been temporarily reduced by 60 – 70%.

Weight Remains a Constant Challenge

By the start of October I was feeling better and more positive. I was not as depressed as I had been when the hip pain resurfaced. I had proven to myself that I could still run even with this problem. I was recording faster average mile splits than ever on my 5 mile runs, and I was not nearly as winded or tired or sore after the long training runs, except for the occasional quad soreness. I was not stopping to walk anywhere near as much during my long runs, and I was getting much more disciplined at pacing and staying steady on my runs.

I was feeling fitter and stronger than I had felt in a long time, however, I was disappointed that I'd gained 3 – 4 pounds since the hip problem, because I had not been exercising at the same level of intensity or duration, but I had not yet reduced my calorie intake.

I was definitely not losing weight anywhere near as easily as I used to. I had regrettably crept back up to 171, but I was determined to get it off and reach my goal of breaking into the 150s before my event in Tempe. It was a fine balance to lose fat, not lean muscle.

I did notice on my Tanita Ironman Body Composition scale that my muscle mass had actually been creeping up and that some of the weight gain was pure muscle. In fact, ever since that 50K ultra, I felt that my legs were stronger and more defined; I just felt more confident with any hill. My legs began to feel like pistons. Whenever I hit a hill, I remembered how I conquered Bulldog Mountain and my legs just sort of took over like they just knew what to do; they'd been there before and this was nothing at all.

I planned to start reporting my weight to David in my weekly updates, just to have a bit more accountability. I understood that I had to be very careful that I didn't do anything shortsighted in terms of radical diets that could jeopardize that hard-earned lean muscle I had paid for in sweat over all those past months.

The Inevitable Emotional Swings

Sometimes I was neither high nor low: just pensive. What was frequently going on in my head was a debate about the time commitment. I started to feel very selfish spending so much time in training and preparation for rides. I felt like it was a colossal waste of time in a purely selfish pursuit. It was especially bad in October 2008, following my biggest week ever for training.

Subject: Callos Update
From: John D. Callos
To: David Warden

Hi David,

I had a dream about you last night. You were telling Coach Friel that I was the biggest complainer you'd ever worked with and that I was always making excuses. I know this isn't true, but the reason for this dream was probably my hip, which was aching all night; I knew I needed to tell you, but was hesitant to do so.

The new medication for the hip is worthless. It is called Vicodin and it has Acetaminophen in it as well, but it doesn't work. So I am going back to the Ultram, even though it makes me dizzy, sleepy and nauseous; just yesterday, I threw up in the parking lot at work. But at least it seems to reduce the hip pain, so it's worth it.

I won't kid you: I did make a mistake and got overly confident and cocky during my run yesterday, trying to set a new half marathon time record. I did it in 1:59, but paid the price. All the rest of the day on Thursday I was tired, very sleepy, and my knees and hamstrings ached; things are still the same this morning.

My plan is to leave work around 1:00 pm and do my 2.5 hour ride in the early afternoon. I better be really lucky today and hope nothing pops up at the last minute to prevent this workout. Tonight is Connor's school football game with their archrival, Mater Dei High School in Anaheim, and I will not miss that game, no matter what.

As for my state of mind, I am a bit down on myself for

being a complete undisciplined idiot and being so sore today. But for the most part, I did keep within the parameters of the workout yesterday except for the last 30 minutes or so.

-John

Toward the end of October, however, I was doing better and my confidence was improving. I started feeling stronger and I felt more prepared than I had been for any other race to date.

On October 27, 2008, I recorded a great 2.5 hour run, averaging about 8:51 per mile and covering almost 16 miles. I've covered 50K in the mountains at 95 degrees, and while it took me 7.5 hours, I did not quit. I had just completed a 106 mile bike ride, and with the buoyancy advantage of a wetsuit, I knew I could manage my way through 2.4 miles on the swim. I was ready for Arizona.

I had dramatically improved my attitude and confidence from earlier in the summer. I had the confidence to get on the starting line in Tempe; deep inside I just knew I could finish the full Ironman.

The Ironman event is about endurance and raw grit, not speed. My goal was to finish like a man, a proud man. An Ironman. I didn't need to set any speed records, although if I broke 14 hours, I would be elated.

I had a hip problem, but so what? Nothing would stop me at this point. I might be forced to slow down a bit and the IT band issue might flare up, but I knew I would finish, even if I had to walk.

I had the endurance and I knew I had the confidence. Those two are a deadly combo. The third leg of that stool was ego. And I could never come home from Arizona having to tell people that I did not finish...regardless of the reason. If I ended up on crutches for a while after the race, that was fine, but one way or the other, I knew I'd finish. My confidence had skyrocketed.

THE 24-HOUR RELAY TEST OF WILL

In 1977 I was running on the Villa Park High School Track and Cross Country teams. One time, a few of us on the team got together and entered a 24-hour relay where each person had to run one mile on the track, then hand the baton off to the next runner, and continue doing that for 24 hours. We started with 8 or 10 guys, but after several hours, many of them quit. Later in the middle of the night, most of the team had left with their parents and by early morning I think there were only two or three of us left on our team. We finished that event but I recall that my last mile was spent literally crawling on part of that track. We'd gone out way too fast early in the event and we never had enough time to recover in between. Our first few legs of the event were in the low 5s, but by the end, the last miles were over 20 minutes.

But we finished. The final few guys never quit. I finished that brutal test and ended up on crutches for about two weeks, but as I recalled that event thirty years later, I knew that I would finish Arizona, even if it meant I'd be on crutches or in a wheelchair for a period of time.

So between my aerobic fitness, confidence, my positive thoughts of having finished each of these events in my workouts and having survived tough times like that 24 hour run relay, I just knew I could finish Arizona.

But just when I was at an all-time high of unstoppable confidence, the worst possible thing happened…I was hit by a car while on my final long weekend bike-run brick prior to Ironman Arizona.

My Bike is Destroyed in a Car Accident

On October 28, 2008, less than four weeks from the start of the Ironman, I was hit by a car while on my bike. I was at about mile 90 of my ride when I was struck at about 3:35 pm. This was the most important workout of the entire year, the last big workout before Arizona. The day called for 112 miles or 6.5 hours on the bike, whichever came first, then an additional run for 1.5 hours.

It was a complete accident and I was not upset with the driver, nor did I harbor any ill-feelings toward her. Accidents happen and I was just thankful and elated to be alive. Period.

I was traveling about 16 mph and was broadsided or T-boned by a very young lady making a left hand turn into a side street. She tried to merge between oncoming traffic and was so focused on the traffic that she did not see me coming. I was just minding my own business and clearly in the bike lane, but there was nothing I could do; there was not even time to try and brake. The moment I saw the car was the exact same moment I saw my bike get pulled under her bumper. There was zero time to react.

I hit the hood of the PT Cruiser, rolled off and, according to witnesses, rolled side over side 15 - 20 times, shoulder to shoulder, somehow settling face-down on my stomach on the sidewalk. The one thing I did remember was this uncontrollable rolling and rolling. Remarkably, my Oakley Radar sunglasses and bike helmet were still attached.

I just lay on my stomach for a long time trying to process what had just happened. I didn't want to move anything and instead, did a mental check on every part of my body before I decided to try to move. I didn't feel any pain at that moment and that really worried me.

Had I severed my spinal column? Was I paralyzed? I was too scared at the moment to think about that. I didn't want to know how bad it was. All I could think about was that my Ironman dream was ruined. I had done so well over the past year, endured so much, and I was just about three weeks away from my final goal and now those dreams lay scattered all over the road in broken bits of carbon, aluminum, plastic and rubber.

Many people had gathered around and were asking me so many questions at the same time that it was hard to process anything. People kept scouring the street and bringing me pieces of my bike and piling them up next to me; I remembered that part. I also remembered people asking me, "Who is David? Who is David?"

Apparently, I kept saying that David would see the workout data and I had to finish the workout, this was the most important workout of the year and my last major brick workout prior to the full Ironman.

The scene was surreal. There were about 50 spectators, an ambulance, police cars, a fire truck, paramedics and the Harbor Patrol. That was a lot of tax payer dollars at work.

The great news, in fact, the miraculous news, was that I barely had a scratch. There were hardly any external signs on my body that I was hit by a car at that speed.

It had been a cold, foggy morning in Carpinteria when I had set out from our weekend beach shack, and I'd decided to wear three, yes THREE, long sleeved shirts, a pair of full-fingered running gloves, and also my bike gloves. All these extra layers were 100% responsible for saving my arms, hands, back and elbows from certain road rash.

The outer bike jersey was really ripped up, but it took the brunt of the asphalt abrasions. The other layers prevented any abrasion at all to my skin. It really was miraculous. And lucky. It was sort of like wearing two pairs of socks for long runs in order to avoid blisters; those extra layers really made all the difference.

Also fortunate was that my feet had sprung out of the toe clips immediately when the car smashed the bike right out from under me, and I was immediately thrown clear; the quick-release pedals and cleats did their job and I had no twisted ankles or broken bones in the lower legs, ankles or feet. In fact, I barely had a scratch on the lower legs despite being thrown, hitting the hood and rolling about 20 - 30 feet. Just amazing.

To be clear, as I was told the story by the eyewitnesses, I more rolled than was actually thrown: I rolled off the hood, rolled down the street. My bike helmet stayed on and my head was not hurt, but my neck was really sore and very stiff and my shoulders ached from taking the brunt of all the rolling. Thanks to Rob Parks, I suffered no head injury of any kind.

Rob Parks is a long-time friend of over twenty years who is also a world-class cyclist. One morning, Rob, Tom Sinclair and I took a quick ride down PCH to the Huntington Beach Pier. While resting for a moment, Rob noticed that my helmet chin strap was dangling too far below my chin. I explained that it was just too restrictive to wear it any tighter. Rob explained that I was a complete idiot and then he personally adjusted my helmet straps to the correct position. He said, "One day John, you'll thank me for this."

That day has come Rob. Thank you. Your action may have literally saved my life.

The first responders to my bike accident were fantastic, they included a male nurse and a middle-aged man who saw the whole thing happen right in front of him as he and his friends were in the car waiting to make a right hand turn. He was shocked that I was alive and breathing, and he took great care of me. I wish I had his name to thank him personally. He kept me calm through it all.

I'm not too proud to admit that I was a bit scared. I really did not want to know how bad the injuries were. I had just laid there for a few minutes and mentally processed all this before I took any physical action to check for injuries.

I did not want to accept any medical attention for fear of the costs. I know that sounds irresponsible, and I did have fantastic medical insurance with Blue Cross, but about 18 months ago my wife needed emergency treatment when she contracted West Nile from an infected mosquito and hardly anything was covered. Despite all of our insurance coverage, I was paying for all kinds of additional non-covered tests, procedures, and drugs for months and months. It even got to the point that they threatened to ding my credit because of a dispute over the ambulance charges which had obviously been inflated. All these additional bills just kept showing up out of nowhere. Doctors I'd never heard of, never met, never knew were involved, were sending us bills. It seemed that all the extra tests that the hospital ordered were not covered and we had to pay for all of those as well. The ambulance ride, everything. Based on her bad experience, I wasn't interested in going through that again.

I tried to stand up (it took two attempts, as I was still a bit wobbly) and I was able to answer the basic questions that the paramedics asked to determine if I might have a concussion. They finally let me decline the ambulance service which was great on two fronts: I'd save the money and I could continue with my workout.

The bike was really trashed. Bits and pieces of carbon and my PowerTap wattage meter broke off and the Specialized S-Works Roubaix SL Carbon frame took a broadside hit and got smashed by the car. A fellow triathlete who had witnessed the accident began reassembling what was left of my bike and putting things back in order so we could see what was going on. He was very concerned that I should not ride the bike as he was certain that the carbon frame was cracked from the direct hit of the car and going under the bumper.

But nonetheless, he did a great job reassembling things and I was very grateful. I was very worried about the bike as well. The wheelset was out of true, but by releasing the brake calipers, he was able to get the rims to spin just enough to miss the brake pads and get the bike back on the road.

When I'd been face down on the ground struggling to figure out what had happened and why, someone had seen the chain on the back of my neck and reached into my shirt to grab my Road ID dog tags. They called my business partner Kevin, who then called my wife. She tried to call me, but I never knew it because my cell phone was crunched and fell apart during the accident. Later, some witnesses at the scene reassembled my phone and it started ringing immediately. The first call was from my wife April.

I will never forget her first words:

"I'm coming to pick you up. It's OVER!"

I didn't know exactly what "It's OVER." meant. Today's ride? My training? My Ironman dream? Biking on the streets? Whatever it meant, I could tell that she was pretty damn serious and more than just a little upset.

I said, *"I'm fine, and even though my bike is ruined, I have to try and finish the workout. Don't come. I will see you in about 45 minutes. This is the most important workout of the year."*

I had a funny feeling that my wife was coming up and that she'd track me down, so I had to plan a quick exit. I thanked everyone profusely because I was so genuinely happy to be alive; crazy as it seemed, I was smiling broadly, just so relieved that I was not seriously injured, or worse.

I tried to act manly and tough for some reason, as if I had an obligation to live up to the Ironman mystique of being tough and the reputation of pushing through the pain and overcoming any obstacle. It was as if I was representing all Ironmen worldwide, and had a standard to uphold. I can't explain it, but I think that other Ironmen might understand.

I grabbed three Tylenol from a stranger, downed them quickly with my Carbo-Pro and took off very slowly in the opposite direction of home. The wheels of my bike were wobbly and the gears could not shift due to the broken derailleur and the jammed/bent brake and shifter lever, but I was determined to try to finish what I had started; I still had to cover another 16 miles to complete the bike portion of the workout.

The fact is, this could very well happen in the Ironman event—I could get banged up in a bike accident during the race, and I would still have to find a way to finish. So I viewed this as just another test.

Time was passing very slowly (plus I couldn't shift gears). Before I knew it, my wife and son had driven all the way up to Santa Barbara from Carpinteria and found me limping down the road.

She drove her new Range Rover right next to me and told me to put the bike in the back of car. I wouldn't do it, but I did stop to talk to her and thank her for caring. I told her the story of what had happened and assured her that I was not injured, but she was worried that I might have internal injuries or a head injury.

She couldn't understand why I was so excited and happy, but just to be alive and unscathed after that accident made me very grateful and energetic. I smiled broadly for a photo that she could send to my business partner to tell him that I was all right.

She followed behind me, which of course any man will tell you is all at once embarrassing (ever had your mother follow you home on your bike as a kid?), exciting (to try and beat her home with only one gear and half a brake), and endearing (to know that someone actually cared so much about me).

As soon as I arrived home, I started making plans for the 1.5 hour run. I changed my clothes and got into my running gear, fueled up, grabbed my water bottles and was off.

The run was quite difficult as I had a new fear of cars that I'd never experienced before. Soon, it got dark and I was very worried about the cars around me. I was tired from the 106 mile bike ride and ended up walking and jogging. I was also very hungry. I stopped by a liquor store and bought a bag of chips, some peanut crackers, a bag of salted peanuts, a 5-hour energy shot and a PowerAde. I ate all this while I was running down the road, pulling items one by one from the plastic grocery bag.

I completed the run on Foothill Road in Carpinteria where there were no lights and it was pitch dark. I used the white lane marker lines as a guide, as there were no street lights and this was the only thing I could see.

It was a long day. A lucky day to be sure. I was, and still remain, very grateful that I was not seriously injured, and I was happy that I completed the entire workout despite the hurdles and challenges of the day.

I knew that if I could finish this workout despite what had happened, I could complete the full Arizona Ironman Triathlon on November 23, 2008.

I had no hard feelings toward the person who hit me, she and her family turned out to be very fine, caring people with the utmost in character and integrity. The girl's father called me the next day and was clearly concerned about my physical condition. He took the time to care, and I appreciated his kind gesture.

It was important to me that he knew that I thought I was fine, and that he should not have any concern about any trumped-up fake injuries, attorneys, neck problems or anything of the sort. This was clearly an accident and I was not about to play any games or further traumatize this young girl or her family.

I was sore and bruised up, but I was delighted to be alive and doing fine. There was no need to settle a score. I would not be part of the problem; I wanted to be part of the solution by demonstrating that we could forgive and forget, that we could be neighborly and all get along even when there was an accident.

The family very quickly understood that my dreams of Ironman glory were at risk and that I had to get my bike repaired immediately because the race was only three weeks away. They quickly paid to have the bike repaired. The damages were substantial, but some of the bike could still be salvaged, such as the Zipp 606 wheelset and the wireless PowerTap 2.4 Power Meter.

I was so grateful that there were no severe injuries and I could be back on my training schedule within a couple of days. If I had to get hit, at least I was lucky enough to deal with a family that understood the importance of my Ironman dream and why I needed to resolve this issue quickly so I could get back on the road as quickly as possible.

So to the young lady I say:

"Please do not feel badly at all. I forgive you completely and am not mad, upset or angry with you in any way."

To her father and family I say:

"Thank you for getting me back on the road quickly and for understanding the importance of completing this Ironman journey with the least amount of interruption."

To all cyclists out there I say:

"Even when you are totally alert, accidents can and will happen. ALWAYS wear a helmet and ALWAYS carry ROAD ID."

In the end, the bright side of the bike accident was that it gave me the confidence that I could finish nearly anything that I set my mind to, even overcoming tough obstacles and hurdles. I felt powerful and ready for anything. Ironman Arizona? BRING IT!

THE AFTERMATH OF THE BIKE ACCIDENT

The emotional high of surviving the bike accident and the feeling of power and near-invincibility quickly faded. I may have suffered a delayed reaction to the stress and trauma of the accident, but I was really shaken up. I had lost my mental edge, my swagger, my confidence.

Subject: Probably Need Help
To: David Warden
From: John D. Callos

Hi David,

I have been very, very hesitant to send this email.

Something is wrong. I don't feel right. I am in a slump. I am operating at a very, very low level.

I am scared and afraid of the event in front of me in just two weeks.

I feel overwhelmed.

I have bad intestinal distress that has kept me very close to home.

I have also developed a case of "restless leg syndrome" and am having a very hard time sleeping. This is a horrible condition, and I don't know much about it or why it has sprung up on me. It is an achy, tingling, pins and needles condition like a billion fire ants crawling just under the surface of the skin on my thighs, knees and calves. Very hard to describe, but suffice to say it's very uncomfortable and makes it absolutely impossible for me to rest peacefully.

I have also been tired and feel like I need to take naps, but have not. General overall malaise has set in, big time.

I am not consciously trying to sabotage the race, but wonder if my subconscious is fighting me.

It is likely fear. The fear of a potential DNF. I do not fear the pain, I fear the humiliation of a DNF.

I am leaving now to do the swim that was supposed to take place on Friday, but due to flu-like symptoms, I skipped 100% of Friday's workouts.

Any words of advice, wisdom, support, encouragement? I do not need a tough talk right now. I am probably harder on myself than anyone could be.

-John

My two hour run that day (make up session for the day before) was a 100% unmitigated disaster. It was the worst I felt in many, many months. I was not thinking straight.

I also stupidly got excited about a new pair of running shoes that were so remarkably comfortable that I thought I would take them on the run. That was an idiotic, totally ignoramus stunt and I knew better. Way better. Was I subconsciously trying to destroy my chances before I even started? Was I looking for an excuse to not even enter the race?

Of course, blisters developed, but at least at that point, I had the common sense to stop running and turn around and get back home before they got too bad. In the early months of my training, I would have tried to tough it out, which would only have made matters worse. Maybe I was secretly hoping that my poor judgment would continue and that I would become so ravished with blisters that I could not possibly even think of entering the race. Who knows?

All I know for sure is that I was miserable.

Subject: Probably Need Help #2
From: David Warden
To: John D. Callos

John,

I expect there may be a few things going on. Is it possible there is still some trauma from your bike accident? All of your symptoms point to extreme stress.

I need you to understand something. Short of disastrous mechanical failure that even the tech van won't be able to solve (highly unlikely), you will not DNF this event.

You are more prepared for this IM than most first-time athletes. I need to repeat this. You are more prepared for this event than I was for my first Ironman, than my other athletes doing this event, than anyone I know who did their first IM.

You are the most dedicated and disciplined first-timer I have ever worked with. And that discipline will end up with results, and that result is you will finish this race, and finish it strong.

You must stop worrying about DNF stop reinforcing this negative visualization. You can create your own reality with your negative thoughts.

Physically, you are there. I don't care if you missed your entire workout this weekend. Yes, it will have an impact, but we are talking in terms of minutes, not DNF.

John, mentally, you need some help.

I need you to spend the next 2 weeks visualizing your day and how it will go. Here is my plan for how the race will go for you:

- Imagine yourself at the starting line. Your bike is good to go, your wetsuit is on. Thousands of other athletes are mingling around you. You strike up a conversation with one or two of them. It is the first IM for another athlete as well, and you talk about your training.
- You get in the water and the cannon goes off. You get

bumped around a bit more than usual and it is crowded, maybe someone even knocks off your goggles and you struggle to put them back on while other athletes are bumping you and swimming all around you, churning you like you're in a washing machine. That's OK, you just have to breaststroke for a while or let your wetsuit keep you afloat while you get the goggles back on and adjust your bearings. Breaststroke for a while and get settled in again. Then get into your steady rhythm just like you've been doing for the past year in your Endless Pool.

- You come out of the swim feeling great. Imagine yourself running to the bike, your family calls out to you "Go John! You are doing great."
- You get on your bike, and this is the best you have felt for months. You feel powerful and strong, the challenge is to not go too hard. You know David will be angry if he sees you went out too hard the first half.
- At mile marker 90 you start to feel some fatigue or maybe even some hip pain, but things are going great. Flat tire? No problem. We can handle that. Chrissie Wellington got a flat at the IM World Championships this year and still won the entire event. She just rested for 5 minutes while her tire got changed.
- Transition to the run and the race is essentially over. You can run/walk this with ease. At T2 the crowd is screaming, your family is there.
- Mile 12 of the run starts to hurt, but it is a good hurt. Less than 2 hours to the finish.
- Mile 22 is very tough, but the finish line is so close.
- Mile 25 is unbelievable; the crowd is going crazy lined up along the street. You are high-fiving hundreds of people.
- You approach the finish line and as you cross the announcer says, "John Callos, YOU ARE AN IRONMAN."
- John, you have essentially already done this in your training. The Arizona IM is just a formality for you at this point.

I need you to visualize THIS version of the event, not your current DNF version of negativity.

-David

On November 11, 2008, the morning I was leaving for the Ironman, I took one last step on my Tanita Ironman Body Composition scale to see how close I came to the weight goal that I had set so long ago.

I was shocked that I just barely came in at under 160 pounds (159.8 exactly).

Weight Goal: ACHIEVED.

Remarkably, exactly to the day, I had met my goal of dropping below 160. That's quite a difference from my high point of morbid obesity at 212 pounds (well, that's when I stopped weighing myself). So clearly, I had lost at least 50 pounds from my high point.

Everything seemed to be lining up for the Ironman and achieving the weight loss goal was a good omen. It had been an amazing journey, and in hindsight, well worth the struggles and sacrifices.

The real goal is not just completing the Ironman race, but rather, staying fit for life. If my goal is just to reach this objective for a single event, I will fail and quickly return to my former fat self.

An important lesson that I've learned in this journey is a lesson about myself. I am a man that needs goals. Goals are what drive me and keep me focused and motivated. Without goals and accountability for their achievement, I tend to drift. And when it comes to goals, I need giant, crazy goals that are shockingly difficult for most people to even fathom.

At that time, I knew I might not meet all my crazy ultra endurance goals, but one thing was for sure: I was going to finish the Ironman.

CHAPTER TEN

EVENTS

The lead-up to Ironman Arizona consisted of many smaller races that were designed to build my skills at pacing and nutrition and to improve my confidence in long events and open water swims.

Over the period leading up to the Arizona Ironman, I completed:

- Four Sprint Triathlons (Carpinteria & Santa Barbara)
- The Los Alamitos 10K
- The Solvang Metric Century bike event (60 miles)
- The Tour de Poway bike race (60 miles)
- The Long Beach Marathon bike race (26 miles)
- The Hono/Kona Ironman 70.3 Triathlon
- The Vineman Ironman 70.3 Triathlon
- The Bulldog 50K ultra marathon (31 miles)

In total, these events helped prepare me for my ultimate objective of completing the full Ironman event in November 2008. In each of these events I learned distinct new skills about racing, pacing, sticking to my race plans, nutrition and proper hydration.

Outlined below are some notes, race reports, lessons learned and observations from select events:

CARPINTERIA SPRINT TRIATHLON 2007

By any measure, this race was a terrific success and a real confidence booster.

My improvements over the previous year were substantial, especially when I considered that I did not do any running over the three weeks prior to the race due to a broken ankle and plantar fasciitis issues, plus I had been sick for two days during the race week. Still, with all of that, my training over the months leading up to this event really brought it all together.

On the swim I learned that I shouldn't over-tighten my mask/goggles. By doing that, I caused the silicon seal to become wavy and let in some water. Water was leaking into my mask, so I thought that my mask was not tight enough. I tightened the mask even more, letting even more salty ocean water into my mask, which stung my eyes. Then it occurred to me what might be going on, and when I loosened my mask that solved the problem. It was interesting how the solution was the exact opposite of what one would naturally assume.

Another important lesson learned was never to let the seal of the mask touch any part of the silicone race cap. Tiny droplets of water could develop there, so it was best to never let the silicone cap slip beneath the seal of the swim mask.

Another challenge was swimming in a straight line without the benefit of lane markers at the bottom of a pool. I swam toward the Olympic distance buoy instead of the Sprint, which took me way off course. However, despite these challenges, my swim time was a full two minutes faster in a 500 yard swim; that was a remarkable improvement for such a short distance, especially with the leaking mask problems.

Also, this time I charged forward without hesitation and got toward the front of the pack. I was no longer afraid of the pack and had confidence in the water. Of course, then my mask filled with water and I was overtaken by hundreds of guys while I treaded water to try and fix the situation. But there was a lesson there, as well as a lesson to steer clear of the buoy, where there was huge amount of congestion with people literally crawling all over each other. I also charged out of the water and ran across the sand; this year I was not dizzy or light headed.

In T1, my bike shoes took a long time to put on, maybe a minute or two. The problem was that they have a dial that must be turned to securely tighten the shoe. It took a long time, but otherwise, I did fine in transition. I wore my tri suit/singlet and race belt with number, under my wetsuit. I just flew through things, except for the bike shoes.

On the bike, I used my Garmin 305 and was glad I did. I didn't grind heavy gears, but I really pushed it going down the hills and made up some time. This is my home town, my home course and I knew where I could really push it, which was a huge advantage. For about the last 5 miles, I was averaging close to 22 – 23 MPH, which is huge for me. I dropped a full two minutes on the bike leg over the same course compared to last year, despite the fact that the bike was where I thought I would actually do worse this year; I was very happy with the bike leg.

On the run, I was dying for the first half mile. Then by mile 1.5 I thought, "You know, I actually feel pretty good overall. I feel OK." I remembered to keep a steady pace, no crazy spurts of speed. I remembered that a measured steady pace was how records were made. At the turnaround I told myself, "OK, I've done this before. This is my race, I know this course like nobody else and I can run this last half a lot faster."

I really picked it up. I remembered my leg speed and dug really deep. I was passing people so fast that they didn't even try to put up a fight. Then at the end, the last quarter mile, I resolved to pass everyone in sight. Nobody was going to beat me. Tears were streaming from my eyes, and I couldn't even imagine how disturbing my finish photo would be with my terribly disfigured and contorted face writhing in agony.

I completed the run in 28:07. I dropped a full 2 minutes on the swim, I dropped 1:30 on T1, I dropped about 2 minutes on the bike, and dropped a full three minutes in the run. Overall, I dropped 8 minutes on the same Sprint course from the prior year. Also, I placed 151 out of 407 people and I placed in the top 37% of finishers overall; I beat over a third of the guys in my age group. Just two years prior, I placed nearly last in my age group.

The prior year I was laid up with ice packs all over my legs and knees. I was shot and in miserable shape. This year, I was fantastic and needed no ice, could easily move around afterward and actually wanted to walk around our small beach town and just keep active. I was full of energy and doing fantastic with no pains, strains or overall fatigue. The base training with Amanda had really paid off, and I was thrilled with the results.

THE WEEKS LEADING UP TO HAWAII

I needed to become acclimatized to the heat I would face in the lava fields of Hawaii, so a couple of weeks prior to the event I'd wear a lot of extra clothes in my workouts to really make it hot and uncomfortable.

I went to Hawaii coming off my worst day ever on a bike just two weeks before, on May 16, 2008. That day was horribly hot (103 degrees) and my hip flexor was really hurting me. I was cursing out loud and shouting at my hip and this whole business of training and this crazy goal of Ironman. The pain was so intense that I was tearing up like a girl in junior high who didn't make the cheerleading squad. My left leg hung limp and was just along for the ride since it was locked into the pedal, and the right leg did 100% of the work; there was no other way, as I was at least 25 miles away from home when this hip pain flared up.

So with that extremely poor bike ride behind me, I went to Hawaii about four days prior to the race. I left my prized Cervelo P3C Time Trial bike at home and shipped over my Specialized S-Works road bike. I knew I'd be far less aerodynamic, but at least the relaxed geometry and position on the road bike would take some of the pressure off the hip and would reduce the flare-ups to the trigger points in my upper trapezoid area.

Despite these issues, I was in good spirits, and determined to succeed and was confident that I'd finish. But I must plainly admit that I was a nervous wreck once I arrived at the check in area and saw the fitness level of those who would be participating in this event.

Race Preparation: Hawaii 70.3

Subject: Hawaii 70.3 Training
From: John D. Callos
To: David Warden

Hi David,

I have booked and confirmed the trip for the 70.3 on May 31st. My wife April and our 14 year old son Connor are going as well.

David, I do not want to disappoint my family.

I must finish that race upright, with dignity and still in fair enough condition to enjoy a few days with them on the Big Island without limping around and complaining that I am too sore to have fun. I would consider it a failure if I was not able to spend time with them following the race because I was too beat up due to lack of preparation or inadequate conditioning between now and May 31st (about 100 days from now).

As Vince Lombardi used to tell his guys, "The more you sweat in practice, the less you bleed in battle."

Having said that, I would appreciate it if you could be absolutely certain that the plan you are putting me on between now and May 31st will be more than enough, without a doubt, to help me accomplish the objectives stated above.

At this point, and with your help/accountability, there is no excuse for me not to be in absolutely optimal condition to meet my goals.

-John

Even though my goal for the race was to just finish, I was nervous about what time I might record in the Hawaii/Kona Ironman 70.3. I had a rough number in mind that I wanted to hit. However, at the same time, I didn't want to feel like a loser if I had a really tough day and failed to meet my projection.

I was thinking that I would like to finish the swim in 40 minutes or less, I would love to do the bike in 3:00 – 3:15, but that could really be a wildcard if my nerve (sciatica) got too crazy, and then I wanted to do the run in 2:00, but that might end up being 2:20 – 2:30 with the heat and if the bike segment was really windy.

So my super-secret goal time was 6:30, but anything under 7 hours and I would be happy. I wanted to beat 200 – 300 participants so that I could walk away knowing that I actually was faster than a bunch of participants; that would be really great.

If I did over 7 hours I'd be disappointed, but the only reason I could think of that could make me go over 7 hours was if the hip and trapezoid trigger point issues caused so much pain that it became unbearable, or if the heat and severe winds totally destroyed me. Or both.

I continued with a rigorous training schedule for the next ninety days, then David gave me an outline of my race week preparation and race day strategy:

Subject: Race week and strategy
From: David Warden
To: John D. Callos

John,
I have updated your schedule:

Wednesday is a 20 minute run, depending how you feel. I would run during the time of day that your actual run will take place in Kona, ~12:00 pm.

Thursday is a 20-minute open water swim. Please do this in a safe place, preferably with other people or a place that has lifeguards.

Friday is another optional open water swim. If you felt your open water swim went very well on Thursday, skip it. If you struggled on Thursday, do it again on Friday. It is very common for your first open water swim of the year to be stressful. Don't worry if this happens on Thursday, just try it again on Friday.

Friday: 20 minute run with some brief acceleration, and 15 minutes on the bike primarily to check your equipment and shift into every gear to make certain everything is shifting properly.

PRE-RACE:

Do lots of positive visualization. Imagine yourself crossing the finish line and hearing everyone yelling and clapping. Don't be intimidated by the other athletes. Everyone always looks leaner, fitter and faster than you.

Try to take in ~800 semi-liquid calories 3 hours before the race (Ensure, applesauce, bananas, hot cereal, or your specific race-nutrition you have been using). Don't take in anything but water for the last hour before the race. Use the bathroom every chance you can get.

RACE STRATEGY:

Swim:
Swim how you have done in training. You are swimming well, and I don't see many problems other than going off course. Mark every 10 strokes, or latch onto another swimmer (best). Make sure this swimmer is not slower than you have been swimming in your training.

Bike:
Start out slowly. Not super-slow, but let that hip warm up for a good 20 minutes. Your HR for the first ~30 minutes is likely to be off the charts because you will be very excited. It will probably be in the 150s for a bit.

After about 30 minutes, try to keep your HR between 120-130 until 2 hours into the ride. At that point, 130-140 is acceptable for the last hour of the ride. Again, it is also dependant on the hip. If the hip kicks in, you have to use your own judgment.

Nutrition is critical. Do whatever you have been doing in your long rides. I believe that this has been ~300 calories per hour. Don't forget to drink as well.

Run:

By this time, HR will become more reliable. Start slow, 135 would be a good place to start. That can gradually increase for the duration of the run, but don't exceed 145 until the last 4 miles. For the last 4 miles, go however you feel. Make sure you take in 100 calories per hour on the run.

I'm very excited for you.

-David

HAWAII 70.3 REGISTRATION AND RACE CHECK-IN

The check-in for Ironman 70.3 was an amazing and intimidating scene. Everyone looked so incredibly fit—literally like cover models for all of the fitness industry magazines.

And there was this peculiar dynamic I witnessed, where so many of the athletes were wearing their race-labeled gear from past Ironman events from all over the world, which intimidated me all the more. It seemed that most were wearing their hats, visors and other M-DOT (The official Ironman logo) gear, and many of them had that incredible M-DOT tattoo.

At that point I decided that when I completed the full Ironman, I was definitely getting that tattoo. It was so awesome and they didn't have to say a word—their M-DOT tattoo did all the talking. Those athletes (men and women) were so incredibly fit.

It seemed that everyone was highly tanned and exceptionally lean with well-toned muscles. I also noticed rather large biceps on many of the men, as well as the sure sign of a dedicated athlete: highly-developed calf muscles, often rippling with veins that had nowhere to go due to the fibrous muscle and were forced toward the surface of the skin.

Many of the athletes came down to the registration area wearing compression shorts, their spandex race gear and very tight race jerseys, which all served to highlight their bulging, rippling muscles and lean physiques.

AND THEN—THERE WAS "THE LOOK"

It didn't matter where you were at the event: in the hotel, in the nearby gift shops, at a local restaurant, in the elevator, down by the beach or the pool. A quick once-over and you could tell in an instant who was here to race.

Their face and neck were lean and they were tan and fit. Check. Their legs were usually tight—not too heavily muscled, but always highly toned and taut. Check. Their calf muscles were well defined. Check. There was a slight hollowness to their face between the cheekbone and jaw. You just could not fake that kind of fitness.

This is the look I call a Triathlete's body. It is a combination of a well-developed upper body from swimming and the lean body of a marathon runner with the developed leg muscles and the calf muscles of a cyclist. There is just nothing else like this kind of fit body, and I was seeing it everywhere I looked. Everywhere, that is, except in my own mirror.

It was intimidating because I did not look like these well-toned, world class athletes, at least not yet. But I couldn't let my expectations be set on achieving a body like many of these guys, because they were literally the best in the world, like right off the front cover of a fitness magazine. And all in one place. It was really quite a scene and hard to believe.

If this was a solo, individual race, then why was I so worried about everyone else? It really shouldn't matter. But I had to be honest with myself: this was a test. It was a race. Period. I could try to hold back and run my own event, but the competitive juices were already flowing and I was already looking for people that I might be able to beat.

If I wanted to go out and do my own individual triathlon, I could do that at home on any weekend. No, this was different. This was the real deal. Perhaps my first Ironman 70.3 should not have been this one, which attracts athletes from all over the world.

We were each out to measure ourselves against others who were also working hard to push themselves past new athletic limits. Without this competition, people would not push as hard, would not be as fit or as prepared.

There are entire industries built around the individual competitive drive in people like me and those who were in the registration lobby that day. Without these races, events and competition, there may not be M-DOT logoed merchandise, race sponsorships, or the aero bike frames and accessories designed to shave seconds from our long bike segment. Athletes just love the thrill of beating other people, of testing themselves.

I knew that this was my first Ironman 70.3 and I might have made a mistake picking this event as my first one, but I really wanted to try and beat some people in this race. The only problem was that I hadn't seen a single person that I thought I might be capable of beating in the race.

Back when I was home, when I was thinking clearly and not so intimidated, I was planning to just finish this event, to compete with no one other than myself and my past times in workouts at home. I would treat this as a catered workout and just be thankful that there was plenty of water all along the lava-lined course.

The real test for me would be whether I could stick to the plans I'd made at home, not the adjusted race plans I seemed to want to make after I had seen how fit and lean everyone was.

I had to stick to my plan and run my own race. I couldn't let these ultra fit athletes intimidate me. I had to remember how far I had come, and that I was totally new to this scene. This was not yet my time; my ultimate goal was Ironman Arizona in November 2008. This event in Hawaii should just be a training exercise.

As the nine-time Ironman finisher from Chicago said when Connor and I ran into him in Hawaii,

> *"Be smart, John. You chose the wrong event for your first half, but now that you're here, make the most of it and be smart. No heroics. Just aim to finish this one. You should measure your success based on whether or not you finish, not your final time or how many people you pass. If you don't finish this one, it's OK, but stay with the sport. If everyone finished this race they wouldn't call it the Ironman."*

I had to stick to my original plan and not be an idiot and start racing people or try to pass them. I had to stay in my zones and keep to my original plan.

"Be smart, John. Be smart." This became my new mantra.

Subject: Race update from Hawaii
From: John D. Callos
To: David Warden

Hi David,

I am here in Hawaii, and man you were right; it is very intimidating.

I have never seen so many fit people in my life. They are like alien beings, a superhuman breed of athletes. Impressive and very intimidating.

Anyway, I do intend to be smart, stay disciplined and

stay within what I know are my safe zones from training. I will not push so hard and risk a DNF. No way.

I am absolutely 100% positive I can finish this race and still take my family out for a nice dinner later that night. It is just a matter of not letting these guys get to me and staying within my very detailed race plan.

If the wind is insane, then I have a plan. If I get a flat or breakdown, I have a plan. I do have a terrible blister that just popped today (new shoes on my last 13 mile run), but I have a plan for raw feet as well.

I have a plan to deal with aggressive swimmers and a back up plan if I get sick along the way on the bike or if my nutrition goes haywire on the run.

I expect the wind to be totally crazy. I drove the course and you won't believe this, but it is totally true...at the turnaround point, there are about ten huge windmills. That gives you a sense of the constant wind situation. But from my recon trip, I know exactly where the wind starts and where it ends. Most likely, there will be 10 - 12 miles of wind. The rest of the course is a lot of rolling hills. The return trip back from the Hawi turnaround will be faster I believe, so a negative split is likely.

The one constant here seems to be the strong trade winds.

Also, it is interesting how the athletes sort of have their game faces on and how they size up one another. I don't look like these guys, so they don't do it to me; I'm not a threat to them at all. But I can watch and observe and it's amazing how they are wearing their tightest shirts, compression gear, Ironman race gear and M-Dot logo'd gear from their various races around the world.

Very cool, very exciting, but also very terrifying. I wish the race was starting in 10 minutes from right now. I really want to get it over with; the anticipation and anxiety is killing me.

I did a swim this morning in VERY rough seas. But as long as you keep looking at the bottom, you don't realize how bad it is. But man, looking from the shore at the swells and the thousands of white caps is really sort of fun and scary at the same time.

I did fine in the rough water. I learned very quickly to only take a breath when the swells lift you high in the water like a bobber—at the top of the swell, never at the bottom, because the white cap might break at the top and crash down on top of your face just as you are taking in a breath. That is exactly what happened to me a couple of times and I learned quickly to only breathe at the top of the swells, never while in the trough of the waves. This is an important lesson that I discovered on my own and never heard of or read about in any of my swimming books.

My bike just arrived with Tri Bike Transport; this is an excellent service. I went over to retrieve it from the racks, but there were a couple of guys standing over it and commenting that: "Whoever is riding this bike doesn't have a clue. Where are the aero bars?" I was so embarrassed that I just kept walking right past my own bike.

That was really a blow to the gut and crushed my confidence. I just walked away with my head hung low and got out of there fast. I will pick the bike up later when there are not so many people hanging around.

Well thanks for everything, David. The race is in just 1.5 days.

I would not be here if it wasn't for you, so thanks again.

-John

RACE REPORT:
HAWAII IRONMAN 70.3

I had a great day, placing 649 out of 1,100. Placing within my age group was another story altogether, a rather sad tale of 62 out of 72, but I did manage to beat 10 guys in my age group.

But this was not the average community Sprint Tri; these guys meant business and they took the race very seriously. So in the end, I beat a few guys in my age group, and I was happy with that. These guys came from all parts of the world and there were very few Ironman 70.3 newbies like me. I even saw Chris McCormack, my hero, in first place on the bike and he was really gritting his teeth and obviously working extremely hard hammering away on his bike, even though there was no one even close to him! That's a real winner, a real athlete. Later, I saw him after he'd already been up to his room, showered, changed and probably had a meal, just about the time I crossed the finish line. I didn't stop to say how inspiring he was to me, or to introduce myself or my family. I wish I had, and I regret that I didn't stop to say hello.

My total time was 6:36 and my super-secret goal was to break 6:30, so I was very, very happy with this result and knew that I was capable of breaking 6:30 on a different course. I had no other issues:

hydration, electrolytes and nutrition were dialed-in 100% perfectly.

The swim went very well, I really wasn't even that tired at all. It was a mad, crazy start and a lot of elbows, shoving, pushing and grappling the entire way. I could have swum faster, but I could not get out of the huge crowds. Swim time was 41 minutes and I was fine with that.

TI took 6 minutes but includes a huge and long uphill run to the bikes. I was fine with this, but it could be faster in the future.

My bike leg was tough. Total time was 3:21 and there was a lot of wind. Later I learned that it was one of the windiest days they have ever seen for the race. My average speed was about 16.1 mph, which does not accurately reflect my true speed because in the headwinds it was about 8 mph, but in the tailwinds on the return, I was doing over 30 mph in some spots. I had been hoping for a total bike time of 3:15 and an average speed of 17 mph.

The hip had been acting up a bit, but was not totally unbearable, and the good news was that the left trapezoid did not affect me at all—what a relief that was.

T2 was about 8 minutes, but at that point, I just sat in a plastic chair in the shade and took my time to change into my running gear; I knew I had plenty of time to make the cutoff, so I just took it all in for an extra minute or so. I also had to put blister pads on my feet due to the raw, oozing blisters that did not recover prior to the race; T2 could definitely be faster in the future.

The run was tough. Quite hot, windy and hilly. Plus, in some parts we were running right in the middle of ancient lava fields, which was less than ideal. I didn't execute my race plan for the run as ideally as I had hoped. I just didn't have it in the legs, because battling the wind in the upright position of my road bike just sucked the energy out of my legs and they were pretty trashed. Total time for the 13 mile run was 2:20—at home I could do the run in 1:59 on fresh legs.

But in the end, I was very happy with the overall results because it went almost exactly according to my plans and the hydration and fueling went perfectly.

I was way too conservative and finished the race with a lot of energy. I could have gone harder and faster; I was capable of maybe a 6:15 even in those conditions. My HR and power data showed that I was almost 100% exactly where I wanted to be in terms of my carefully orchestrated race plan.

The reason why I was slower overall was that I was too worried about all the stories I'd heard about people bonking and blowing up. I had too much at risk, too much on the line to risk a DNF. It was just too important to have the insurance of finishing, so in retrospect, I did not push as hard as I was capable of because I really didn't know what to expect.

Immediately following the race, April said that I didn't even look that tired; I was tired, but not exhausted. I was very excited and happy just to have finished this huge milestone on my way to the full Ironman. That night, I had a great dinner and raced my son Connor in some sprints on the golf course; he easily won by a large margin, or to use his phrase, he "dominated" me.

Later that night, both of my knees ached and I had to put an instant ice pack on the left knee (here we go again with the LEFT side.) But that was it.

The next day, I was not sore at all. The only thing that hurt were both quads. This was consistent with all of my 12 - 15 mile training runs, and in 1.5 days, they were no longer sore.

There was nothing that kept me from moving around and hanging out with my family. I was just great. So my plan came together perfectly: I got the experience of a very tough race, I finished in a low risk way, I achieved my goal time and I was able to still spend plenty of time with my family without limping around and constantly complaining about my injuries.

The only thing that was bad were the blisters. Partly because— and I have never read about this anywhere in any Tri training book— the volunteers who were mostly the retired folks living on the island (and very well meaning) threw water on us because it was so hot. They were just throwing buckets of water or dousing us with huge sponges full of ice water. And as a total rookie, of course I loved it and kept encouraging them to splash me even more; the cool water on my head and back just provided great relief in that heat.

That is...until my socks became completely soaked through, my shoes filled with water and my insoles became drenched. Every step was "squish, squish, squish." When I could no longer take the squishy, water-logged shoes, I took them off and tried to wring out my socks, but to no avail. I just couldn't get all the water out of my shoes, insoles and socks. Plus, all the tape and blister pads I'd carefully applied in T2 just came right off with all the water.

So this was a total rookie mistake, and I had to run about 8 miles in totally soaking wet shoes when I already had two huge, open-sore blisters. As you can imagine, this only made things much, much worse.

As for the overall run, I was disappointed that I could not get my average speed to my target, which was a one minute band of between 8:30 and 9:30 for each of the last 10 miles. My idea was to run the first three miles very slow, and not pay attention to the speed, then the last 10 would be between 8:30 - 9:30 each. But I just could not maintain that pace.

I just lost the desire and killer instinct to push hard enough to achieve those numbers. I knew I was falling behind and for some reason, I just lacked the courage to push through the pain of the blisters in order to hit those numbers.

But in the end, I was delighted with the overall results. The interesting thing was that David's workouts for me were much harder than any single portion of this race. I worked much harder in his assigned workouts than I ever did during the event, and that was backed up by both my power and HR data. That was what I wanted to do, and I was glad that it worked out that way. I did not want to push harder in this race than in my daily workouts. My numbers clearly revealed that I had been cruising, just running a very conservative, low risk race to ensure a finish. Now that I knew I could finish a 70.3, I could be much more confident in future events.

A couple of other things: I wanted to find a tri suit I could wear from start to finish and not have to change in T1 (the swim to bike transition)—that would save time.

I also needed a watch that gave me both HR and pace per mile data on the run, and which I could also wear in and through the swim and not have to change in T1.

I did beat plenty of people with my road bike, and the gearing really allowed me to get up some hills I might not have tackled so readily on the TT bike, but in the long run, I might have saved some time if I were on the TT bike, especially because I would not have been in such an upright position as I battled the strong Hawaiian trade winds.

I did note that the bike was a very weak event for me. While I was never passed on a downhill, I was always passed on the uphill sections and level ground. I was so weak on the uphills that I knew we'd need to incorporate more hill training to improve my climbing strength and raw power for future events.

Another thing I took away was that I didn't look like all those other athletes. These guys are lean, but at the same time, had very well defined muscles. I noticed that my chest/pecs were heavier and beefier than most, and that my arms seemed skinny compared to everyone else. I had a thicker mid-section too. I felt like I should commit more time and focus to weight training and daily core exercises. I also needed to recommit to a more disciplined diet in order to reduce excess fat. Most of these athletes had very little fat and it was clear that I still had a lot of work to do.

VINEMAN IRONMAN 70.3 IN SONOMA, CA. IN JULY 2008

My second Ironman 70.3 Triathlon took place in California's wine country. I beat my Hawaii Ironman 70.3 time by 45 minutes and I was extremely happy with that result—positively elated.

When I finished in Kona, I felt great, not that tired at all. That was because I played it safe. I was holding back, not knowing what to expect on my first 70.3. Now that I knew what to expect and had completed the event once, I was ready to push things a bit harder this time.

I arrived two days prior to the event to settle in and drive every mile of the bike course. That was a good idea, as it was a very technical bike course and I felt better knowing what to expect on the narrow, winding and rolling roads coursing through these beautiful Napa/Sonoma vineyards. I got lost twice while trying to follow the course in my car, so it was actually a great idea to preview the bike course in advance.

On race day morning I rose at 3:45 am with three separate alarms (2 watches and my cell phone alarm). This was a wetsuit-legal race as the water was less than 78 degrees. An up-and-back route in the shallow Russian river was much easier than the open-water melee of the Hawaii Ironman start, and I had plenty of clean water (no one was swimming in front of me or crawling on top of me). Swimming up current was no big deal at all compared to my Endless Pool workouts at home, and the return trip with the flow of the water seemed effortless.

One remarkable incident was that a huge catfish swam right into me during the race. The fish was so big, and it hit me with such speed and force that it nearly knocked the wind out of me. At the time I had absolutely no idea what had happened and was pretty startled to say the least. The Russian River is so dark green that I could not see the fish that hit me and was completely surprised. The unexpected hit, combined with the powerful thud when it collided with my chest, really shook me up.

Despite the run-in with the giant fish, I finished the swim about 5 minutes faster than the Hawaii event. The transition from the swim to the bike took four minutes and the bike leg went well. I pushed the bike harder than I had planned, and I broke somewhat from my race plan. I let my ego push me a bit as I tried to average 19.5 mph. I finished the bike about 20 minutes faster than Hawaii.

One interesting note was that my toes were nearly frozen on the bike. It was cold and I was not wearing socks. So when I transitioned in T2 and started running, the exact feeling was that of running with my feet frozen inside of two blocks of ice. I literally had no feeling at all—someone could have hammered spikes into my feet and I would probably not have felt any pain. It felt as if my feet were so brittle that they were going to literally shatter.

The hard effort on the bike really took its toll on the run; I paid the price to be sure, but that was fine. On the 13.1 mile run, I seemed to average just under a 10 minute mile, but was surprised by how many hills there were. I walked many of them. I also made it a point to walk the aid stations. Since Gatorade really makes me cough, I stuck mostly to water. I picked up the pace toward the end of the run and passed dozens and dozens of people in the last mile. That told me I probably did not push hard enough during the middle of the run. I also learned that it was sort of poor form for an age-grouper like me to sprint the last bit of the race trying to pass everyone. Apparently, that rookie move was sort of poor sportsmanship, but I really didn't know any better.

I was very, very happy with my race results. No shoulder pain, no trigger point pain in the aero position and no hip pain. I just ran out of energy on the run and my legs were pretty much shot from the harder than normal bike. I set new power records on that ride, which proved to me that I was likely pushing too hard. But with all of that, I still recorded a very good time, shaving about 45 minutes from my first 70.3 Ironman, which was only about 50 days prior to this race.

My confidence skyrocketed based on these results.

THE BULLDOG 50K ULTRA MARATHON RUN IN MALIBU, CA. IN AUGUST 2008

In August 2008, I completed the 50K (31 mile) Bulldog ultra marathon run in the mountains above Malibu, CA. in 7:29.53. In no way did this seem or feel like 7.5 hours on the trail. The day went by so quickly that it only seemed like a 3-hour run.

This was the most extreme test of willpower that I have ever experienced. The Bulldog ultra marathon course winds through the mountains between Malibu and Agoura, with a combination of hiking trails, dirt paths and fire roads. There were also two stream crossings, but we were able to hop on rocks and avoid getting our shoes wet.

The two-loop course had extreme elevation gains (about 9,000 feet in total) and we were well above the clouds when we reached the summit of Bulldog Mountain. It was pretty amazing to have such a huge elevation gain so quickly, running through and then above the clouds.

The hardest part of this event was not the distance at all—in fact, I could have gone much further if it were on level ground. This was not a test of endurance, but rather a test of willpower and smart hydration, electrolyte intake and fueling. As the temperature was in the mid 90s, the heat had a major impact.

As an Eagle Scout, I am always prepared, but in this case, perhaps too prepared. I was quickly spotted as a newbie due to the size of my hydration pack, which was bulging with my eleven essentials, a full medical kit, full nutrition kit, electrolyte capsules, extra hat, poison oak remedy, sunscreen, toiletries, and so on. I was fully prepared for everything. Everything except the steep downhills.

The hardest part of the day were the impossibly-steep descents. One might think that running down the face of mountains would be a lot easier, some might even say effortless, since it was just like letting gravity do its work. But the painful reality was that when the road got too steep, every step was a painful, toe-jamming, knee-grinding torture test—at least it was for me. It was also high risk for slipping on loose dirt/gravel as well as the dreaded black toenail from the toes repeatedly slamming into the front of the shoes.

Despite my ample study and preparedness, I was not expecting so much pain from the downhills. While I couldn't compete with younger men and women in terms of speed, it seemed that these ultra marathon and ultra endurance events were a great equalizer because speed did not play as vital a role as did endurance, hydration and on-the-trail nutrition.

Despite the insanely steep elevation gains/losses, I finished in good time. I never ran out of wind from running because I stuck to my race plan as much as possible. I had no hydration problems, no nutrition issues, no injuries, no falls (remarkably) and my hip held up fine as well. The real issue was the extreme downhill grades which just totally pounded away at my knees like a sledgehammer and jammed all my toenails with each step.

I had no permanent injuries from this race, but having said that, after the race I could hardly move. The soreness was in my quads, not really much in my calves or hamstrings. I guessed that the soreness was due to the quads taking the full brunt of the downhill load—imagine riding your bike down a very steep hill and having to brake to keep control of the bike. That was exactly what I think my quads were doing to absorb the downhill shock and to keep me from quickly getting out of control with downhill speed. So my quads took the full brunt of constant braking and two days later, I could not walk up or down steps without grunting audibly.

The only other area where I was sore was in the shoulders in the area where the straps of my hydration pack were carrying the weight of all that water for 7.5 hours.

LESSONS LEARNED FROM THE BULLDOG ULTRA MARATHON

I would definitely do another ultra marathon, but probably not this one.

This was not really an ultra marathon in terms of a run, it was like an adventure race because the grades were so steep that it was extremely difficult to run up or down the steepest of these grades. I could go the distance to be sure, but the steep grades just were no fun at all and ruined the experience. It took an extreme physical toll on my knees, toes and especially my quads. I think I'd rather do a 50-mile run on more gradual grades, rather than this 31-mile run where the grades are so steep that I could not even attempt to run in many spots. The Bulldog 50K is a beautiful site and venue, but for me, it's just too hard on my knees.

Another lesson learned was that I had to get the weight of my hydration pack down. Perhaps I could carry more water on a waist belt system and only the bare essentials on my back. The constant jostling of about 10 - 12 pounds on my back for over 7.5 hours was very rough on my shoulders and they were very tender for about a week afterwards.

As long as I could stay injury-free, these ultra marathons and extreme endurance events were going to be my focus. I really did enjoy these crazy events that seem impossible to complete. The more extreme, the more interesting and exciting they were to me.

Also, I noticed that these extreme events did not attract as many people as the Ironman 70.3. In the Bulldog 50K there were only about 150 participants. People were friendly, supportive and helpful. These events were not about extreme competition, but rather, a brotherhood of mutual respect, pride and feeling of accomplishment just for finishing. In these extreme endurance events, anyone who just managed to finish was a winner; I'd found my niche.

So now my goals were fixed solidly on finding a 50-mile race to complete—but only sometime after the Arizona Full Ironman in November 2008.

CHAPTER ELEVEN

IRONMAN

RACE VENUE CLIMATE ACCLIMATION

Many months prior to the Arizona Ironman, I had the opportunity to take an early morning detour on a business trip to Phoenix and run on the exact Ironman course that I would be racing in Tempe. That was a great chance to experience the actual course and the local weather conditions.

The course followed the man-made Tempe Town Center Lake, then went inland. One thing I experienced during this run was that it was VERY dry weather. I went through 64 ounces of water in 1:25 and during the final 20 minutes I had no water at all. Also, it was much brighter than anywhere else I had been, so I decided that I would need very dark sunglasses. Most of the course was on concrete but there was an option of running about 15% of the time on sand, dirt, grass and crushed granite.

I did eat a lot on this run, having 2 or 3 GUs and some Cliff Shots, but I didn't have a breakfast before that because it was just so early in the morning and the hotel restaurant was not yet open. One great lesson from this scouting expedition was that even though it was not much hotter than home, it was significantly drier and that caused me to drink much more water than on any other workout. I learned that temperature alone was not the only factor; one also had to carefully consider the humidity and overall climate. Prior to developing race day hydration plans, I learned to take into account the local weather conditions of the race venue.

RACE HARD
OR ENTER JUST TO FINISH?

Leading up to the Ironman, I was haunted with a single question that led to constant internal debate, and which still has never been full resolved to my satisfaction:

Am I quitting, giving up, and actually a loser for entering a race just to finish?

Should I go full-tilt and compete at my highest level, taking every risk and competing at the redline level in order to really test my ability and see what I'm made of?

Aren't I just giving up by playing it safe and entering just to finish?

These questions plagued me constantly.

Those who are not intimately familiar with Ironman have no idea about what a good time would be, and frankly, don't care about the final time. All they want to know is, "Did you finish?" I have rarely been asked about my finish time for any of my events. To most people, finishing is enough.

David Warden, my coach, had great confidence in me. Based on all of his science, technology, spreadsheets and experience, he was very confident I could achieve a time that to me, seemed wholly unobtainable. But as Napoleon Hill is credited with saying, "Whatever the mind can conceive and believe, it can achieve."

I believe more strongly than most, in the remarkable power of a positive mental attitude. However, when participating in Ironman or ultra endurance events, I have my own take on this saying, which now reads:

> "*You can achieve whatever you can conceive and believe... with proper training, hydration, nutrition, rest, coaching, the discipline to stay within proper HR zones, and barring any unforeseen mechanical issues with the bike, heat-related health issues, hyponatremia issues, dehydration issues, repetitive-motion injuries, and frankly, just about any freak accident that could happen at literally any point in the race.*"

A positive mental image is vital, but the reality is that it can only take you so far...at some point, you need to do the work and you need to be prepared.

SEVERE PRE-RACE JITTERS AND CONSEQUENCES

In the weeks leading up to the full Arizona Ironman event, I was extremely anxious. I was worried about unanticipated problems that could hit me at any time during the race.

In the swim event, the water could be so cold that your muscles would cramp up, in some cases causing extreme pain. One could also get kicked in the head, get scratched in the opening turmoil, get their mask pulled off, step on a sharp rock or glass and lacerate their foot before they take even a single stroke.

On the bike, mechanical issues could quickly sideline your progress. Flat tires were to be expected and planned for. In the 2008 Ironman World Championships in Kona, the reigning champion Chris McCormack (Macca) was sidelined for the entire race after he broke a cable that could not be fixed in time to keep him competitive, so he dropped out of the race near Hawi.

Macca's derailleur cable was routed internally, that is, within the frame so as to minimize wind drag. When something like this breaks, one needs special tools, even under the best of conditions. Even the guys in the technical support van with all the tools said that it would take them at least 20 minutes to repair the problem. They called for another race van that had more tools, but by that point, his race was over. If the reigning Ironman world champion had to drop out, any one of us could break a chain or have any number of mechanical issues or crashes that would lead to a DNF.

Finally, in the run, one could trip on an elevated gap in a sidewalk. Trust me, after 112 miles on the bike, one can tend to lose a bit of concentration—and any small misjudgment, or turning a glance toward an excited spectator, and one could find themselves face-first on the asphalt or lava rocks.

Running tends to be the event that brings out the muscle cramps and GI problems for the day. At this point in the race, most of us mid-packers were not competing; we were just hanging on to finish. And you really feel terrible when you see someone just coming apart at the seams with debilitating leg cramps, vomiting, diarrhea and horrendous gas and stomach cramps. This is a horrible way to end your day, especially if it hits you early in the run and you still have 20+ miles to run, jog, walk or crawl.

All these potential problems swirled through my mind in the week prior to the event. My mind raced with every conceivable potential problem I might experience; it was tough to rest or sit still.

And all this planning (actually, worrying) caused a horrible GI problem that forced me to stick close to home. This became a terrible cycle, because the more I was at home, the more time I had to sit and think and plan. This only created more stress and worry, leading to more GI problems.

The worry and jitters were caused by an intense desire to finish. To have come this far and have gone through so much—all the money, all the training, all the doctor's visits, all the weekends away from family on 6 – 8 hour workouts. And to come home with a DNF...I just could not bear the shame and embarrassment; a DNF would be a devastating blow after so much hard work and sacrifice.

I knew that logically, a certain number of participants would always DNF and it usually had very little to do with their preparedness, fitness or planning. Their DNF would be due to situations largely beyond their control. So no matter how much I planned, there was still a chance that I could be one of the DNFs.

IRONMAN ARIZONA
RACE PREPARATION

The week before Ironman Arizona, my hip was killing me. I was going back to the doctor for one last Cortisone injection right into the hip socket (bursa sac) just prior to the race. I was also getting my 6th round of Cortisone into my upper trapezoid area to numb the last of the trigger points. The trigger point pain was 90% better, which made my cycling far less painful and much safer because I was finally capable of turning my head to look over my shoulder for oncoming traffic.

David advised that perhaps it was the right time for me to take the super powerful anti-inflammatory for my hip that was prescribed by Dr. Jeffery Ho. This particular drug is called Ketorolac and is often prescribed post-surgery.

David's main concern was that Ketorolac might increase the risk of hyponatremia during the race. But with my hip still hurting, he thought I should start taking it for 3 days prior to the event so that the inflammation could go down before the race, still leaving enough time to allow the drug to leave my system by race day. Thus we'd hopefully have the inflammation down, but the NSAID would not be active in my system during the race.

My hip pain was not the only problem I had before the race.

The extreme level of mental stress and anxiety I was feeling about the race was due largely to the fear of letting David down after he took such a risk on an over the hill, hugely overweight executive. I knew that he had confidence in me, and I did not want to let him down. I wanted to be sure that I would definitely finish this event. It was unacceptable to even consider the possibility of a DNF (Did Not Finish).

I ran over the numbers literally hundreds of times...even in the shower and in my sleep. I could see a way in which it might even be possible to break 14 hours for the full IM event. But the more I thought about times and the more I ran through the numbers, the more anxiety it caused me. The risk was that if I pushed really hard to try and meet certain times, I would be increasing the chance of bonking and a DNF. So it was really a conundrum that caused a lot of stress.

I've seen even the pros get escorted off the course. Ironman world champions Chris McCormack and Normann Stadler both had races where they blew up and quit; Luke McKenzie, another pro triathlete, literally blacked out and recorded a DNF after finishing the bike leg. I was certainly not a podium contender, but it was possible that I might blow up if I pushed too hard. These pros had been pushing hard to win, but I would be pushing hard just to try and meet a particular time. But I did not want this to cause me to potentially blow up, bonk, crater, detonate, and worst of all, DNF.

If I looked at this event as a "catered long workout," as Bob Babbitt says, I had all the confidence in the world that I would definitely finish. It was only when I started thinking about these goal times that I really started to get anxious.

I could remember just a few months prior, I had very serious doubts about my ability to complete a 70.3; now that distance just seemed like an extended workout and finishing a 70.3 no longer held much mystique or generated any excitement for me.

As for the full IM, I was at a point now where I was 100% certain that I could go the distance on my own. I wanted to cross that finish line standing tall and proud. And I needed to get over the internal pressure that I was putting on myself.

When I told David about this high level of anxiety and self-imposed stress, he assured me unequivocally that he had absolutely no expectation of me other than to finish. He would give me very specific power zones that would be well within my means and not be aggressive at all, and they would be "finish strong" zones without risk of flaming out. Perfect.

Leading up to the Ironman Arizona in mid-November 2008, I turned off the heater in my Endless Pool in order to make the water very cold and simulate the environment I'd face in Tempe Town Center Lake. I also used my wetsuit in my Endless Pool to make certain there would be no chafing issues.

It was so much easier and way faster to swim in my Endless Pool with a wetsuit. I swam 1.9 miles in 50 minutes like it was just a warm up. It was fun and almost relaxing. I had a fantastic wetsuit by Xterra, but I learned that I needed to aggressively rub a lot of body glide into the nylon fabric at the back of the neck to avoid chafing in the race. I was not that worried about the swim portion of the race. It would not be easy, but I was confident I would hold my own.

My new bike was awesome, too. It was a great machine and I loved it: a Specialized S-Works SL2 with the new SRAM Red grouppo. Even though I wouldn't have the Cervelo P3C TT bike, which is extremely aero, I was much more confident in the bike leg because I would be far more comfortable on my new road bike.

David also gave me some solid advice on how to pace myself and he established a reasonable race strategy that would keep me well within my established power and HR zones. His strategy was to stick within the ranges I had been keeping throughout all my long training days—that way, I could be confident that if I stayed in these ranges, it would be just like any other workout that I'd done many times before on the weekends.

Subject: Power and Pace for Arizona IM
From: David Warden
To: John D. Callos

John,

I have scrutinized your workouts over the last few months and have the following recommendation. This is a conservative approach to your cycling and running pacing strategy for Sunday's Arizona Ironman. It is based on a goal of finishing, not racing.

Bike:

The course is conveniently split into 3 loops. This makes it easy to split the pacing.

- First loop of 37 miles: Maintain 135-150 watts. Do not exceed 190 watts at any time, even avoid 190+ when passing. You will feel like you are not going fast enough. Save it for the last third.
- Second loop: Maintain 145-160 watts. Do not exceed 190 watts at any time, even avoid 190+ when passing.
- Third loop: Maintain 150-170 watts. Do not exceed 190 watts at any time, even avoid 190+ when passing. This last loop has a wide window to allow you to race a little stronger if you feel good.

This strategy will have you averaging anywhere from 143-160 watts for the entire ride. You have consistently put out an average of 160 watts on your long rides with a one hour successful brick run immediately following those long rides. This is less than what you have done in training, and the lower level of an average of 143 is extremely conservative based on your past performance. You averaged 183 at Vineman (and you are a much better cyclist now than you were then), therefore a 143-160 average for a full IM is a safe bet.

To give you a contrast of what I would recommend for a more aggressive approach, I would have you averaging 165-175 watts for the entire ride. I am having you go 15% slower than what I would normally recommend based on your abilities. This should help minimize the potential of a hip flare up during the race.

Run:

First 20 minutes: 9:30 per mile pace. High cadence of 85+. The first 20 minutes will lock you into your cadence for the rest of the run. You will tempted to go harder that 9:30 because you'll feel so good from the lower than normal power on the bike. Don't.

20 minutes to 6 miles: 9-10 minute pace. I know that is a wide window, so split the difference at 9:30 if you feel good, but allow yourself some room up or down.

Miles 6-12: 9:00-9:30. Now you can pick it up. Race is over at this point. If you made it this far, it's a done deal even if you have to walk it. Still, don't take any risks and stick with this pacing.

Mile 12-18: 8:30-9:30. Pick it up slightly again.

Mile 18+ Anything goes, but no faster than 8:00 miles until the last 3 miles, then sprint if you feel like it. Very unlikely that you will feel like going that fast, but you do have permission.

Nutrition, nutrition, nutrition. You've got to keep eating on the run, ~200 calories per hour.
-David

MY IRONMAN RACE STRATEGY

My strategy was simply to finish at all costs, under all circumstances and regardless of the pain or setbacks. There would be no turning back in Tempe. There would be no sitting down to rest or regroup. I would continue under all hardships until I crossed that line or was ejected from the race due to a life-threatening medical incident or failing to meet a cutoff time.

What this strategy meant was that I would be participating at the lowest possible level of risk. I would under-perform by design, keeping my watts, HR and pace below the levels that I normally achieved in training. Not because I was a quitter and didn't want to test myself, but because I would never quit under any circumstances. By participating at a level where I would minimize the risk of a bonk, a blow-up or other stress related issue, I was substantially reducing the chances of a problem that could lead to a DNF.

So I had the plan in mind and I knew I had to maintain the discipline to stick to it. That meant: not worrying when people passed me, and at all times, fighting the normal temptation to speed up and catch that guy right in front of me.

But even with the plan firmly in place and my coach totally on board to support me and to yell out at me to "slow down and stick to our plan" if he found that my splits were too fast, I was still nervous.

Only after I created an extremely detailed packing list of everything I would need, and then packed everything, quadruple checked it to make sure all the gear was labeled and put into separate Ziploc pouches and categories based on each event, was I finally able to rest. (See Appendix for my packing lists)

Nutrition and Hydration Plan

It has been said that "nutrition/hydration" are the fourth event of Ironman triathlon. If you don't get those right, your first three events (swim, bike, run) won't matter at all.

For a mid-packer like me, the Ironman triathlon will take anywhere from 12 - 17 hours. During that amount of time, one burns far more calories than they can possibly replace with food or liquids. One also sweats and loses not only vital fluids, but also vital nutrients and electrolytes. Without a systematic way to replace fluids and calories in the right quantities, the right timing, and the right types, one will be setting themselves up for a potential disaster, including life-threatening reactions.

I had been practicing and honing my nutrition and hydration techniques for the better part of a year. While I moaned and griped about the amount of time it took to prepare everything for my long rides and runs, I knew it was vital that I paid close attention to these matters.

I had been very fortunate and generally avoided any kind of GI distress in workouts and races. This was not due to great genetics or a solid gut, but rather, to using precise measurements and quantities of the world's best proven endurance-formula products. Without getting into all the science, it's important understand that you can't just go out on the road for 12 – 17 hours and plan on drinking water and eating a few snacks; that is literally a recipe for disaster.

My clear preference is the line of products from SportQuest in San Diego, CA. Working with a food scientist at SportQuest, they developed a formal training and racing nutrition/hydration protocol for me that was based on my age, weight, BMI (Body Mass Index) and other factors that influenced my hourly caloric intake/absorption as well as electrolyte replacement. I followed their protocol exactly, and had zero problems of any kind during the race. It was absolutely perfect.

About 4 -5 days prior to the race, I began a carbo-loading protocol that included their Carbo-Pro powder product. In the morning and evening I took 2 scoops of Carbo-Pro in a glass of water. It is tasteless and not syrupy-sweet at all; just perfect. This quantity was the theoretical carbohydrate equivalent of two pounds of potatoes per serving.

RACE DAY NUTRITION STRATEGY

The morning of the race, I got up at 2:00 am and had two PowerBars and washed them down with a Carbo-Pro drink and went right back to bed. Then I got up at 4:00 am and had another two scoops of Carbo-Pro along with the capsules detailed below.

During every hour of the bike and the run, I drank a product called CarboPro 1200 which contains 1,200 calories of carbohydrate in a 16-ounce bottle. I took 300 calories each hour by marking the correct amount of product on the outside of my bike water bottle for each hour. That way, I could just sip the product until I reached the hour-marker on the side of the bottle. This was a great idea—I highly recommend it and I even called the company and asked them to make their own bottles with these markings.

While on the bike course, I still drank plenty of ice water, about 30 ounces per hour. The water was supplied at aid stations about every 10 miles. So I started with one 22 ounce bottle on my bike and one water bottle filled with CarboPro 1200, which was enough for about 6 hours. I supplemented my nutritional needs with several bananas and half a bag of salted nuts. That was it for my seven hour bike segment.

But for every hour on the bike, I also had a supplement strategy as follows:

I had prepared three small plastic bottles of the nutritional supplements I would need. I applied a small piece of medical tape along the inside edge of each bottle to ensure a much tighter fit than normal, otherwise the bottle caps would pop off and all the supplements would fall out in my bike jersey and get mixed up. Since many of the supplements looked alike, there would be no way to tell them apart if they'd been mixed together, and that would have been a real problem.

As a side note, I learned these things by trying them during my long workouts. It's especially important to test everything well in advance of the race, and to never try anything new on race day.

Every hour, on the hour, I took at least the following:

- 2 capsules of V02 Max
- 3 capsules of Recover Amino Power (Glutamine, and Amino Acids)
- 3 capsules of Thermolyte (Essential salts and electrolytes)
- Every third hour, or whenever I felt the need, I would also take 1 or 2 Motivator capsules which are similar to a caffeine tablet, but actually more like a couple of Red Bulls in caplet form.

That was at least 8 capsules every hour on a seven hour ride (in total, well over 60 capsules on the bike) and another 45 capsules on the run. That was well over 100 capsules while on the bike, plus handfuls in the morning before the race and also in the transition areas.

I would gulp about a mouthful of CarboPro 1200 every 15 minutes or so and quickly follow that with ice water. When it came time to take the 8 – 10 capsules per hour, I would use the CarboPro 1200 to coat them in the syrup-like liquid to help get them down without the risk of any getting stuck to my very dry throat.

TECHNIQUE TO MINIMIZE SUPPLEMENT CONFUSION

Now to take all those capsules and not get mixed up about what I did or did not take, I developed a technique worth sharing:

I had three small plastic bottles in my bike jersey; these bottles are made by Fuel Belt and are designed for race-day supplements. I labeled each bottle with the contents and how many capsules I was to take each hour, on the hour. I put all three bottles in the back of my jersey pocket, and I would take out one bottle at a time, take the prescribed number of capsules, and then transfer that bottle to the opposite pocket (I have three pockets in the jersey). So one by one, I would transfer the bottles from the left to right.

This may sound a bit overdone, but trust me, when you are hot and tired, you may not be thinking as clearly, and so to avoid any potential confusion, I followed this technique, and this pocket transfer process worked perfectly.

I also took Pepcid AC and two Mucinex tablets during the race. The Mucinex was critical for me because it helped me avoid coughing and kept the windpipe and throat clear of mucous, which could really be a big problem for me, especially with thick, syrupy products.

I avoided Gatorade completely because it makes me cough. It is just too sweet for me and whenever I got the urge to take a bit of Gatorade, I would always regret it. The only liquids I accepted on the bike were pure, ice cold water and the CarboPro 1200 that I brought from home. That was it.

On the run, I kept to the same strategy. While offered all kinds of things to eat and drink, I rejected them all, knowing that I had the right strategy. I rejected all fruits, all GUs, all PowerBars, all cookies, literally everything.

However, toward the end of the run and when it got colder and pitch dark at night, I did accept some warm chicken broth by the cupful, which was absolutely fantastic. The only other thing I accepted that was not part of my pre-race planning or nutrition program were small Dixie cups full of stick pretzels. In hindsight, my cravings for salty pretzels and chicken broth clearly indicate that I needed to be taking even more Thermolyte capsules. In fact, I could not get enough salt into my system for about 3 – 5 days following the event.

In the end, I was absolutely delighted with my nutrition and hydration results. I would give myself an A+ for this plan, although the real credit goes to the scientists at SportQuest/Carbo-Pro. In my opinion, they are simply the best at what they do. Period. Yes I could have used more Thermolyte, but I never got sick and besides the swim, suffered no cramps and no GI problems whatsoever.

RACE DAY PREPARATION

I slept pretty well the night before despite getting up at 2:00 am for a meal (plan on about 3 – 4 hours for the meal to digest pre-race), and then got up at 4:00 am to head over to Tempe Town Center.

I was scared and nervous and anxious all at once. It was just like you might feel before you step onto a stage with hundreds of people in the audience, or perhaps how you might feel when you're driving home from a great New Years Eve party, and then see flashing red lights at a mandatory checkpoint. The fear, the adrenaline, and the anxiety...that was what it felt like.

Sure, I knew I had done everything I could have done to prepare, but I really did not feel like jumping into that freezing water on that very cold morning.

It was totally dark, but out of nowhere, my great friend Kelvin Shields showed up to surprise me. Having Kelvin there was fantastic because he knew the ropes of Ironman. Kelvin once served an internship with the Ironman organization during the late 90s and having him there was exactly like having your best man at a wedding. He took care of all the details so that I could focus on getting ready. He had arrived at the venue even before I did, and he had used that time to scout out the drop off points and more importantly, to learn the lay of the land for race number body marking and other early morning, pre-race essentials.

I cannot overstate how important it is to have someone like that to assist on race morning. I never would have understood the importance of this without Kelvin there, but let me assure you, if you ever want to attempt this endeavor, do yourself a huge favor and have someone assist you on your first Ironman in these early morning hours, especially if they have experience with the event. Your day will go much smoother.

THE CANNON GOES OFF AND THE 2.4 MILE SWIM BEGINS

It was very cold in the morning and everyone seemed to be shivering, even many of the bundled-up spectators. It was incomprehensible that in just about an hour or so, I would be in that freezing water fighting it out with over 2,200 other very nervous athletes for 2.4 miles.

Kelvin helped me with the wetsuit and made sure that we used a lot of Body Glide lubricant in the back of the neck where it could rub your skin raw due to turning your head to breathe on every other stroke. This is really an important thing to remember: you cannot use too much Body Glide at the back of the neck.

My plan was to be the last person to jump into the water. The reason for this was that as 2,200 other athletes all jumped in, it would force us toward the middle of the lake, and my plan was to be on the far inside lane. In order to do that, I thought I should enter last, and then I would swim the 200 yards or so up to the starting line.

Despite my detailed plan, I did not count on the fact that so many people would actually force me to the very back of the pack. What that meant was that once the cannon went off, I still had to swim nearly 200 yards just to get to the starting line. Whoops. That was not a good idea after all; I'll never make that mistake again.

The swim was a mess. It was extremely hard to make any kind of forward progress with so many people clawing and scratching and bumping. For about 5 minutes, many of us at the very back of the swim start were just treading water waiting for the pack to open up and give us enough room to stretch our entire bodies out lengthwise so that we could actually start swimming. I lost at least 5 – 10 minutes on my swim time due to this mistake of starting at the back of the pack. I am a relatively strong swimmer, but that morning on my first Ironman attempt, I lacked a bit of confidence in the water.

I can swim in a really straight line due to the fact that I had spent a year in my Endless Pool practicing swimming with my eyes closed to see if I could hold a line. Regrettably, most people couldn't swim a line, so what happened was that I would be going straight, and then out of no where I would get T-boned by someone swimming wildly off course. At one point, I got so tired of this that I started swimming with my head out of the water looking for open lanes to swim into. Once I found an opening, I'd quickly accelerate to claim the hole before it quickly closed up on me.

DROWNING SCARE DUE TO CRAMPING

That was when disaster struck. At about the 1.75 mile point, I got T-boned, lifted my head to find an opening and immediately started a very quick and aggressive stroke at a very fast pace. That was when my right leg cramped up severely from the combination of very cold water and rapid acceleration. By the way, the same thing happens to me when I accelerate rapidly to try and make it through a green light on my bike. It's that sudden burst of power and speed that seems to trigger this cramping, and with the extremely cold water that day on the swim, both the cold and the sudden burst of speed conspired to give me the worst calf cramp of my entire life.

The cramp was extremely painful and could not be controlled. I had no option but to stop and immediately grab that calf muscle. It was seizing up rapidly and caused another cramp in the instep or arch of my foot. I could not move; I was totally immobilized and people were swimming all over me. If I grabbed the cramping muscle, I would sink and at the same time I lost the ability to push swimmers off of me; for a fleeting moment of panic, I honestly thought they were going to drown me. I tried to swim with the left leg only to get out of the extreme traffic, and then that leg cramped at the same time. I started to sink again, but the buoyancy of my full wetsuit prevented me from going completely under.

Let me sketch the scene: I needed both hands to grab the cramping muscles that were seizing and causing unbearable pain, but as I grabbed the muscles, I would lose the ability to push the other swimmers off of me, so I would get dunked and sink because I could not kick with my cramped-up legs. But if I took my hands off the muscles to try and paddle and pull myself up to the surface, the muscles would immediately seize up again and I'd start sinking. And even the slightest movement of the legs would immediately re-trigger the cramping. Either way, I was just bobbing around in extreme pain, getting hit and dunked under and basically totally unprepared for this worst-case scenario. You really cannot plan for this kind of thing.

I finally got to the point where I just dragged my legs behind me, motionless. Finally, after about 3 to 4 minutes, I was able to get the pain to subside. As a side note, later that night after completing the race, I slept very poorly with bad dreams that I was drowning in the swim; it was really that close with all that cramping.

The pain was so bad and the cramping so intense that three days post-race, I was still walking with a limp due to the cramp in the calf muscle. It was actually a pulled muscle that had microscopic rips and tears just from that aggressive and uncontrollable cramping.

The next problem with the swim was that the water was so incredibly cold that even the two swim caps that I was wearing were not enough. I had brain freeze for about 20 minutes and the pain was like a splitting migraine headache.

I thought my race was over at this point. I literally thought I should just swim to the side and get out; my day was over, my dreams crushed. I lifted my head to see how much further I had to swim and was totally demoralized when I saw how far away I was from the final bridge. But I just kept thinking about that emergency Imitrex pill I had stashed away in one of my special needs bags or my bike jersey. If I could just hang on long enough to find that emergency Imitrex, I might be OK. So I slowed down, tried to keep my head out of the water and kept heading toward the swim finish.

When I got to the end of the swim I had to climb up about 15 steps of a ladder/walkway out of the concrete channel. My legs immediately seized up from the cramping, but after about ten seconds of light stretching, I could keep going.

The great news was that once I got into the changing tent, the heat from dozens and dozens of athletes and volunteers made my headache go away literally within minutes. I was fine.

My transition time in the changing tent was much longer than my worst case scenario, but at the time, I could not have cared less. I was just out of the water and I was thankful to be alive.

So 15 minutes in transition and I was out on the bike.

BIKING THROUGH THE DESERT

David and I had a plan to go very easy on the bike segment in order to avoid anything that might trigger a hip reaction. The hip problem had been a recurring issue for the past 15 months and was our biggest concern in planning for the race. We did not want to do anything that might trigger this, so we dialed back my average watts to be far lower than anything I had ever done in training. Basically, I could do that ride as an easy afternoon joy ride, and that is exactly how I treated it.

I didn't care if people passed me and I didn't ever try to catch anyone. I just stuck to my plan. I was a little below my planned wattage numbers and perhaps could have gone faster, but I just didn't want to risk it. My average HR for the bike was only about 122, which was extremely low for a race.

Then, at about 70 miles into the bike, I had another tough issue. I started to feel some tension and some aching on the left knee at the Iliotibial band (IT band).

The IT band is a ribbon-like band that extends from the outside of the thigh over the hip and knee, and is connected again just below the knee. The band helps to stabilize the outside of the knee during exercise and it moves from behind the femur to the front as you bend your knee in walking, running, climbing stairs, and cycling. This long fibrous band gets tighter with age and athletic activity. To keep it supple and reduce the risk of injury, one must be proactive with certain stretching and strength exercises. Usually, as in my case, there is not much warning before the IT pain hits. The continual rubbing of the band over the outside of the knee can cause the area to become inflamed and results in shooting, often debilitating pain.

My case was caused by a combination of taking shortcuts with stretching over the past 15 months (i.e. very little to none) and a problem with my bike seat adjustment. Less than a month prior to the Ironman Arizona, I was hit by a car while cycling and my bike was destroyed. By the time we got the new bike built, there was no time to do a proper fitting and then, to test that fitting on a long ride. The bike was fit, I put it on my rooftop bike rack and I was off across the desert to Tempe.

As it turns out, the seat was too high and because my left leg is shorter, every pedal stroke was pulling on the IT band far more than ever. By mile 70, I knew we had a serious problem and the damage had already been done; I immediately stopped to lower the seat, but by that point, it was too late. This was an injury that I was familiar with. At the first sign of this IT band trouble while on the bike, I literally said to myself, *"John, this is going to get really ugly!"*

The remainder of my bike would be painful and my run would be a disaster.

The only way to relieve IT pain is to immediately stop what you are doing. There is no other way. And the more you try to do once the pain starts, the worse it will get, because every rotation of the pedals and every step or stride in running only makes it worse. At that point, I knew for certain that the pain and inflammation would only get worse throughout the day and night.

If I had completed an Ironman prior to this event, then this would have been the signal to immediately stop and drop out of the race after the next loop through town. But I would not consider that option today—I might not finish before the deadline, but I wasn't ever going to quit.

So I did the only thing I could do with a goal of finishing: I dialed back my power/watts to the minimal level that would still help me maintain about a 15 mph average, and unclipped my left leg for long periods, just to let it hang. Of course this caused more strain on the right side because I was pedaling with only one leg, but at least it helped save the left. This decision would end up costing me on the bike, giving me about a 7-hour bike split, but it would still leave plenty of time (perhaps 8 hours) to jog, walk or crawl through my next event, the 26 mile marathon.

I struggled through the bike and finished in just over 7 hours; I was relieved with that time considering how much I had to ride with just one leg. The run was next and was usually a strong event for me. I enjoyed running—it was simple, pure and often just relaxing.

But today would be different.

THE MARATHON

I changed into my running clothes and attached my Nathan hydration belt that was preloaded with 4 hours worth of CarboPro 1200. Then I was off and running, high-fiving my coach as I passed him right out of the tent.

The race plan was to do 9:30 miles for the first six miles and no faster, no matter what. Regrettably, I was having a really tough time just with the 9:30 miles. And with every single stride the IT band was rubbing, rubbing, rubbing. It was getting worse with each stride.

Finally the pain became unbearable and the band had swollen to the point where it was causing my knee to lock-up and click. The swollen band was interfering with the free movement of the knee joint. I had to improvise. I needed ice to try to reduce the swelling, but there was no way to jog or walk while bent over at the mid-section trying to hold a handful of ice cubes on my knee.

Just the day before, I had purchased some compression socks at the vendor expo. These socks rise above the calf muscles and are very tight. The theory behind compression socks is that they cause constriction, which forces blood into the area to provide more oxygen to aid the muscle and to carry away waste products such as lactic acid and ammonia.

But since I wanted to wear my own socks for the run, I purchased a modified compression garment that just covered from the ankle to the bottom of the knee. These compression garments had been proven for decades in hospitals for post-op recovery and were now leading-edge technology for endurance sports.

I suddenly got the idea to pull my 2XU compression sock up over my knee. That would give some support to that area. It wasn't the intended use for the product, but improvisation was what I needed at this point; I literally had no other option. The idea worked a little, but I was getting the feeling that it was just pressing the IT band even harder onto the outside of the knee, perhaps even making the situation worse.

So I decided to take off the other compression sock and put them both onto the same knee, one right on top of the other. Then when I arrived at the aid stations every mile or so, I had them load ice right in-between the two compression garments. They were so tight that they easily held the ice in place, and since the ice was sandwiched in between the garments, I could just leave it there without worrying about frostbite or other damage from direct contact between the ice and my skin.

The ice inside the compression garments worked incredibly well and literally saved my race. There was no possible way that I could continue with my strong run as we had so carefully planned, but at least I could reduce the IT band pain and hopefully get close to finishing before the deadline. My only goal at that point was to make it to the next aid station in order to get more ice. I was not thinking about how many more miles I needed to run, just the 'next' mile. Aid stations were every mile so that meant in about 11 minutes or so, I could walk a bit and jam more ice into the compression socks. That was all that was going through my mind.

Other than the IT band issue, I really had no other problems on the run. Certainly under different conditions I would have run significantly faster, but I was happy just to be moving at that point.

THE GOING GETS TOUGH

The sun set quickly and soon it was pitch black. Even though I was shuffling along, I was still passing hundreds of people during the run portion of this event; many of them were walking at that point.

When I was passing the walkers I felt sorry for some who were really very ill and suffering from severe GI problems. Some of these people were world class athletes, and most were in way better physical condition than me, but they were just having a horrible day.

One brave warrior in particular was thin as a rail and an obvious champion. He'd speed by me, then pull over to the side and violently throw up, then speed by me again, only to jump out of a Porta Toilet, and this went on for 12 miles. He was in such agony, but he finished, and I was proud that he finished in front of me because he earned every bit of that. He was a real champion, a winner, a hero. In better times, I'm sure he'd likely finish in the top of his age group.

But there were others who I passed that were just walking and enjoying themselves, just chatting away. They knew that they'd finish sometime that day if they just kept walking. I did not have as much respect for that group as I did for the guys who were really suffering but somehow finding the drive, the pure grit, to continue.

For some reason, I was inspired to make up my own mantra on the run as I was limping and gritting my teeth from the IT band pain. I said to myself over and over again:

> *"You will never learn what you are capable of doing by just walking. Don't phone it in. You saved yourself for this. David Goggins doesn't quit. You planned for contingencies, now work your plan."*

I could have phoned it in by walking or limping, but I would not have learned as much about my drive and my ability to endure pain and my resourcefulness to improvise. If I had walked, I never would have been forced to come up with the idea to use compression garments to hold ice over the IT band.

THE FINAL LOOP

The last 10 – 13 miles I often had tears streaming down my face from the pain of the IT band, but I was not going to walk the entire way.

I certainly did walk though, no question about it. I walked through the aid stations for water, pretzels and ice, lots of ice for my knee. The ice was enough to get the swelling down so that the knee would not lock up and that was all that I needed to finish.

From about mile 10 to mile 22, things were really bleak. I couldn't believe that I had been out on the run course for a full 5 hours. I really don't understand how I did that. There was no ego out there, no heroics. I really don't know what happened or how I did it. I did not black out or anything like that, and I remember the aid stations and certain aspects of the course, but I still have no idea how I was able to go the distance; it was a blur. It felt like someone picked me up at mile 10 and then just dropped me off at mile 22.

Once I saw the mile 22 marker, I knew I would finish. My home course was a five mile loop around Cal State Long Beach. I could do that loop in my sleep, after a large dinner, after a couple of beers, basically anytime and under any condition. So when I saw that I only had five miles to go, I was very happy and I think that raw emotion got me through the rest of that race.

THE LAST 200 YARDS TO REACH MY GOAL

When I came down the finish chute, I was surprised that my son Connor jumped out and ran beside me. I kept telling him, *"Connor, you cannot run beside me and pace me, I will get DQd."* I literally pushed him away and told him to get out of the chute, fearing that I would get into trouble and they wouldn't give me credit for finishing the race.

But then I remembered that an athlete could have one family member under the age of 18 run alongside them at the finish. And what I didn't know at that time was that my great friend Kelvin Shields had made arrangements for Connor to run alongside me and that Connor had the approval and the markings to allow him to do so.

But despite my urgings to get out of the chute, Connor stayed right there with me the entire 200 yards or so and I am SO HAPPY that he did. I would have always regretted it if he had pulled out like I had urged him to do.

I suppose that I did not have my full wits about me at that point in the evening when I kept telling him not to pace me. With only 200 yards to go, I don't think anyone would have said this was an unfair advantage, but at that time, nearly 14 hours into my race and nearly 18 hours into my day, apparently my thinking was not crystal clear. So I am delighted that he stayed there right with me and I cherish the video of Connor crossing the finish line alongside me.

JOHN CALLOS...
YOOOOOOU... ARE AN IRONMAN!

As I crossed the finish line, I heard the announcer say what I had been planning and silently saying to myself on the toughest workout days over the last 15 months:

"John Callos...YOU ARE AN IRONMAN."

WOW, that was fantastic. Just absolutely incredible.

I collapsed into the arms of two volunteers who draped a Space Blanket over my shoulders, gave me a finisher's medal and a T-shirt.

My wife, coach, son and Kelvin were instantly on the scene. I was a bit lightheaded and sort of just collapsed to the ground—not from musculature soreness or tiredness, but from all the emotion leaving my body. It was an amazing release and the realization that I had accomplished the toughest goal that I had ever set out to achieve in my entire life.

I just could not process or fathom that I had actually completed this endeavor. This was the same event that I had watched countless times on DVD and thinking that these men and women were super beings. It just seemed absolutely impossible, yet I had just completed the event.

It just didn't register that I had completed the same race I had watched so often on those Ironman DVDs, and frankly, it may always be hard to process.

FINAL THOUGHTS ON THE RACE AND THE YEAR OF TRAINING

So I finally achieved my goal of completing a FULL IRONMAN, crossing the finish line with the support of my wife, my business partner Kevin Kelsey, my son Connor, my great friend Kelvin Shields and of course, my coach David Warden.

My goal had been to treat this event like a long workout, nothing more. I had way too much time and emotion invested in this endeavor to engage in a high-risk strategy of racing for the best possible time; essentially, the plan was to be disciplined and frankly just cruise the 140 miles.

It was a very long day to cover 140 miles, and if one rejected their race plan, lost focus and discipline, it could spell disaster. I was now experienced enough from two prior 70.3 Ironman events to know that I had to stick to my race plan—and I was glad that I did, because disaster struck on the swim, the bike and the run.

Despite the problems, I still had a terrific event (again, finishing was my goal, not racing). I finished within 2 minutes of my projected time, breaking 14 hours with a total race time of 13 hours, 58 minutes.

In the swim, I finished in the bottom 40% of my age group; in the bike I was way back, finishing in the bottom 10% of my age group, and in the run, I finished in the bottom 40%. Overall, I finished in the bottom 25%; essentially 75% of all participants finished in front of me. I crossed the line in front of 600 other entrants, but behind 1,585 Ironmen.

In 2008, I completed three Ironman events. Two of these events were the half Ironman, which is known as the Ironman 70.3.

Training for the full Ironman was exponentially more work than just training for the 70.3. It was many times more complicated and difficult and time-consuming. Those who have trained for and completed the full Ironman would know the difference.

You cannot just read about it in a book to understand it; you really need to live it. You need to understand the discipline, the sacrifice, the struggle and the enormous number of training hours this endeavor requires.

Completing the 70.3 does not make one an Ironman. And as a finisher of two half-Ironman events as well as a full Ironman, I now understand the difference.

I could understand why my completion of the Hono/Kona 70.3 in May 2008 and the Vineman/Sonoma 70.3 in July 2008 were great achievements, but certainly not Full Ironman efforts. To understand the difference, one needed to complete the full 140.6 event.

All these months of training, and it all came to an end in just 13 hours and 58 minutes. That may sound like a long day, but it really only felt like a 3-hour workout. At mile #2 of the run, I was thinking, *"Over 24 more miles to go? No way!"* But before I really knew it, I had somehow progressed to mile 22 and only had less than 5 miles to go.

At that point, I knew that I would be an Ironman that night.

Chapter Twelve

LESSONS

Discipline, Patience and Focus

I have learned incredible lessons about training, nutrition, weight control, healthy living and triathlon. But I have also learned important lessons about business, life, relationships, time management and many things about myself and my true abilities. This wasn't just an event; it was a process. It was a huge commitment and ongoing test of willpower and discipline, and at the end of this journey I took away several life lessons.

So many times, especially toward the end, I felt that this Ironman dream was a colossal waste of time. I told many people about the toll this training took not just on me, but on my family, friends, business and even hobbies. In fact, training for the Ironman took over nearly every aspect of my life, and that is a mistake I hope not to repeat in the pursuit of other great endurance challenges.

It took 10 – 15 hours a week for training and I usually spent another 8 – 20 hours each week for prep work, maintenance, workout downloads and updates of data, as well as analyzing my workout data, preparing nutrition for the workouts, special nutritional supplements, stretching, massage, doctor's visits, journal entries, online research, keeping up with the latest in training, taking my bikes into the shop, socializing at the bike shop, reading books and the monthly editions of all the magazines...the list goes on and on. I was an actual example of living the "Ironman Lifestyle."

It took a year of focus and discipline—often getting up at 4:30 am, doing double workouts, running at 9:30 pm with a headlamp and a flashlight, even running down Pacific Coast Highway to Seal Beach, then up the San Gabriel Valley River bed at midnight (no joke), all in order to get the workouts done.

WORKING THROUGH THE PAIN

I started this journey with a very low pain threshold and really struggled with the amount of suffering involved in training for the Ironman. Many days I was so sore that I would just skip a workout altogether. Ultimately, I had to come to grips with pain and I realized that if I was going to achieve my goal then I would have to be courageous and just learn to "suck it up" and work through the pain.

Once I made the decision that I would complete my workouts even if I was in pain, things started to change. I learned about different kinds of pain and different levels of pain. There is sharp stabbing pain, electrical shock pain, dull aches and then there is just old fashioned muscle soreness. Over time, I learned to tolerate greater amounts of pain, but sometimes it was just too much. I'd often say to myself, *"This is literally insane! Why would anyone continue with their workout when they are in so much pain?"* Yet there I was, trying to work through the pain and gut-it-out.

Much of this pain was the result of constant blisters and my plantar wart problem, where the pain is often so intense that I'm limping and wincing with each stride. Sometimes I even laugh out loud at how incredibly painful it is with each step. But after about 5 – 10 minutes, the pain starts to fade and the area goes numb, allowing me to complete the workout. My rule of thumb is to start very lightly and give it just ten minutes. If the pain is getting worse, then I turn around, but in most cases, the pain will have subsided, and then I can finish my workout. I call this my "Ten Minute Rule."

The Ten Minute Rule

There will times when you remain sore and stiff for one to three days following a tough workout. This soreness can be caused from an especially rigorous strength training session, a strenuous run, hill work on your bike or even sore shoulders from swim intervals. If you are so sore that you don't feel like working out, try the ten minute rule. Even though you are very sore and don't feel like you can do it, go ahead and continue with the workout as planned, but instead, start out very slowly. In most cases, the aches and pains will subside within ten minutes and you'll be able to manage the rest of the workout. However, if you feel sharp, stabbing pain or electrical shock-like jolts, do not continue.

This ten minute rule has saved many of my workouts on days when I thought that there was no possible way that I could complete the run or strength training session because I was just so sore. It's the same on the bike. If I've been off the bike for a week or longer, the first ten minutes back in the saddle can be very painful.

The Sit Bones and Going Numb Down There

At the lower part of the pelvis are two rocker-like bones that carry much of the weight of the upper body when we sit on a bike saddle. When sitting, the pelvis transmits our upper body weight onto these two small bones called the ischial tuberosity, commonly referred to as the "sit bones." Sometimes the pain of getting back in the saddle is rather intense, but if I follow the ten minute rule, the pain usually subsides and I'm able to ride for hours without even a hint of discomfort. Much can be done to relieve this pain with a proper bike fit, including: adjusting the saddle position, the handle bars, the brake hoods and the stem height.

While on the subject of the saddle and sit bones, we have to discuss the common newbie issue of nether region numbness. One day I was riding up a steep grade and staying in my saddle for a very long time. I felt a very odd sensation and quickly realized that I had gone completely numb in my nether regions; literally 100% loss of any feeling whatsoever. Needless to say, I totally panicked! Fearing the worst, I immediately pulled over to the side of the road, and within a few minutes the numbness went away completely.

The numbness was caused by prolonged saddle pressure and compression in a portion of the male anatomy called the perineum, an area that lies between the sit bones. What happens is that the nerves in the perineum are being pinched and pressed while blood flow is reduced to a mere trickle. Imagine laying a drinking straw on the top of your saddle and sitting on top of it. The straw collapses as it is crushed by your weight. Well the same thing happens to the artery carrying blood down there. That's why it is absolutely essential to get out of the saddle about every ten minutes or so in order to encourage blood flow and prevent numbness. The first time this happens, you'll never forget the experience; it's rather frightening the first time.

WHEEL SUCKERS AND DRAFTING

One of my routine bike workouts is to take the San Gabriel Valley Riverbed Trail from Seal Beach up to the huge Santa Fe Dam in Irwindale. The dam is 34-miles inland from my home in Long Beach and the weather can be dramatically-different in just that short distance.

The challenge with this particular ride is that if I leave too late, which is often the case, the onshore ocean breeze picks up and literally pushes me up the riverbed, giving me perhaps a 2 – 3 mph advantage. As the day progresses and the heat picks up, so too, does the wind. The problem is that every time I get that wind advantage for the ride up to the dam, I foolishly think that I'm having a terrific day and feeling very strong. I often try to push it and set a new speed record. But two hours later on the return trip home, the wind has picked up dramatically, and now it's blowing directly in my face. It can blow ferociously in the mid to late afternoon, and there is no protection of any kind when riding high atop the trail.

One particular trip back from the dam, I was battling heat in the mid 90s and very strong headwinds. I had foolishly tried to set a new speed record to the dam and was really spent. Cursing at the stupidity of pushing so hard on the trip up to the dam, I was struggling in the small chain ring in my easiest gear, yet barely making any headway. The struggle into the headwind was harder than climbing a steep hill. Out of instinct, I turned at one point and noticed that a guy had been hanging right on my rear wheel, literally just inches from me. He was using me as a windbreak to allow him to cruise along while I took the full brunt of the headwind. I looked him in the eye and he said nothing. I was incensed that he just snuck up on me and was sucking my back wheel, riding for free while I was doing all the work.

Despite being very tired, I tried to get this guy off of my wheel by speeding ahead with everything I had left, but as long as he stayed in my slipstream, it was impossible for me to lose him. I turned around and he just gave me a wry smirk, which really set me off. I told him to pull around me and get off my wheel. He continued to smirk and wouldn't move. It finally got to the point where I was literally yelling at him to get off of my wheel. He said that he was tired and needed the break. Tired? Heck, I was a lot more tired than he was and I had come a lot further. But more than anything, it was his attitude that he could just sneak up behind me and that I should just pull him along and do all the work. Had this been a rider in trouble or distress, I would have gladly done literally anything to help him, but this joker was nothing more than a freeloader who was drafting behind me, literally just cruising and being pulled along in my slipstream.

THE SCIENCE OF DRAFTING

Drafting behind another cyclist can make a huge difference in terms of the energy required to maintain the same speed as the front rider. As the cyclist in the front pushes through the air, a region of reduced air pressure is produced behind them as they force the air molecules apart. The air molecules are unable to reform immediately behind the front cyclist which is what creates an opportunity for the cyclist in the second position. This reduction in air pressure creates a small area immediately behind the front cyclist where the air starts to move a bit forward and can actually help pull along the second cyclist if they get close enough to the rear wheel of the front rider. This is what's called a slipstream and when one cyclist rides very closely behind another, they are said to be drafting. The greatest drafting benefit comes when one is within about 4 – 6 inches of the wheel in front of them. Any further than 6 inches and the drafting benefits decline rapidly.

Drafting is used to reduce the amount of energy that is required to sustain a speed equal to the front rider; it offers a significant advantage to the person being pulled along in the slipstream of the front rider. In wind tunnel tests using meters designed to record power and watts, the rider in the second position has been found to be using 40 – 60% less energy to travel the same speed as the front cyclist. In addition to cycling, drafting is used for significant advantage in auto racing, speed skating, swimming and many other sports. But in the Ironman Triathlon there are significant penalties for drafting because it offers such a competitive advantage. Triathlon referees strictly monitor the cyclists throughout each race and penalize riders who are taking advantage by drafting and that's why I never draft in workouts; I want the full benefit of plowing ahead in the face of the wind and doing the extra work. Anything less is really taking the easy way out for me because I cannot draft in the race.

Yet this joker on the riverbed trail had no problem drafting behind me and he wouldn't get around me. Finally I just pulled over and stopped. He did too. He would not proceed into the wind on his own. I got out my cell phone and pretended to make some calls until he finally ventured out into the wind on his own. With that, I jumped on his tail and drafted right behind him yelling at the top of my lungs for him to be a man, take his pull and show me what he had. I taunted him mercilessly by yelling, *"Is that all you've got?!"* I got him so worked up (or scared) that he went out really fast, totally burned out and then as he pulled over gasping, I took the opportunity to blast by him so quickly that he had no chance to bridge the gap and I dropped him.

This was a stupid move on my part and I used very poor judgment throughout that long ride. But it is an example of how the adrenaline can really get flowing and how quickly tempers can rise when out on a long hot ride when people are tired, dehydrated and not thinking as clearly as they would be in a business setting or another environment.

Running on Different Surfaces

As a young athlete in high school, I could run on anything. However, starting-up again at the age of 45, I realized that a lot had changed. Now, running on concrete sidewalks was like pounding my knees with a mallet and running on a steeply-graded asphalt road shoulder would twist my ankles. I really needed to figure out the best place to run or my running days would be over before I even got into full stride.

I reasoned that running on the golf course or any field of grass would be the best solution, but I was horribly wrong. I have found that running on grass is perhaps one of the riskiest things I could ever do on a run. Grass fields, golf courses and the grass medians along roadsides are filled with hidden potholes and just an invitation for a rolled or twisted ankle. The problem is that the lawn mowers cut the grass all at a level height, but the potholes, gopher holes, drainage ruts and such are often completely hidden in the tall grass. My rule of thumb is generally to avoid running on grass unless it is cut very short and I can clearly see any ruts or holes. If the grass is too long, I will stay on the road – it's just not worth the risk of a twisted ankle. However, if I must run on the grass I am extremely cautious and look very carefully for any differences in shadows, color or the slightest indentations. I've learned from experience that a dark patch of grass often hides a depression where excess water has gathered, allowing the grass to grow faster and healthier. Thus, dark patches are to be avoided as they often hide holes and ruts.

My preferred running surface is a crushed granite pathway or trail. These are hard to find, but once I find a great trail, I tend to stick with it and return often. We have a wonderful series of trails in Carpinteria that start along the Salt Marsh and continue through the State Park, along the ocean and on the bluffs toward Rincon. When I cannot find my preferred crushed granite trail, I look for any dirt surface. I've found another great trail near my home in Long Beach along the side of the San Gabriel Valley Riverbed. This dirt trail runs alongside of the bike path that I know so well and allows me to run up to twenty miles with only occasional stretches of asphalt. The only frustrating thing about this trail is that the sections we share with the equestrians have been ground into soft-powdery dust and are totally unsuitable for running.

My preferred running surfaces (in order) are:

- Moist dirt trails (no mud)
- Crushed granite trails
- Dirt trails
- Rubber tracks at Universities and High Schools
- Very low cut grass
- Asphalt
- Hard-packed, level beach
- Concrete (absolutely last choice)

RUNNING ON RAILROAD TRACKS

I enjoy running on the dirt paths that typically run parallel to train tracks. However, this can be difficult when the dirt trails are covered in places with lots of loose gravel.

I was running alongside the tracks one day as part of a 13-mile run in Carpinteria. I was tired, my legs felt very heavy and I kept stumbling on the gravel. I noticed a nice dirt path on the other side of the tracks, so I decided to cross. As I stepped onto the wood railroad ties I was surprised at how they would flex and absorb the shock of each stride. It was a relief from the long day, so I started to adjust my stride to try and run just on the wood ties. I got into a rhythm with the music coming from my iPod and it became a challenging game to land each foot in unison with the beat of the music. It was trancelike because it required extreme concentration. When the song changed, my rhythm was immediately disrupted and I suddenly came to my senses, realizing how foolish I had been. My eyes were totally focused on the wood ties, my music was blaring and I was concentrating on everything but the oncoming trains. The story has no dramatic ending with me diving to safety from the oncoming train, but it could have been a very serious situation if I had tripped, or if I never heard an oncoming train at the blind corner near the entrance of Sandyland and Santa Claus Lane.

I still run alongside the tracks all the time, but never on the wood ties and I am extremely cautious about ever crossing the tracks, especially during long runs or on my brick workouts when my legs are heavy and I'm tired from a long day on the road.

IT BAND SOLUTION

I struggled with constant IT Band issues and then finally found a cure that really works. This is the most painful therapy imaginable, but if you work through it, your IT Band issues can be solved. I purchased a hard foam roller from a Relax the Back store, but you can get them online and also at yoga shops or at your local gym. Use that foam roller on your IT Band, rolling slowly over the area from the top of your hip, your gluteus area and then all the way down the outside of each leg to just under your knee. That will cover the entire length of the IT Band.

This will be extremely painful if you currently are suffering from IT Band issues, but if you stick with this over time, the pain will get less severe and ultimately you'll be able to use this roller with no pain whatsoever. I know that if you are currently suffering with IT Band issues, you'll think that the pain is so severe that it is literally impossible to continue with the exercise; just do whatever you can, even just a few minutes several times each day. Little by little you'll find that this gets easier over time. In my case it took about sixty days for the pain to subside. I'm now 100% free of any IT issues and the foam roller remains an integral part of my routine as a preventative measure.

This will hurt. A lot. But it will get better. You must work through this and in 30 – 60 days you will find relief, but you must be consistent. I found that several times daily was best.

LESSONS LEARNED ABOUT TRAINING

The most important lesson I learned about training was to try and get the workouts done in the morning, no matter how early it means that you'll have to get up, no matter how dark, cold, or wet.

If you don't get all the workouts completed, it's not the end of the world and you shouldn't stress out about it too much. However, if you make it a habit to let your training slide by skipping workouts or fudging your times in your training journal, this will come back to haunt you. Show up at a race unprepared and you'll pay a much higher price than a little less sleep from time to time. It's just not worth it. I would much rather pay the price in training than to suffer in a race or risk disqualification for not meeting the cutoff times throughout the course.

The important thing to remember about this endeavor is that no one can ever do it for you. Your equipment won't make a significant difference; your coach can't do the workouts for you and no amount of 'positive thinking' can properly condition your muscles and cardiovascular system to endure 12 – 17 hours in race conditions. There is no place to hide. We all know if the other guy really did work out hard all year long. If you take short cuts in nutrition or training, everyone knows because you just cannot fake it for 12 – 17 hours out there in the desert or on the lava fields. Either you do your work all year long or you will pay dearly. No amount of money can buy your way out of this. Either you pay your dues in sweat during dedicated training or you will pay the price on race day; that's a guarantee.

So to actually participate in an Ironman event with men and women of all ages who have made similar sacrifices is unique; there's this mutual respect of what we've all been through to reach this point.

We have a bond like a fraternal order, and the price of admission is discipline, long hours of training and for many, pain, suffering and injuries.

You have to do the work in order to cross that line. If you don't, you're not an Ironman. But as long as you pay your dues in training and maintain daily discipline, you will likely have what it takes to finish, and when you do, you are in the club for LIFE.

We all know what we had to do to prepare ourselves in training; there's this knowing glance. You just know. If this guy tells you that he has done an Ironman, you instantly give him props and respect because you just know what he has been through. The pain, the sacrifice, the cost, the agony, the discipline, everything. You just cannot fake your way through one of these things. It's the real deal.

This isn't like a 10K where you can probably hang tough for 45 minutes to an hour. This is a 12 – 17 hour day; you must be prepared and if you try to fake it, you end up in the hospital or an ambulance with IV bags attached to each arm and leg. This is an absolute fact, and I have personally seen it many, many times right on the course. In Tempe, I heard at least three ambulances and I saw at least two athletes on the bike leg, deep in the desert, with IV bags in each arm as they lay prone on the ground. There are no guarantees that training alone will be enough, but if you pay your dues, this is an achievable goal.

No doubt, it's tough. Damn tough. But if one is disciplined, it is possible. Not for everyone, but if they do work hard enough, they have a great shot at it.

To be sure, not everyone finishes. If they did, then they wouldn't call it an Ironman.

STOP TO ENCOURAGE THE NEWBIES

From a distance, I saw him struggling in the center median. I slowed down so I could observe him. I noticed he was an exceptionally large man and he was really having a tough time. I, on the other hand, was feeling great and effortlessly keeping about an 8:30 pace. He'd run about 20 seconds, then walk for a minute or longer.

I turned off my iPod and ran up beside him to encourage him.

"Good morning. How ya doing?"

He could barely respond because he was so out of breath.

I slowed to a jog and said, *"I've been there, man. I give you all the credit in the world. I know it seems tough right now, but soon, you'll be running the entire time and you'll drop a lot of weight. I've already lost close to 50 pounds."*

I explained that the Galloway running method suggests that for newbies, a run-walk protocol is just fine and if done properly, can provide nearly the same aerobic benefit as running the entire time, but with a much reduced chance of injury. (see: www.JeffGalloway.com)

His reaction was fantastic. He was just so appreciative that someone had stopped to encourage him. He had been pretty embarrassed to get out there and often had been the victim of rude and hurtful comments or honking car horns passing by. But he kept at it. And he was extremely grateful that an "athlete" would stop to give him a few kind words.

To this guy, I looked slim. To him, I was running at breakneck speed. To him, completing a couple of half Ironman events and a 50K ultra marathon would be inconceivable and unobtainable dreams. They were for me, and at my heaviest, I was still maybe 75 pounds lighter than he was that morning.

But if he stuck with it, I knew he could achieve these milestones as well. Plus, his self-confidence and self-worth would skyrocket.

I've since made it a point to encourage anyone who is struggling or obviously new to sport and fitness. The heavier, the bigger, the older... the better. I will always slow down or stop and encourage them.

I really have to hand it to some of these people. They are absolutely huge, yet they are out there doing something. They are trying. They are working hard. Sometimes I see guys well over 300 pounds on beach cruiser bikes struggling on the riverbed trail. An hour or two later, on my return trip, I will see them again, still at it. Still pushing hard.

These guys really deserve the encouragement and they get that from me, along with my ultimate respect. I have a really soft spot in my heart for these guys, because I WAS one of them. So I can totally relate.

I cannot relate as well to the finely-tuned, 6% body fat athlete who has always been active and fit. I certainly respect their discipline and all the inevitable pain to maintain that level of fitness—but these finely-tuned athletes have absolutely no idea about being fat.

They don't understand the humiliation, the shame, the ribs and barbs and hurtful comments, the embarrassment when your belly bounces around as you jog, the way your pectorals actually bounce around like female breasts, the huge spare tire that encircles your entire waistline.

These are humiliating issues that big people deal with every time they step out of the house and try to do something about it. I don't care if they are walking, riding a beach cruiser or at the gym doing yoga, spin or weights. It is still embarrassing and humiliating.

For them to receive a positive comment or some encouragement from a person who embodies everything they are hoping to achieve can mean the world to them. To get encouragement from a honed and finely-tuned athlete can keep them on a high for days.

I really believe that no workout is so important that I cannot slow down for just a minute or two, ask them how they are doing, tell them how much I respect what they are trying to achieve and to offer encouragement. I will tell them that I've been there, I personally know how tough this part of the process can be and I know that they will be successful if they are patient and disciplined.

If you are an athlete, take the time to encourage those who are working hard and struggling to get in shape and improve their fitness. I think this just makes the world a better place for all of us.

Caution Regarding Prescription Drugs

My training was supervised by one of the finest coaches, who utilized a very specific scientific approach to slowly building me up for this event. Despite our best efforts not to take any unnecessary risks that might increase the chance of sustaining an injury, I still encountered terrible problems. Through this journey, I saw more doctors and took more prescription medicine than in all the past thirty years combined.

Nearly all of the doctor's visits, treatments and medications were an attempt to treat the symptoms of the same problems that never really went away. These problems included:

- A knotted mass of muscle tissue in the upper trapezoid area that was extremely painful and often prevented me from turning my head to look behind and over my left shoulder.
- A very serious hip pain and related nerve pain that shot down my left leg and severely restricted many types of activities and which also greatly impacted my ability to sleep peacefully, or at all.
- IT band problems, typically in my left knee, but immediately following the Ironman, both IT bands became severely inflamed and extremely painful, completely sidelining my running for at least five weeks.
- Bleeding hemorrhoids, most likely from the very long bike

legs toward the last months of my training for Ironman Arizona.

- Ongoing blister problems and a terrible plantar wart that shot pain through my left leg with every stride and would not respond to any treatment. This was ultimately operated on just a few days following the completion of the Arizona Ironman, and still had not healed ten weeks later.

Most of the medicines that were prescribed were anti-inflammatories (NSAIDs). These medications were not habit forming, but taking them during races and heavy workouts is known to be risky.

Some of the other medications, however, were very strong narcotics. I really had no choice. I could not continue due to the extreme pain. There was no such thing as just being tough and working through the pain when it got to that level. My only choices were to immediately stop training for Ironman, or to find some kind of medication that would relive some of the constant pain.

When it came to the strong narcotics, I was very worried about developing a habit with these medicines and from time to time, I would stop taking them cold-turkey, just to see if I was developing a reliance upon them.

It has been well documented that people with an addictive-type personality may be at potentially greater risk to develop a dependency or habit with prescription narcotics. This has happened in some very highly-publicized cases such as Rush Limbaugh, Betty Ford, Cindy McCain, Elizabeth Taylor and hundreds of others. These people became addicted to the medicines that were prescribed to them by their very well-meaning family doctors, who had every intention of trying to relive their pain.

As a triathlete who had already become obsessed with my Ironman goal, I knew I had a somewhat addictive Type-A streak and I was very careful to discuss this with my doctors before any medicines were ever prescribed. Not only was I concerned about drug interactions but also about possible dependency. In every case, we opted for a lesser quantity and the least powerful drug that would allow me to complete this journey.

Some of the drugs made me sick and sleepy, some made me constipated, some had other undesirable and unanticipated side effects. Some seemed to do absolutely nothing at all. Some took a long time to start working, such as the NSAIDs.

However, some seemed to work exceptionally well, such as Ultram. I took it just before bedtime in order to allow me to sleep relatively pain-free. The only problem with this particular pain killer was that it made me dizzy and nauseous.

It's vital to work with all of your doctors and to tell them all the different medications that you are taking (I used to bring all the bottles to each doctor).

When a medicine didn't work for me, or if one of my doctors prescribed a different kind of medicine in an attempt to get at the same problem, I would ask the doctor to go through all of my pill bottles and physically remove any pills that I should no longer use. Then they'd destroy the pills. The last thing I wanted was 10 – 15 different bottles filled with pills that did not work. I was glad when the doctors eliminated certain medications and took those bottles away for destruction.

After Arizona Ironman, I went at least ten weeks without taking any of the prescriptions I was taking before the race; nothing. I dumped every single one. There was some pain in the hip and especially the IT bands, but I was relieved to find that I could go this long without craving pain medicine or NSAIDs. I was functioning perfectly well without any of them and so I concluded that I had no physical or psychological need or craving for these prescriptions.

Once I return to daily training, I may have to go back to taking certain NSAIDS and pain medicines, but if I do, I will continue to be extremely cautious about avoiding or minimizing the risk of dependency. When narcotic painkillers are the only way to go, I will continue to seek the least potentially addictive medication and take them only in small quantities for limited periods. I have been so cognizant and concerned about potential dependency issues that I probably do not take the medicine as often as I should. However, a potential prescription drug dependency is just not worth the risk to me. I'd rather endure a bit more pain and lower my risk of dependency.

Final Remarks on This Journey

What seemed completely impossible at first, a goal far beyond my reach, has now been achieved. I completed the full Ironman triathlon within the time frame I set and I met my weight loss goal of getting under 160 pounds.

Even several weeks after I had crossed that finish line at the Arizona Ironman, I still didn't know how I did it. I still had a hard time recalling much of the day and struggled to comprehend that I actually completed the full event. It just hadn't sunk in yet. I wonder if it ever will.

When I look back on all the preparation, planning and workouts, the injuries, the doctor's visits, the stress and the constant suffering from injuries and treatments, I wonder if it was really worth the struggle. I've said many times before that this endeavor was a "colossal waste of time" and many days it really did feel that way.

There was a heavy price to pay. A heavy toll. And while I have not yet been asked whether it was worth it or not, I think that it was.

Not for the actual bragging rights, which of course are substantial, but more for what I have learned about myself and what I have become in this process.

At first I thought I would make the Ironman Triathlon part of my lifestyle and would do this forever, but now I really don't know. I seem to have lost something in the attainment of the goal. I seem to have lost some of the courage it required to suffer through so much pain and some willingness commit the incredible amount of time to the ultra endurance endeavor.

I have been trying to get back into the groove, to find the drive and the passion to get back into training again. One thing I've learned about myself is that I am no good at maintaining the status-quo; I must have huge, new goals and challenges. Maintenance is not my bag and if simply maintaining health were my objective, I would certainly fail. I've learned that I'm just wired in a way that requires a massive commitment for extremely challenging goals.

So what's next?

THE ULTRAMAN: A 318 MILE, 3-DAY ENDURANCE EVENT

I have my sights set on the Ultraman, which is a 3-day, 318.6 mile individual ultra endurance event held in British Columbia, Canada. Entry is limited to 30 solo participants and is by invitation only.

The first day includes a 6.2 mile swim, immediately followed by a 90 mile bike event. The second day is a 170 mile bike event, and the third day is a run that consists of a double marathon (52.4 miles). Each participant is required to have their own personal crew that follows them throughout the entire event. This requires a lot of planning and very detailed preparation, which is something I learned I really enjoyed during the Ironman process.

Do I have what it takes to complete the Ultraman? Where will I find the passion and the drive and the grit to embark on another crazy journey? Will my body hold up under the incredible amount of additional training I must endure to prepare for this event? Will I even be invited to compete in the Ultraman in 2009?

I don't yet have the answers to any of those questions. The most important one being, where will I find the passion to pay the price necessary to prepare for this event?

The answers to these tough questions are yet to be determined, but may one day be available in my next book:

"From Ironman to: What the Hell was I thinking!"

CHAPTER THIRTEEN

GRATITUDE

THE INFLUENTIAL PEOPLE
WHO CONTRIBUTED TO THIS ACHIEVEMENT

There are so many people to thank, all of which have made important and significant contributions in their own way, that this list is quite long. Please know that there is no particular priority assigned to the order in which names appear. However, Scott Gower appears first because I met him at the very first community triathlon event I ever attended in our small home town of Carpinteria, and so we begin with Scott:

SCOTT GOWER
AT WWW.GOFORITSPORTS.COM:

Scott is a world class endurance athlete and about the nicest guy you'll ever meet. Connor and I met Scott many years ago while he was setting up for the Carpinteria Sprint Triathlon. We helped him pitch his tent and set up his multisport gear for sale. I was very interested in this gear and the sport, and Scott...well, he was the fittest man I had ever seen, and still is. He encouraged me to try this sport sometime. I NEVER thought I could do this, ever, but he encouraged me and gave me a running cap that I still wear today (Tri). Scott remains an inspiration and I follow his races closely, most recently, a top-10 finish in the Hawaii Ultraman World Championships in 2008. Scott has been a great friend and a source of incredible inspiration. Scott is a very friendly, very helpful and extremely supportive man. If you are ever within 100 miles of his shop, or you see him at any of the race venues, please stop by; you'll be glad that you did. Just watch out...a ten minute encounter with Scott Gower could literally change your life.

DAVID WARDEN:

David's Tri-Talk Podcast is fantastic. I really enjoy all the research and the science behind each show. David has an upbeat, high energy approach with contagious enthusiasm that really gets me pumped; he is an excellent communicator. While he is currently working on a book and numerous other multisport adventures, you can still listen to his podcast at www.Tri-Talk.com. I am so lucky to have David as a coach. Not only is he a great athlete and coach, he is a devoted husband, a terrific father and a role model to thousands. He was booked up with athletes but took me on as a special experiment. He kept me motivated, and it was the accountability to a world expert that forced me out of bed at 4:30 am. David, thanks for believing in an over the hill, middle-aged former athlete who hadn't done a thing in 25 years. You, more than anyone, got me over that finish line at Ironman Arizona, literally the biggest accomplishment of my entire life. Even with the great level of respect I have for you as a world-famous coach and communicator, I value our friendship even more.

STEVE RUNNER
AND PHEDIPPIDATIONS PODCAST:

Steve has produced a fantastic Podcast. He does an incredible amount of research on many of his topics and he's got the guts to have an opinion. He is an average guy like the rest of us and it's easy to relate to his struggles, injuries and setbacks as he pursues his goal to break 4:00 hours in the marathon. Steve and I have corresponded regularly and despite the fact he gets hundreds of listener emails, he still took the time to offer me encouragement. Steve's podcast is just fantastic, but he's also just a terrific guy and a wonderful father. If you listen to his podcast you'll see how he interacts with his family; it's really touching. Listen to his podcast and you will be both entertained and inspired: www.SteveRunner.com

BOB BABBITT
AND THE COMPETITOR'S PODCAST:

Bob has such a great way about him, and while we have never met, his interviews and podcast have been a source of learning, humor and inspiration. I would love to meet Bob at some point. This is a truly outstanding Podcast. He and Paul Huddle have entertained and educated me throughout my entire journey. I strongly recommend and endorse the Competitor's Podcast. I listen to his stories and podcasts over and over. I read his Competitor magazine and his books. If you are going to pursue endurance sports, you need to get plugged into Bob's podcast. He is just so upbeat and has an incredibly approachable way about him that gets his guests to really open up. And the great thing is that all the world's best endurance athletes really open up to Bob, so you get a wonderful view of what they face and endure. I absolutely love this podcast and am certain that if you are pursuing endurance sports, you'll be as eager as I am for the release of each week's interview. www.competitorradio.com

DR. JEFFERY HO:

After over one year of seeking solutions to constant pain in my upper back, he relieved the pain with Cortisone injections. We knew we finally hit that knotted trigger point when the muscle had a violent, involuntary spasm that nearly pushed the needle right back out of my back! Seven treatments of wet needling finally got this pain under control and allowed me to get my 6 - 7 hour training rides complete on the weekends. Dr. Ho also found the right mix of NSAIDs and pain relieving medicines to reduce the pain in my hip. Further, he and his staff made all kinds of accommodations to fit me in for last minute consultations or for urgent pain problems. It took me nine months to find him, but you can call him direct at (562) 424-8111.

ERIC WEBER:

As a world class water polo player, he taught me a few moves that may have literally saved my life in the open water swim where up to 2,200 raging lunatics were all grabbing and climbing over one another at the first buoy turn of each swim.

DAVID JOCHIM:

As a world class Triathlete, he was perhaps one of the most open and coachable IdeaBridge clients; he really understood coaching. But his level of fitness was the greatest inspiration to me. He had completed many Ironman events and hearing his stories made me dream of one day completing my own triathlon. Thanks, David. It's one thing to read triathlon magazines, but it means so much more to actually know and work with a real professional triathlete.

KEVIN KELSEY:

The world's greatest business partner and a great friend. He made allowances and clearly took up the slack when I was out training 10 - 15 hours a week. He helped me develop fitness scorecards and weight loss progress charts. He helped me set up technical equipment and he calmed my nerves many times when I'd come back from my early morning bike rides really heated after being cut-off by aggressive drivers. These Ironman finishes would never have been possible without his support all along the way. In fact, Kevin is so rock solid and reliable, it is his name and contact information that I carry around my neck at all times on my Road ID dog tags. When I was hit by the car and was unable to speak for myself, Kevin got that first call and contacted my wife. To say "thanks" seems wholly inadequate. But I am incredibly grateful and appreciate all of the support. Thank you Kevin, for everything.

CHRIS BARSH:

My great friend and cousin-in-law. I am just so lucky and fortunate to have him in my life and appreciate our time together more than words can ever express. Chris, thanks for the encouragement the day prior to my first Ironman 70.3 race in Hawaii (that was huge) and thanks for helping me in my carbo loading weekends at our Club in Carpinteria. Chris cares, and it shows. He's genuine and sincere. I am so grateful to have Chris in my life and I appreciate all of our time together as we raise our families together in Carpinteria on the weekends.

CONNOR WILLIAM LATHROP CALLOS:

He has sacrificed a lot during this process. I might have been around more often if I was not training as much and I hope that he will one day understand that a small part of this effort was to set an example for him that whatever you really believe in and work hard toward achieving, you can accomplish. If I could finish an Ironman Triathlon, Connor, you can literally do anything that you set your mind to. Literally anything. Thanks for getting up at 3:00 am in Kona to encourage me when I was up worried about my first 70.3. Your encouragement of, "You've got this Dad!" stayed with me the entire race and every day since. Then when you ran alongside me at the Ironman Arizona, that was the highlight of this entire process! I was so nervous that I'd be DQd because you were pacing me, but then I realized that Kelvin must have made all the arrangements. I am so glad that you crossed that finish line with me, together, and we have the finish video which I will cherish forever. Thank you Connor.

My Wife April:

Most guys would love to have the kind of wife that is totally supportive and never gripes about all the training and hours away from home. You never complained a single time and you accommodated my schedule. You even let me convert the entire west wing of our home (about 1,000 square feet) into my training facility and Ironman headquarters. This endeavor took a tremendous amount of time, especially on the weekends, but you never, ever made me feel bad or guilty in my multi-year pursuit. You never complained about the cost of the Endless Pool, all the bikes or the race fees. You never asked to look at my credit card receipts or to account for all the money I spent on equipment. More than anyone, you had to endure my groaning, complaining, bad days, restless nights, early morning alarms, constant injury reports and so much time away from home. But through it all, you remained encouraging and completely supportive of my efforts. Thanks for the understanding, support and flexibility, dropping me off 15 miles away so I am forced to run home, and really pushing me out the door when I would have definitely skipped the workouts. I really appreciate you getting up at 4:20 am to take me to the Tempe venue and I was thrilled that you and Connor were right there at the finish line at 10:00 pm. April, thank you so much.

Amanda McCracken:

As my first coach, you did a great job to get me out of Seat 2A and kept me injury free with the right balance of fun and adventure that I needed. Circumstances beyond your control forced us to part, but we remain in contact and I'm grateful for your ongoing support.

Joseph Otting:

As one of the busiest people I know, you have managed to make time to stay fit. Your example made me eliminate the excuse of not having enough time. If you could make time to stay fit, there was no excuse for me, or for anyone. Not only that, but your encouragement in 1999 to start my own consulting business, led to the formation of IdeaBridge and many millions of dollars in revenue from clients around the globe; that all started 100% due to you. As one of the owners of a business, it was somewhat easier for me to break away when needed to do this training, so in large measure, your encouragement to start IdeaBridge also contributed to the flexibility I needed to train for Ironman. Thank you Joseph, for being an inspirational role model and for encouraging me to follow my passion of helping senior business executives and their companies improve their performance and reach their full potential. My life has changed for the better for knowing you.

MARK GANZ AND SLT:

The Washington offsite was a productive session focused on developing a tight set of operating principles that would serve as a leadership and strategic guidepost for the senior leadership team; one of those principles focused on personal health. The principle regarding health deeply resonated with me. Within one year of this offsite, I had lost about 40 pounds, completed three triathlons and many road races, including two Ironman 70.3s and a 50K ultra marathon. The impetus to embark on this lifestyle change was largely set at that offsite. And now, years later, I am delighted to see you and your entire team continuing to walk-the-talk with your own commitments to personal renewal and encouraging others throughout the company to do likewise. Your support of these initiatives is a visible sign that the goal of healthcare transformation starts by transforming our own attitudes about health, personal responsibility and the commitment to risk moving from the comfort of the status quo.

SURF CITY CYCLERY
IN HUNTINGTON BEACH, CA:

Sean, TJ and especially Mike, you guys have been absolutely fantastic. Getting into the sport initially, I was really taken advantage of by other shops who sold me all kind of gear and gizmos that I didn't need. You guys reeled in my spending and set me straight on great quality bikes. Mike was very patient with fitting me time and again, and he took a personal interest in tuning my bikes to perfection. The lightning-quick replacement set-up with the new Specialized S-Works Roubaix SL2 following my bike accident was fantastic. I highly recommend Surf City Cyclery. Please visit them if you are in the Orange County area. www.SurfCityCyclery.com. These guys are the real deal. They are like family to me and I trust them.

CARBO-PRO AND SPORTQUEST:

"GR" you are the best and your entire line of products simply rule! John Dufournet, a Performance Specialist at SportQuest, personally designed a custom race and training protocol for my hydration and nutrition needs. I have now converted to only SportQuest products, including CarboPro 1200 and all of their supplements. These products work synergistically to minimize the risk of hyponatremia and dehydration, as well as speed the recovery time from tough workouts. I am a huge fan. Call them, and more often than not, you might even be talking to my friend and the owner, "GR" who is very well known throughout the world of endurance sports. Whoever takes your call will be very knowledgeable about the products and how to use them; their customer service is fantastic. I tried all the others, but SportQuest is the best product I've found for my training and racing. I support them 100% and I have never had problems of any kind when I used their products as directed. People were detonating all around me in the last stages of Ironman Arizona, and I felt really horrible for them. I couldn't help but think that had they only been using a custom nutrition and supplement protocol from the experts at SportQuest, they may not have been suffering so much. The world's best athletes use Carbo-Pro, even my personal hero David Goggins, and for good reason. These products are fantastic. Find them at www.Carbo-Pro.com.

DR. ROBERT WILCHER
KILLER B FITNESS IN SANTA BARBARA:
(805) 448-2222
robert.wilcher@gmail.com.

Bob, you were the first person who gave it to me straight-up and told me that losing weight would be very hard work, that there were no shortcuts. You told me it was going to hurt if I wasn't in shape, but that it would get easier once I got in shape. You told me I really needed to start burning about 1,000 calories per workout and you introduced me to a nutritionist to get my diet under control. You were instrumental in getting the process started with significant fat loss and increasing my core fitness.

DOUGLAS H. RICHIE, JR., D.P.M.
SEAL BEACH, CALIFORNIA
(562) 493-2451

I had been dealing with a horrible plantar wart virus for over 15 months. I tried every over-the-counter remedy, I went to multiple doctors, I had the wart surgically frozen, burned, even surgically removed; nothing worked and the wart always returned. Finally, I found my way to Dr. Richie who holds multiple U.S. Patents and maintains an A-list of Hollywood celebrity clients and Olympic athletes. With a special blend of potent medicines that he would apply directly to the area, Dr. Richie was able to eliminate this problem forever. I could not possibly offer a stronger endorsement. By the way, his special blend cannot be purchased over the counter: he has it custom-mixed for him by a pharmacist and it includes a blend of: Salicylic acid, Podophyllum and Cantharidin. This was an extremely effective procedure and my only regret is that I did not find him sooner! If I had, I would have avoided over two months of an open-wound following the operation to remove the wart and I would have saved countless hours complaining and updating my blog about all the problems with this single issue. When you are finally ready to fix your foot problems once and for all, then go to the best and call Dr. Richie at (562) 493-2451.

DAVID ALLEN
THE WORLD'S LEADING PRODUCTIVITY EXPERT:

From the moment you hit the scene nationally with the break-through article in Fast Company magazine, I have been consistently using your methods and applying them in business and life. I've attended many of your seminars, read all of your books, listened to your podcasts and had the great pleasure to speak and correspond with you many times, including our lunch at one of the seminars. Without your GTD methodology and how I have applied it to managing all the moving parts of business, family and training, I may not have been able to complete my Ironman dream. I am a huge supporter and endorse your methods constantly. I am constantly directing people to your company at www.DavidCo.com.

KELVIN SHIELDS:

About 5:05 am race day morning, in the pitch dark of pre-dawn, Kelvin Shields somehow found us. Kelvin had driven all the way out to Tempe from Los Angeles and was there to support me for the entire race day. He had arrived at the venue around 4:50 am and never left the area until after he had personally packed my gear into my car and saw that my family and I were settled and ready to go. That was somewhere around 10:00 pm post-race. It was perhaps the single greatest act of selfless support and friendship that I have ever experienced. He was there at every turn of the entire event, from getting me set up on race morning, to the moment I exited the swim, and all the turns in the bike race and the run. He was there at the finish line and even arranged for Connor to run the last 200 yards with me. He also put some motivational messages for me up on the electronic board so that every time I ran by, it triggered a motivational message to help keep me going strong. Those little electronic messages were so important at miles 7, 16 and 23 of the marathon. How do you thank a friend like that? Words cannot express the gratitude. Kelvin and I go way back to the mid-90s when, as an executive with the Franklin Quest Organization, he helped me organize dozens of projects and lots of ideas that I really didn't know what to do with. He was so successful at getting me organized and dramatically more effective that I did everything I could to lure him away from Franklin and come to work for me. He finally relented and those were some of the greatest and most productive years of my banking career. Today, Kelvin is back at his former company, now called FranklinCovey, and he is one of their most successful professionals, maintaining accounts, selling new ones and ensuring that executives have every possible tool and technique available to be their most effective while focusing on what matters most. He certainly worked wonders with me! I only wish that others could know the very deep sense of joy that comes when you have a true friend like Kelvin Shields. Thank you, Kelvin. 140.6 times. Thank you.

CHAPTER FOURTEEN

ENDORSEMENTS

MY FAVORITE RESOURCE BOOKS FOR TRAINING:

I have purchased thousands of dollars of books on health, diet, nutrition, cycling, Navy SEAL workouts, running, ultra running, swimming, and everything ever published on triathlon. Despite these hundreds of books, I find myself continuing to return to the same core books that really seemed to resonate with me. Here they are:

RUNNING BOOKS:

Galloway's Book on Running
by Jeff Galloway
Published by Shelter
- A classic. I love his run-walk methodology.

Total Heart Rate Training
by Joe Friel
Published by Ulysses Press
- You'll need to understand optimal training zones and this book explains it well.

Ultramarathon Man
by Dean Karnazes
Published by Penguin Books
- This is the one that started it all. Dean is awesome. His first book is best.

Fixing Your Feet
by John Vonhof
Published by Wilderness Press
- A must. Buy it.

The Runners' Repair Manual
by Dr. Murray F. Weisenfeld with Barbara Burr
Published by St. Martin's Griffin
- A constant bedside companion. Incredibly valuable tips on problems from running.

TRIATHLON BOOKS:

Years of the Ironman Triathlon World Championship
by Bob Babbitt
Published by Meyer & Meyer Sport
- This is the history of the sport. A must.

The Triathlete's Training Bible
by Joe Friel
Published by Velo Press
- As the name says, this is the bible for all things triathlon. Buy the most recent edition.

Going Long
by Joe Friel and Gordon Byrn
Published by Velo Press
- Training for Ironman distance by two of the best in ultra sports

Going Long-2nd Edition
by Joe Friel and Gordon Byrn
Published by Velo Press
- I've listed both editions because I read them both. Easy to read and digest. Excellent.

Ironstruck...The Ironman Triathlon Journey
by Ray Fauteux
Published through Lulu Enterprises www.lulu.com
- A simple read with fantastic insight and deep perspective. I love this little gem.

CYCLING BOOKS:

Zinn & The Art of Triathlon Bikes
by Lennard Zinn
Published by Velo Press
- I take this to every race. This is the only bike repair and fitting resource I need.

Bicycling Medicine
by Arnie Baker, M.D.
Published by Simon & Schuster
- Diagnose cycling-induced aches and issues. I had plenty!

Training and Racing with a Power Meter
by Hunter Allen and Andrew Coggan, PH.D.
Published by Velo Press
- A great resource to understand how to get the most from Power Meter training.

Bicycling Magazine's 1,000 All-Time Best Tips
edited by Ben Hewitt
Published by Rodale
- A quick read at any time. Just flip to a page for a quick tip. I love it.

SWIMMING:

Triathlon Swimming Made Easy
by Terry Laughlin
Published by Total Immersion, Inc.
- This book got me started with Total Immersion swimming. Strongly Endorsed.

INSPIRATIONAL VIDEOS/DVDS:

Some of my indoor training rides were as long as 7 full hours on rollers. On long days like that I really needed some quality entertainment to keep me going. Just watching a TV is not going to keep you going and pushing hard, but watching any of these DVDs can keep you pumped for hours and hours. There is simply no limit to the number of times that I can watch any of these particular DVDs and not fail to be totally inspired!

- *Running the Sahara*
Documentary film on the only non-stop run across the Sahara Desert. I think that runners Charlie Engle, Ray Zahab and Kevin Lin showed remarkable grit and indomitable spirit in their 111 non-stop day run. I'm following Charlie in Badwater, his run across America and all his ultra endurance adventures.

- *What it Takes*
Documentary film on professional triathletes preparing for Ironman. I lent this to my dad to give him a sense of what I was doing training for Ironman. He was stunned. It is interesting, but many

people have no idea what is truly involved in our training; this movie is a realistic portrayal of what we do.

- *Running on the Sun*

Documentary on the Badwater 135 in Death Valley. You will not believe the heat and the harsh environment of this run. The people are real characters. It takes a special breed to go after this event.

- *The Runner*

Documentary on running the world's longest trail in record time. California's Pacific Crest Trail is the world's longest, non-stop hiking trail and David Horton runs all 2,700 miles of it, in record time.

- *Distance of Truth*

Another compelling documentary film on the Badwater 135 in Death Valley.

- *Ironman World Championships in Kona*

The editing is amazing. The human interest stories on the athletes can be both compelling and heart breaking all at once. Get any year. I watch these over and over again; they never get old.

ADDITIONAL FILMS AND TRAINING DVDS:

I have found all of the products from the following companies to be high quality and very helpful in my training. I have about 20 DVDs on various training topics and workouts from just these two companies and attest that all of their programs are very high quality:

www.EnduranceFilms.com

www.Spinervals.com

SPONSORS, PRODUCTS, SUPPORTERS AND PERSONAL ENDORSEMENTS

I wholeheartedly endorse, recommend and personally use every one of the products, services and podcasts outlined below and stand behind them all with a long record of complete satisfaction:

- Nutrition & Supplements (Carbo-Pro)
  www.CarboPro.com

- Endless Pools. Awesome.
  www.endlesspools.com

- Total Immersion Swimming.
  Taught me open-water swimming!
  www.totalimmersion.net

- Road Bikes: Specialized S-Works series
  www.specialized.com

- Distance Running Hydration System
  www.nathansports.com

- Rooftop Racks for Bikes
  www.yakima.com

- World's Best Espresso Machine
  www.nespresso.com

- My local Bike Shop in Orange County, CA
  www.surfcitycyclery.com

- David Warden and Tri-Talk Podcast.
  Great facts, research and science.
  www.tri-talk.com

- Indoor Bike Training Rollers
  www.kreitler.com

- Online Training Software, Journal and Tools
  www.trainingpeaks.com

- The Garmin 305 HR Monitor and PGS Watch.
  www.garmin.com

- Ultra Running Experts & Products
  www.zombierunner.com

- Phedippidations Running Podcast.
  Steve Runner is the man!
  www.steverunner.com

- The Competitors Podcast.
  www.competitorradio.com

- SRAM Red:
  Bike Component Grouppo
  www.sram.com

- Wattage Meter and HR Monitors (PowerTap 2.4)
  www.cycleops.com

- Zipp are my Deep Dish Race Wheels
  www.zipp.com

- Castelli Cycling Apparel is my all-time favorite
  www.castelli-us.com

- Computrainer Indoor Computer-based trainer.
  Best in the world.
  www.racermateinc.com

- HWD1000 - Haier Ventless Washer/Dryer Combo. This is just awesome!
  www.compactappliance.com

- Zoot Tri Shorts
  www.zootsports.com

- 2XU Triathlon Shorts
  www.2xu.com

- Nike Running Gloves
  www.Nike.com

- Newton Running Shoes
  www.newtonrunning.com

- Road ID Emergency Information Dog Tags. A must.
  www.RoadID.com

- Waterproof Note Pads
  www.riteintherain.com

- The Note Taker Wallet by David Allen
  www.Davidco.com

- Oakley Radar Sunglasses
  www.Oakley.com

APPENDIX

Ironman Triathlon Race Day Checklists

Some might say that I can tend to be obsessive with details and planning. I do enjoy planning and research and when I couldn't find a comprehensive packing list for my Ironman events, I decided to keep detailed records of everything I needed and packed. I augmented this list by doing a comprehensive research project to try and determine if I had missed anything.

This checklist is likely the most comprehensive packing list an Ironman athlete might ever need.

PAPERWORK:

☐   Hotel reservations
☐   Car reservations
☐   Map to hotel
☐   Plane tickets
☐   Race confirmation papers
☐   Bike shipping confirmation
☐   USAT card (check for current date)
☐   Race plan and estimated splits
☐   Written nutrition plan
☐   Event maps and times

- ☐ Passport (check for current date)
- ☐ Photocopy of insurance, license, USAT card (laminated in plastic)
- ☐ Instruction manuals for all electronics

SWIM EVENT:

- ☐ 2 pairs swim goggles; one pair must be tinted for bright sun
- ☐ 2 nose clips
- ☐ 2 sets ear plugs
- ☐ Anti-fog solution
- ☐ Chamois for mask
- ☐ Wetsuit
- ☐ Ear drying solution
- ☐ Silicone cap
- ☐ Neoprene skull cap (if cold water)
- ☐ Body Glide (for back of neck)
- ☐ Heavy plastic bag w/race # (to ditch last minute items)
- ☐ Throw-away, super inexpensive flip flops

BIKE EVENT:

- ☐ Helmet
- ☐ Sunglasses with hard case
- ☐ 3 tubes with extra long valves already taped
- ☐ Brand new patch kit
- ☐ 4 cylinders of CO_2
- ☐ CO_2 micro inflation tool
- ☐ Mini, hand tire pump
- ☐ Toolkit for hotel room
- ☐ Toolkit to carry on bike
- ☐ Bag for bike tools
- ☐ Bike gloves
- ☐ Sweatband/headband
- ☐ 3 tire levers

- ☐ Extra valve stem extender
- ☐ Extra threaded nuts for rim
- ☐ 3 water bottles and lids
- ☐ Bike shoes (check cleats)
- ☐ Rubber bands
- ☐ Black electric tape
- ☐ PowerTap meter
- ☐ PowerTap HR chest strap
- ☐ Foam ear plugs
- ☐ Chamois Butter

RUNNING EVENT:

- ☐ Lightweight cap/visor
- ☐ Tri suit (shorts, top, extras)
- ☐ Heavy running socks
- ☐ Running shoes
- ☐ Fuel/hydration belt
- ☐ Garmin 305 watch
- ☐ Garmin 305 HR chest strap
- ☐ Garmin charger
- ☐ Timex Ironman watch
- ☐ Running gloves (gray)
- ☐ Road ID Tag
- ☐ Race number belt

MEDICATIONS:

- ☐ Pepcid AC
- ☐ Cortaid
- ☐ Celebrex (NSAID)
- ☐ Lidoderm patches
- ☐ Tylenol PM
- ☐ Prep – H
- ☐ Ketorolac 10mg
- ☐ Celebrex

- ☐ Meloxicam/Mobic/Voltaren
- ☐ Ultram ER 50 - pain
- ☐ Excedrin
- ☐ Imitrex (migraine)
- ☐ Advil liquid gel caps
- ☐ Sunscreen
- ☐ Body Glide
- ☐ Deodorant & toiletries
- ☐ Hand wipes
- ☐ Toilet paper
- ☐ Anti - diarrhea pills
- ☐ Mucinex for coughing

NUTRITION:

- ☐ Carbo-Pro Powder
- ☐ 3 - CarboPro 1200
- ☐ Recover Amino Power
- ☐ Cliff Shots
- ☐ GU packets
- ☐ Thermolyte Caps
- ☐ Vantage VO2 Max
- ☐ Motivator Caps
- ☐ Recovery Drink
- ☐ Bags of salted peanuts

MISC:

- ☐ Zip ties
- ☐ iPod, charger & 2 headphones
- ☐ Transition bag
- ☐ Small chamois for glasses
- ☐ TP and hand wipes
- ☐ Sewing kit
- ☐ Gel tape for bars
- ☐ Extra bar plug

- ☐ Pad of paper and pens
- ☐ Camera w/charged battery
- ☐ Massage stick

SPECIAL NEEDS BAG - BIKE:

- ☐ 2 - extra tubes
- ☐ 2 - extra CO2
- ☐ Bag of salted peanuts
- ☐ Extra Thermolyte caps
- ☐ 8 oz of CarboPro 1200

SPECIAL NEEDS BAG - RUN:

- ☐ Extra socks
- ☐ Bag of salted peanuts
- ☐ Safety pin for Blisters (also one in visor or cap)
- ☐ Small anti-chafing stick
- ☐ Lip balm/chap stick
- ☐ Sunscreen
- ☐ Emergency blister kit and patches

T-1 BAG for BIKE:

- ☐ Very thin socks
- ☐ Race belt and number
- ☐ Bike shoes
- ☐ Bike helmet
- ☐ Bike jersey (gloves, etc.)
- ☐ Towel to dry from swim
- ☐ Swim Ear alcohol drops
- ☐ Sunglasses
- ☐ Emergency first aid kit (in jersey)

T – 2 BAG for RUN:

- [ ] Thick, dry socks
- [ ] Running shoes
- [ ] Running hat/visor
- [ ] Small anti-chafing stick
- [ ] Long sleeve shirt
- [ ] Small tube chamois lotion
- [ ] Hydration belt (fully loaded)

OTHER ITEMS:

- [ ] Nutrition: CarboPro 1200
- [ ] VO2 Max Caps
- [ ] Thermolyte Caps
- [ ] Small plastic bag for race day supplements
- [ ] Protein powder
- [ ] Shaker for protein powder
- [ ] iPhone charger
- [ ] Safety pin for blisters
- [ ] Rags for chain and bike
- [ ] Medium-sized towel
- [ ] Spray wax to bike clean
- [ ] Casual clothes
- [ ] Warm up suit/jacket for pre-race cold morning
- [ ] New batteries already installed in everything
- [ ] Instruction manuals for PowerTap and Garmin
- [ ] Replacement batteries for PowerTap and HR straps
- [ ] Sunglasses in case
- [ ] Foam roller for IT band
- [ ] Bike repair manual
- [ ] Anti-chafing nip guards
- [ ] New permanent marker sharpie
- [ ] Hole Punch to put all handouts/materials into a race binder

- ☐ Extra plastic bag with name and
  race number to stash pre-race warm ups

EMERGENCY KIT
for BIKE and RUN (in small plastic Ziploc bag):

- ☐ 1 Mucinex (for coughing)
- ☐ 2 Anti- diarrhea pills
- ☐ 15 Thermolyte Caps
- ☐ Safety pins (1 in hat, 1 on jersey)
- ☐ Chapstick
- ☐ Micro-sized body glide
- ☐ 2 Pepcid AC
- ☐ 4 Excedrin
- ☐ 2 Imitrex 100 mg.
- ☐ Keep all of this in bike jersey or tri shorts at all times

INDEX

SYMBOLS

A

B

C

D

I

O

P

R

S

T

U

V

W

X

Y

Z

JOHN D. CALLOS

John D. Callos is President & CEO of IdeaBridge, LLC where he advises CEOs and their direct reports on leadership issues relating to executive effectiveness, accountability, corporate strategy, and growth. His work involves confidential advisory services, speaking engagements, executive coaching, facilitating strategic planning offsites, team building and training. He is a frequent keynote speaker in the areas of: leadership, execution & accountability, personal achievement, change & organizational effectiveness, and corporate growth strategies.

Based on his experience as told in Iron Ambition, John delivers an inspirational speech for large organizations, titled: "From Seat 2A to Ironman: Applying the Disciplines of Ironman Training to Accomplish the Unthinkable."

John was raised in Orange, California. As a youth, he earned the rank of Eagle Scout while being very active in soccer, cross country and track. In 1980 his performance in track led him to the CA state semi-finals for the 2-mile event. He graduated from the University of Southern California with a business degree and emphasis in the school's Entrepreneur Program.

The Callos family has made Long Beach, CA their home for nearly 20 years. When he's not meeting with clients or developing new program materials, John will likely be found training for his next ultra endurance challenge or spending time with his wife April and son Connor at their weekend beach shack in Carpinteria, CA.

Feel free to contact the author:

John D. Callos
President & CEO
IdeaBridge, LLC

Phone: (800) 986-1230

www.JohnCallos.com
www.IronAmbition.com
www.IdeaBridge.com

email: John@IronAmbition.com

3547632

Made in the USA